THE MARS ONE CREW MANUAL

Belongs To:

Rich Pchanene

THE MARS ONE

CREW MANUAL

KERRY MARK JOËLS

DESIGNED BY ALEX JAY

BALLANTINE BOOKS
NEW YORK

Also published by Ballantine Books

The Space Shuttle Operator's Manual
  by Kerry Mark Joëls, Gregory P. Kennedy,
  and David Larkin

Acknowledgments: Dave Criswell, California Space Institute; Jim French, Jet Propulsion Laboratory; Ted Maxwell, Center for Earth and Planetary Studies NASM; Vic Vykukal, Glen Carle and Trieve Tanner, NASA/Ames Research Center; Joe Loftus, R.F. Baille and Wendell Mendell, NASA/Johnson Space Center; Stan Kent, Lockheed Missiles and Space; Kathy Fish.

Library of Congress Cataloging in Publication Data: 85-90578

Joëls, Kerry Mark, 1946–
  Mars one crew manual.

  "A Del Rey book."
  I. Title.
PS3560.0245M3   1985   813'.54   86-6178
ISBN 0-345-32747-0 (hdcvr)
ISBN 0-345-31881-1 (pbk)

Cover design by James R. Harris
Patch design by Mike Hinge
Patch illustration by Paul Hudson

PHOTOS AND ILLUSTRATIONS
Paul Hudson: Title page spread; 1.4.1–1.4.2; 1.4.3–1.4.4; 1.4.5–1.4.6; 2.6.1; 3.0.1–3.0.2; 4.0.1–4.0.2; 5.0.1–5.0.2; Gatefold*

Mike Hinge: 1.4.7–1.4.8; 1.4.9–1.4.10 (line art); 1.4.11; 1.5.1; 1.6.4; 2.1.3 (waste management unit, fecal collector, urine drawer); 2.2.1 (lavatory unit); 2.2.2; 2.2.3; 2.3.2 (food storage diagram); 2.4.1; 2.5.1; 2.5.2 (monitor and cameras); 2.7.1.; 2.7.2; 2.8.1; 2.8.2; 2.9.1; 2.10.1; 3.1.2; 4.2.2 (penetrator); 4.3.1 (satellite); 4.3.2; 4.3.4 (top—Mars airplane TV survey); 4.4.3–4.4.4; 4.5.8–4.5.9*; 4.6.9; 4.7.1; 5.2.2; 6.3.2; 6.4.1

Kerry Joëls: 4.5.12–4.5.13

Barry Schein: 2.3.3; 2.9.2

Alex Jay: 4.1.2; 4.3.5; 6.2.1

H. C. Vykukal: 5.2.5 (manipulative arm)

Brand Norman Griffin: Rover design: 4.5.8–4.5.9; Gatefold

All other illustrations and photos derived from NASA sources.

Manufactured in the United States of America

First Edition: November 1985

10 9 8 7 6 5 4 3 2 1

July 1, 1995

Dear Crew Member:

Congratulations on your selection to the Mars One crew. You are about to realize one of the greatest dreams of mankind—to visit another planet, Mars. Through you, all of us will share this momentous event.

This manual is your flight reference guide. It contains basic flight information, important training data, and reference material. Remember that this manual will have to last the length of your mission, over two years, so treat it well.

This crew represents every major race of humans. You are all diverse and extremely well qualified. The energy and intelligence you bring to this project, however, will not be sufficient for success. Attitude and training will be even more critical. Study this book as though your life depends upon it, for it may.

Again, our congratulations to you. Our hopes ride with you.

Sincerely,

UNITED NATIONS
MARS EXPLORATION AUTHORITY
(UNMEA)

This chapter provides an overview of your mission. It outlines flight plans and introduces you to the major hardware components. It also describes preparation procedures and staging areas. The chapters following it will provide specific detail on your craft and the mission ahead.

1.0.1

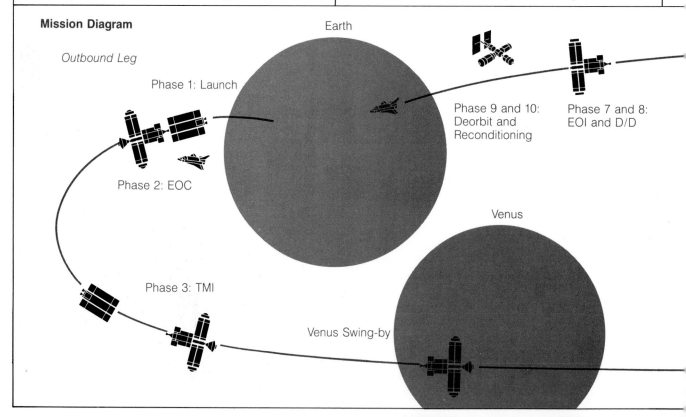

Two great debates raged during the last decades of the nineteenth century: (1) Is there life on Mars? (2) Can man fly? In each case experts argued on both sides.

Regarding the Mars question, American astronomer Percival Lowell insisted that the straight lines across the planet's surface that were reported as *canali* by the Italian astronomer Giovanni Schiaparelli in 1877 were, in fact, canals for distribution of water on a desertlike planet. Unfortunately, *canali* should have been translated as "channels" not "canals," since the latter implies construction and therefore intelligence. Like others, however, Lowell concluded that these observed planetary features were constructed canals, not natural phenomena.

The debate continued with Lowell and others opposed by such notable scientists of the period as E. E. Barnard and naturalist Alfred Russell Wallace.

In 1900, a prize of 100,000 francs was offered by Anne Guzman, wife of a wealthy industrialist, to the first person to make contact with extraterrestrials from anywhere but Mars. That is how sure people were that the "canals" on Mars actually existed as the product of an advanced civilization. As late as 1963, British astronomer G. A. Hole named features on the planet he thought were canals. These names appeared on official maps of the International Astronomical Union until unmanned spacecraft flew by Mars and silenced the controversy forever. There were no canals.

Ironically, the case of the canals was solved by the successful resolution of the second debate. In 1896, astronomer Samuel P. Langley pioneered heavier-than-air flight with a steam-powered model plane he called the "aerodrome." He also corresponded with two brothers from Dayton, Ohio, the Wrights, who also were bent on flying. Orville and Wilbur Wright methodically calculated, designed, tested, learned, and redesigned.

In October and December of 1903, Langley failed to get a full-sized, piloted aerodrome off a houseboat on the Potomac River. While the public ridiculed him for his folly, the Wrights flew. The Wrights had constructed the first practical airplane. Their triumph spurred America and Europe into the era of aviation.

During this same period, Robert Goddard was dreaming of still another way to fly—with the rocket. In the second half of the twentieth century, the rocket technology Goddard pioneered and the industry born of the Wright brothers' efforts became the bases of the space program. At first, only small automated boxes were hurled above the atmosphere, but men soon followed—to orbit, to the Moon, now to Mars!

Your voyage to Mars will answer many of the questions raised by the same unmanned spacecraft that settled the canal issue. Like lunar science in the Apollo era, the capability you bring to a mission is much more than can be gained by a bevy of unmanned systems. This mission has been planned to maximize scientific information while minimizing risk to the members of the crew. Safety features and procedures have been carefully worked out, but when you are over 40 million miles away from Earth, nothing can be certain. This type of mission requires the strongest motivation and cooperation.

Your mission consists of ten major phases: (1) Launch to Earth orbit; (2) Earth orbit check-out (EOC); (3) Trans-Mars injection (TMI)/Mars coast; (4) Mars orbit injection (MOI); (5) Mars orbit and surface activities (MOSA); (6) Trans-Earth injection (TEI)/Trans-Earth coast (TEC); (7) Earth orbit injection (EOI); (8) Decontamination/debriefing (D/D); (9) Deorbit and Earth return; and (10) Medical evaluation and reconditioning.

The Mars One mother ship has been preassembled

in Earth orbit by crews from the space station. Twenty-eight Shuttle launches, six Ariane VII launches and five USSR G1 launches were necessary to lift all of the components to the proper orbit.

The expanded mission outline is as follows:

Phase 1: *Launch to Earth Orbit*
You will be transported from the Kennedy Space Center at Cape Canaveral, Florida, to the space station.

Phase 2: *Earth Orbit Check-out (EOC)*
You will have two weeks to complete activation of the main ship and check all systems and components.

Phase 3: *Trans-Mars Injection (TMI) and Coast*
Once check-out is complete, the ship's main engines will push you out of Earth orbit. This maneuver is called Trans-Mars injection (TMI). With the exception of a short engine burn for midcourse correction (the adjustments of your trajectory), this is the last firing of the main engines until you achieve orbit at Mars. The Mars coast phase will last 350 days. During this outbound period, a heavy schedule of training will be maintained. One hundred sixty-one days out the ship will swing by Venus. This trajectory is more efficient and will give the crew a dry run for the Mars approach. It will also provide new information about this sister planet. (This part of the mission will be covered in Section 3.)

Phase 4: *Mars Orbit Injection (MOI)*
As you approach Mars, a series of precise maneuvers and important activities is required. To orbit Mars, you must reduce velocity by reversing the ship and firing the engines in the direction of flight. This procedure slows the ship and permits capture by Mars's gravitational field. Failure of the engines at this point would send the ship beyond Mars on a path from which rescue would be difficult, or impossible.

Phase 5: *Mars Orbit and Surface Activities (MOSA)*

Once orbit is established, the most intense period of activity begins. Operations are divided into two parts: orbit activities and surface activities. The mother ship now becomes a space station, while the lander, the Mars Excursion Module (MEM), takes the surface exploration team to the planet below. The stay at Mars will be only 30 days, and the surface party will have only 24 days to complete their mission.

Phase 6: *Trans-Earth Injection (TEI) and Coast (TEC)*
The next critical engine burn will propel the ship out of orbit and position it on a trajectory for Earth. During this return leg, considerable time will be spent analyzing the results of the exploration. The total return coast time will be 260 days.

Phases 7 and 8: *Earth Orbit Injection (EOI) and Decontamination/Debriefing (D/D)*
Returning to Earth orbit requires a final critical engine burn. The parking orbit will parallel a special decontamination station where final reporting and debriefing will take place. At this point, the Mars One crew will have been away from Earth for over one and three-quarter years. This short readjustment period will be important preparation for the crew's physical and emotional adaptation to life back on Earth.

In addition, care must be taken that the crew can safely come in contact with other humans. Isolation produces potential immunity problems, and we are still not completely certain there are no life forms on the martian surface capable of causing problems on Earth. (For further information, see Section 5.)

Phases 9 and 10: *Deorbit and Reconditioning*
Deorbit by return shuttle and final reconditioning are the final phases of the voyage. You will have been living without benefit of gravity for two years. The parades and receptions will have to wait until you get your "land legs."

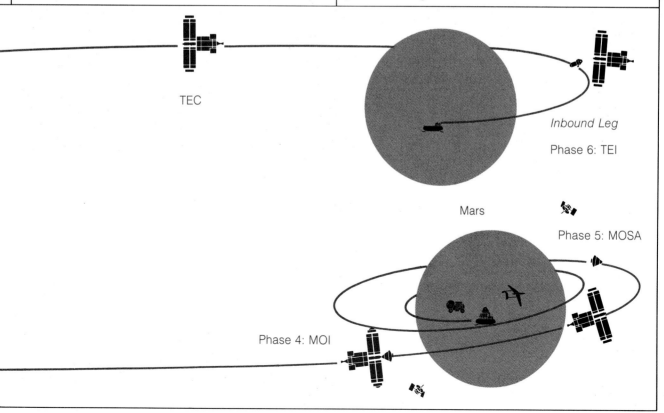

TEC

Inbound Leg

Phase 6: TEI

Mars

Phase 5: MOSA

Phase 4: MOI

In 1987 an international conference was held in Boulder, Colorado. The conference drew representatives from twenty-one nations, including the European Space Agency (ESA) countries, five Warsaw Pact countries, India, and Japan. A consensus emerged from the meeting that a manned Mars mission was of such potential value to astronautical and space science that it should be pursued at ministerial levels. For a variety of political and economic reasons, the USSR and ESA quickly agreed to lay the groundwork for a multinational venture. In 1988, the issue surfaced in the American presidential campaign as part of the US effort to maintain its leadership in space. The United States voted support for the manned Mars mission (M3) when ESA agreed to supply modules for the US space station on a near-cost basis, reducing the US expense by several billion dollars, and ensuring the European module as the prime design element in the Mars expedition vehicle.

Eager to take part, Japan offered to supply customized electronic components and to share the high-speed computer technology necessary for mission support. The US was given overall mission coordination and the USSR was given scientific coordination.

In 1991, the first components of the US space station were launched, and hardware preparation began in earnest. Major design and construction work was assigned as follows:

TMI Stage: USSR
Propulsion: US, Japan, India

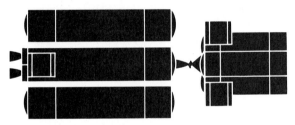

Mars Excursion Module: US

Mars Rover: USSR

Satellites and robotics: ESA, Japan

Mars One Overall Structure: US
Mars One Main Modules: ESA
Mars One Science Module: USSR

EVA Suits (Space): USA, USSR
EVA Suits (Surface): USA

Also in 1991, an overall authority for the mission, the United Nations Mars Exploration Authority (UNMEA), was established by the United Nations and a draft treaty, the Mars Mission Cooperation Treaty, was signed by 117 member nations. The UN set up an information agency and scientific advisory committee to disseminate results.

A problem developed when forty-three nonaligned nations introduced a resolution that each major continent and racial group should be represented in the crew. This was resolved when agreement was reached that members of various races could be represented by crew personnel who did not come from the home continent (for example, an Afro-American could represent Africa). Thus, the US was given an extra slot. The US, ESA, and the USSR were to have had three slots each, Japan one, and a possible international selection was reserved for the final slot. The US also agreed to share one of its slots with Canada.

Launches of components for Mars One, as it was then called, began in 1993 with a target assembly completion date of November 1995. The launch window was for early 1996.

The international nature of the mission required considerable planning to include each major ethnic group. The Mars Mission Cooperation Treaty prescribed representation by crew members from every continent. Three major signatories, the US, the ESA, and the USSR, were to select nine of the eleven crew members. (The US received one extra slot to permit racial representation.) Their selection had to include people of direct descent from Africa, Latin America, and Asia. The following list provides a breakdown of the final representation:

Mars One National/Ethnic Composition

1. US: Caucasian
2. US: Latin American
3. US: Afro-American
4. US: Canadian (Caucasian)
5. ESA: British
6. ESA: West German
7. ESA: French
8. USSR: Eurasian
9. USSR: Slavic
10. Japanese
11. Indian

Four crew members are female, seven are male.

Mission Command Structure:

Mission Commander: US
Mission Pilot: France
Mission Science Officer: USSR
Mission Science Specialist #1: India
Mission Science Specialist #2: Great Britain
Mission Science Specialist #3: West Germany
Mission Science Specialist #4: US
Lander Commander: USSR
Lander Pilot: US
Lander Science Officer: Japan
Lander Science Specialist: US

Mission Command Structure

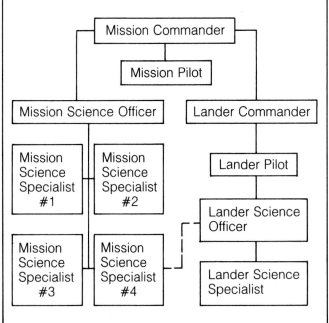

Education (Total Degrees)

8 *Ph.D.'s/M.D.'s*
3 Physics
2 Geology (planetary)
2 M.D.
1 Astronautics

8 *Master's degrees*
2 Aeronautical engineering
2 Electrical engineering
1 Mechanical engineering
3 Geology

11 *Bachelor's degrees*
3 Physics
2 Biology (pre-med)
3 Engineering
1 Psychology
1 History
1 Mathematics

Crew Hobbies and Interests

6 Music (playing)
11 Music (listening)
11 Sports (5 soccer; 4 basketball; 8 jogging; 4 tennis; 4 swimming; 2 mountaineering; 4 scuba; 5 skiing; 3 ping-pong; 2 judo)
4 Writing (poetry)
6 Electronics
3 Painting
9 Photography (2 cinematography/video; 8 still)
2 Crafts
8 Collecting (4 stamps; 2 coins; 5 rare books/art)
6 Modeling (4 rockets; 3 railroads)
4 Gardening
5 Computer programming
2 Antique refinishing
4 Auto racing
11 Travel
10 Flying (10 private pilots; 6 jets; 5 soaring; 10 instrument; 7 multi-engines)

Crew Ages (as of January 1, 1996)

Average age: 39.5
Youngest: 26
Oldest: 51

Religions

3 Roman Catholic
3 Protestant
1 Jewish

1 Hindu
1 Buddhist
1 Muslim

Other Facts

6 Former Boy/Girl Scouts/Young Pioneers
3 Only children
8 First-born children (includes only children)
6 Born in large cities
5 Born in small cities/towns

The Mars One is comprised of two spacecraft: the Main Ship (MS) and the Aerocapture Vehicle containing the Mars Rover (MR).

The main ship is the primary vessel for the voyage. It consists of two propulsion sections, four pressurized modules, two pallets for deployable payloads, various storage tanks, and the Mars Excursion Module (MEM).

The two propulsion sections are the major bulk of the main ship. The larger is the Trans-Mars Injection (TMI) stage which comprises almost 60 percent of the total departure mass. This stage has the job of boosting the entire assemblage out of Earth orbit. It then separates and goes into orbit around the Sun. This means that the engine on the second stage will have less mass to push against and, therefore, will require less fuel for its maneuvers. Like the first stage, this second stage engine uses the Space Shuttle Uprated Engine (SSUE). This engine is 20 percent more powerful than the original Space Shuttle Main Engine (SSME). The second stage engine is a critical component since it must fire three times: first, to slow the main ship into Mars orbit; second, to leave Mars's gravitational field for the trip back to Earth; and, finally, to slow the main ship back into Earth orbit.

Main Ship Side View

TMI Stage

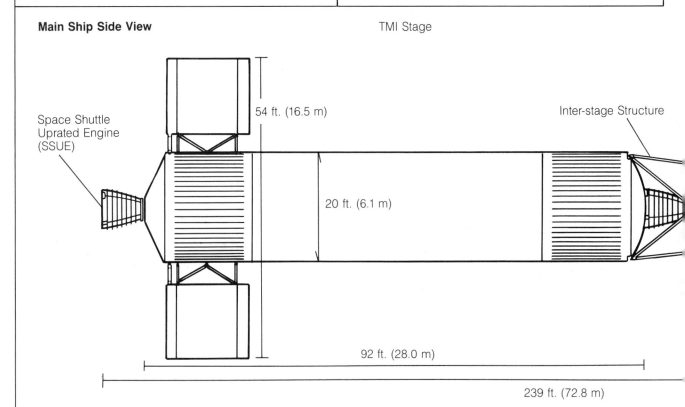

Space Shuttle
Uprated Engine
(SSUE)

Inter-stage Structure

54 ft. (16.5 m)

20 ft. (6.1 m)

92 ft. (28.0 m)

239 ft. (72.8 m)

Propulsion Stage Fuel Tank Assembly Side and Rear Views

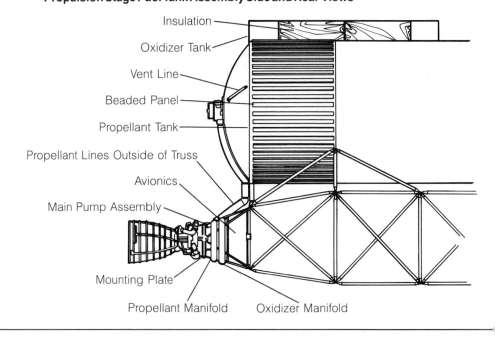

Insulation

Oxidizer Tank

Vent Line

Beaded Panel

Propellant Tank

Propellant Lines Outside of Truss

Avionics

Main Pump Assembly

Mounting Plate

Propellant Manifold

Oxidizer Manifold

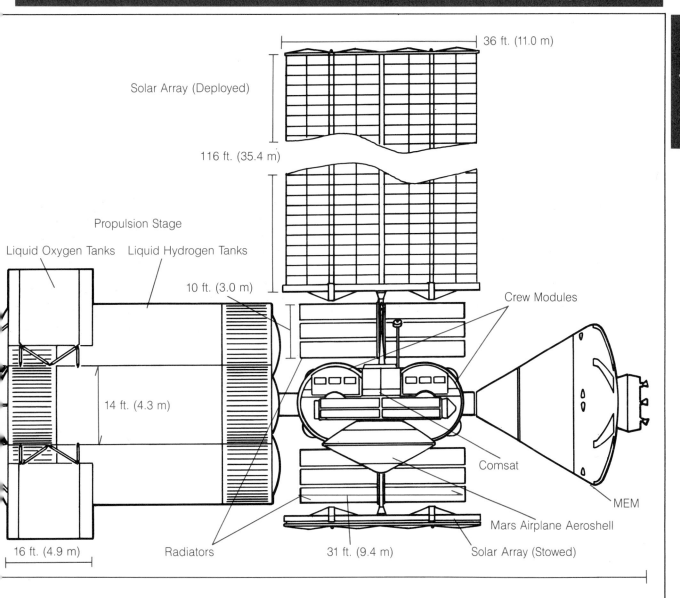

Solar Array (Deployed)

36 ft. (11.0 m)

116 ft. (35.4 m)

Propulsion Stage

Liquid Oxygen Tanks   Liquid Hydrogen Tanks

10 ft. (3.0 m)

Crew Modules

14 ft. (4.3 m)

Comsat

MEM

16 ft. (4.9 m)

Radiators

31 ft. (9.4 m)

Mars Airplane Aeroshell

Solar Array (Stowed)

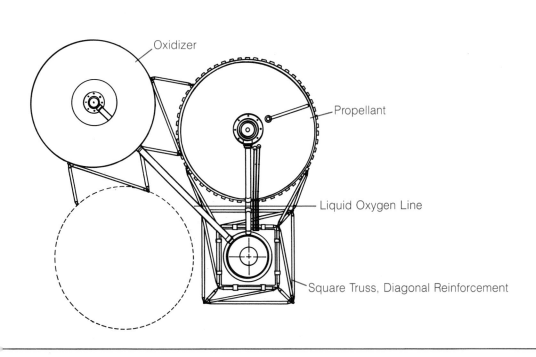

Oxidizer

Propellant

Liquid Oxygen Line

Square Truss, Diagonal Reinforcement

These engines are powered by liquid hydrogen and liquid oxygen. The aluminum tanks containing this fuel are arranged forward of the engines on each stage. The three largest tanks were lofted by the USSR G1 vehicles. The smaller tanks, organized in clusters to simplify the plumbing necessary to feed fuel to the turbopumps, have been ferried in the Shuttle cargo bay.

There are also two Habitability (HAB) modules, a Laboratory (LAB) module, and a Storage module. Each module is 50 feet (15.2 meters) in length and 14 feet (4.3 meters) in diameter. Each module weighs 80,000 pounds (32,300 kilograms) fully loaded. This varies slightly from module to module.

Each of the modules is connected to a docking assembly, which connects them to a central tunnel. The docking assembly has six hatches; four connect to the tunnels, one connects to the Mars Excursion Module (MEM), and one is an extravehicular activity (EVA) port that allows the crew to go outside the craft for any necessary repairs.

Main Ship Top View

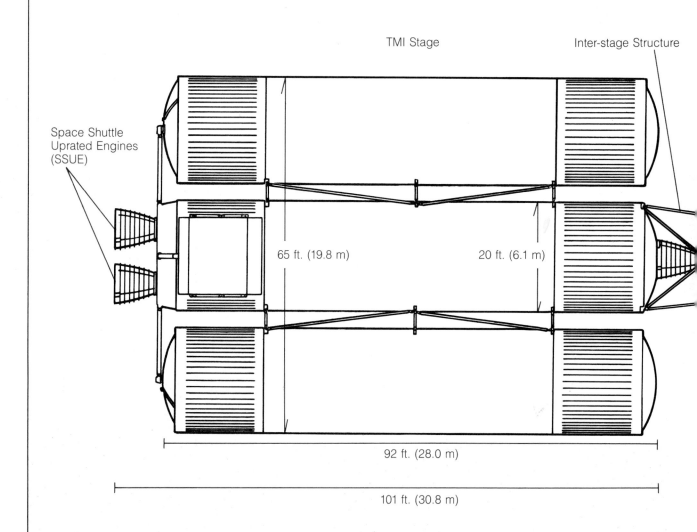

TMI Stage

Inter-stage Structure

Space Shuttle
Uprated Engines
(SSUE)

65 ft. (19.8 m)

20 ft. (6.1 m)

92 ft. (28.0 m)

101 ft. (30.8 m)

239 ft. (72.8 m)

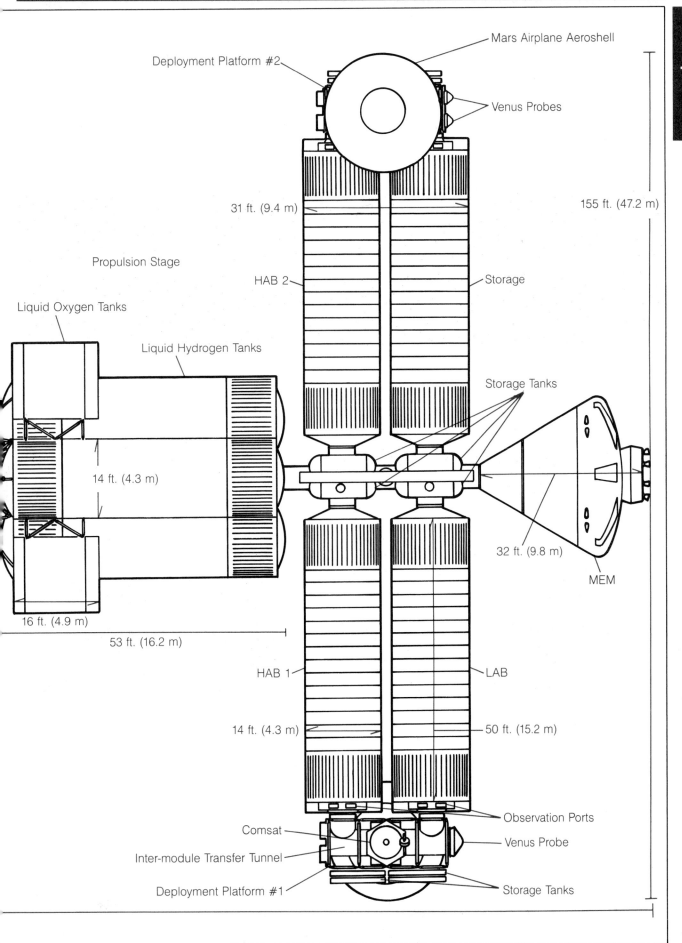

Mars Airplane Aeroshell

Deployment Platform #2

Venus Probes

31 ft. (9.4 m)

155 ft. (47.2 m)

Propulsion Stage

HAB 2

Storage

Liquid Oxygen Tanks

Liquid Hydrogen Tanks

Storage Tanks

14 ft. (4.3 m)

32 ft. (9.8 m)

MEM

16 ft. (4.9 m)

53 ft. (16.2 m)

HAB 1

LAB

14 ft. (4.3 m)

50 ft. (15.2 m)

Observation Ports

Comsat

Venus Probe

Inter-module Transfer Tunnel

Deployment Platform #1

Storage Tanks

Outboard of this assemblage of tunnels and modules are mounted two deployment platforms. Each platform contains one Mars Airplane, a comsat, an assortment of Venus atmospheric probes, and Mars hardlanders and surface penetrators. The MEM protrudes from the front of the MS with its thermal shield pointed forward. The MEM, as well as the modules and tanks, has a thin micrometeoroid shield to protect the MS from these salt-sized particles found throughout the solar system. Although they present no major threat to the ship, these particles can cause pitting and some erosion over a period of time.

The aerocapture vehicle consists of an aerobraking shell and a boost stage to escape from Earth orbit. This vehicle carries the Mars Rover (MR) and requires only enough fuel for TMI, relying on its shape and the frictional drag of the martian atmosphere to slow it into Mars orbit.

Aerocapture Vehicle Side View

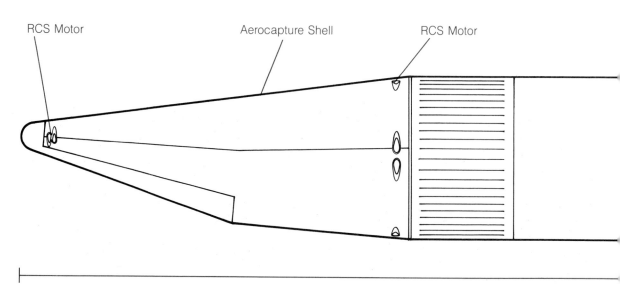

RCS Motor   Aerocapture Shell   RCS Motor

115 ft. (35.1 m)

Deployment Platform

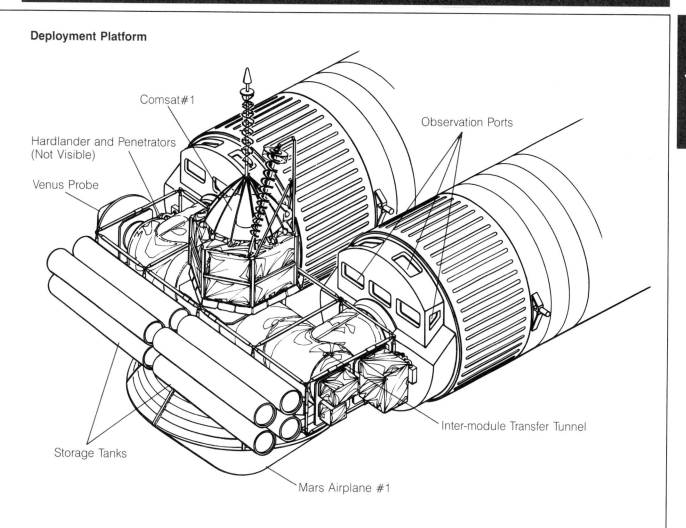

Comsat#1

Hardlander and Penetrators
(Not Visible)

Venus Probe

Observation Ports

Inter-module Transfer Tunnel

Storage Tanks

Mars Airplane #1

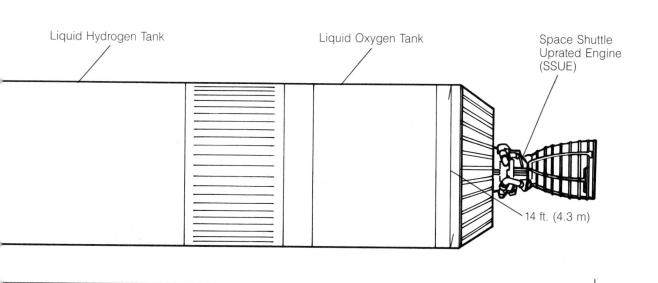

Liquid Hydrogen Tank

Liquid Oxygen Tank

Space Shuttle
Uprated Engine
(SSUE)

14 ft. (4.3 m)

Control Center

The top portion of each HAB module is the Control Center. Each HAB module control center is identical, and each can perform all functions necessary for the operation of the main ship. The main computers are located in the control center, allowing the center to be a communications control room and a classroom for training and simulation. An airlock hatch connects the center to tunnels leading to other modules.

The control center is divided into three work-station areas. The command station is for the mission commander and pilot (or for the lander commander and pilot). The science station is for the chief science officer. The experiment stations are for the science specialists. Each station has computer input and output capability, a Reaction Control System (RCS) control panel, an environmental control system panel, and communications and navigation instrumentation.

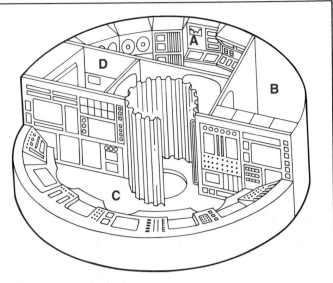

A Science Station **B** Suit Storage **C** Command Station
D Experimental Station

Health and Hygiene Deck

The Health and Hygiene (H & H) deck consists of the Health Maintenance Facility (HMF), the shower, the lavatory, and the waste management (toilet) compartments.

The health maintenance facility is a combination infirmary, exercise area, and health diagnostic center. It contains an array of exercise and medical equipment (see Section 2). It can also be used for in-flight emergencies. The shower, lavatory, and waste management compartments are also described in Section 2.

The HMF takes up about half the deck area, with the other half divided roughly in thirds for the other functions. The deck is 7 feet (2.1 meters) high and has three communications stations and extra ducting to remove unwanted odor and humidity.

A Exercise **B** Diagnostic **C** Infirmary **D** Shower
E Lavatory **F** Waste Management

Wardroom

The wardroom in each HAB module is a communal room for meals, meetings, entertainment, and some class activities. The galley area is for food preparation and storage. Video monitors and a portable computer port allow the area to be used for training, group telecommunications, and showing videodisc movies and other programs. Should an emergency arise, the crew from the other HAB module can use the wardroom as sleeping quarters.

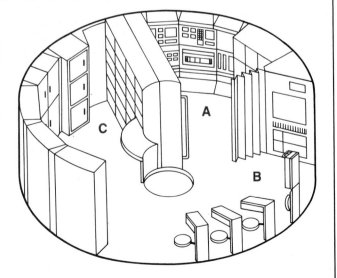

A Group Activities **B** Recreation **C** Galley

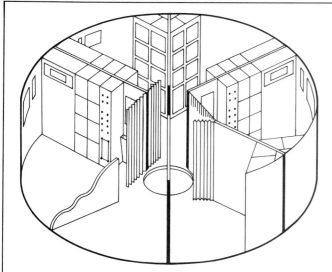

Personal/Sleep Compartment

Each of the two HAB modules has color-coded sleep compartments. Yours will be assigned at the beginning of the mission. Each compartment is wedge-shaped, measuring 7 feet (2.1 meters) along the main wall, 5 and 5½ feet (1.5 and 1.6 meters) along the side walls, and 2 feet along the sliding door. There is a 3-cubic-foot (.09-cubic-meter) storage cabinet on one side and a small 1.5-cubic-foot (.045-cubic-meter) cabinet near the door. The sleep restraint is on the same wall as the small cabinet. A heavy Velcro-secured curtain provides privacy. The 8-foot (2.4 meter) ceiling makes the room a bit more spacious, and the back wall has a tack board for pictures, charts, or other personal items. There is a communications substation in each compartment with a headset, an alarm, and a small digital readout with emergency codes.

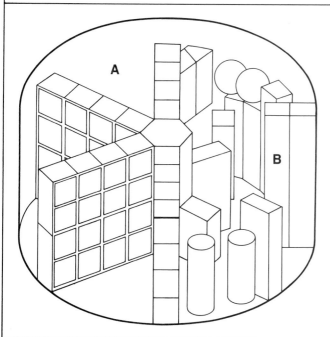

Storage/Life Support

Below the sleep center is a combination storage/life-support area. The life-support area contains your air-handling equipment, your electrical distribution center, your water-treatment equipment, and your solid waste pretreatment equipment. The chamber has soundproofing and the machinery is specially mounted to reduce noise and vibration.

Four banks of storage cabinets are also included. They contain emergency rations as well as normal food stores, hygiene supplies, and personal effects. The storage areas are spaced similarly to the storage module. One bank of cabinets opens to the life-support area. This group of lockers contains spare parts, maintenance information, and tool kits.

An observation area which permits visual inspection of the deployment palette is located near the hatch area at the end of the compartment.

A Storage **B** Life Support

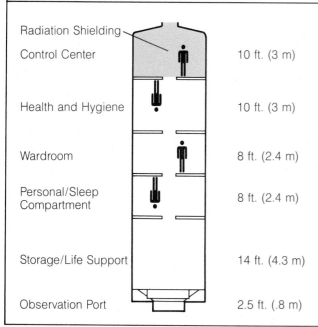

Radiation Shielding	
Control Center	10 ft. (3 m)
Health and Hygiene	10 ft. (3 m)
Wardroom	8 ft. (2.4 m)
Personal/Sleep Compartment	8 ft. (2.4 m)
Storage/Life Support	14 ft. (4.3 m)
Observation Port	2.5 ft. (.8 m)

Radiation Protection

In space, you are outside the Earth's protective magnetic field and atmosphere. The radiation levels from solar protons and electrons and cosmic rays could be extremely hazardous. While this mission will expose you to radiation, two things will minimize your exposure. First, the Sun will be in what is called a "quiet period." This means it will be less active and have fewer harmful flares. Second, each HAB module control center is specially shielded against solar flares. Along with lead shielding around this section, a coil system creates a low-level magnetic field, which stops many of the most harmful particles.

Dosages of radiation are measured in REMs. Current safety limits allow 300-REM exposure over an entire adult life. Normal exposure on this trip should be less than 70 REM; the shielding is therefore essential to stop the penetration of dangerous solar flares, which can be measured up to 100 REM. With the shielding, however, it is hoped that you will have a total radiation exposure of less than 150 REM, well within safety limits.

Laboratory Module

Unlike the HAB modules, the Laboratory (LAB) module is laid out along the long axis. Similar to early space station modules in configuration, the LAB module has larger work areas than the HAB modules.

At the entrance to the module is the same airlock found in the other modules, with spacesuit storage nearby. This storage area contains LAB and other supplies and is separated from the large LAB section by an airtight door. The LAB itself looks like a traditional room. Instrument racks line the walls in this 10-foot (3 meters) by 25-foot (7.6 meters) room. The nine-foot (2.7 meters) ceiling and extra floor space allow storage of life-support equipment. At the far end of the LAB module are two separate compartments, a storage area and an isolation area, which can serve as a small laboratory if necessary.

The LAB module can also be reconfigured for habitation in an emergency situation.

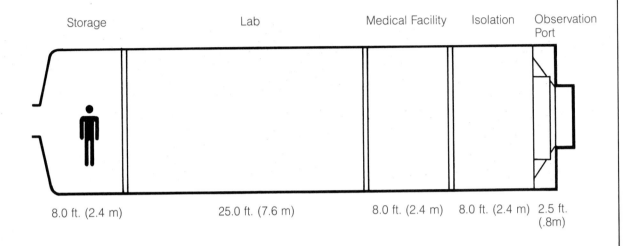

| Storage | Lab | Medical Facility | Isolation | Observation Port |

8.0 ft. (2.4 m) 25.0 ft. (7.6 m) 8.0 ft. (2.4 m) 8.0 ft. (2.4 m) 2.5 ft. (.8m)

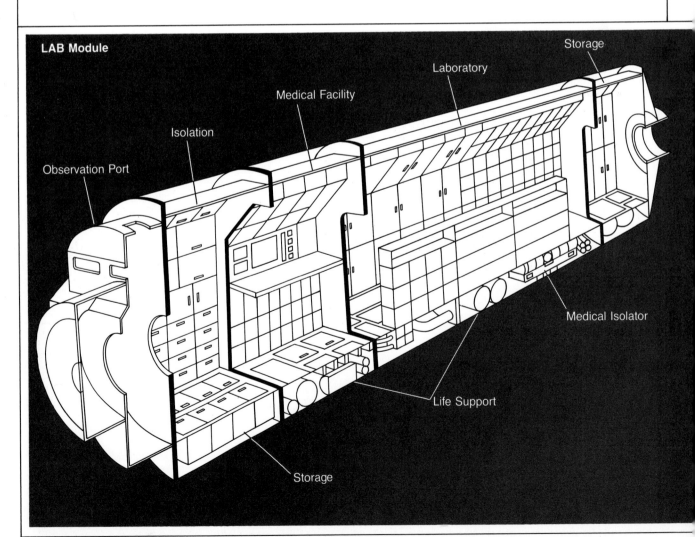

LAB Module

Storage
Laboratory
Medical Facility
Isolation
Observation Port
Medical Isolator
Life Support
Storage

LAB Module during construction.

LAB Module Trainer.

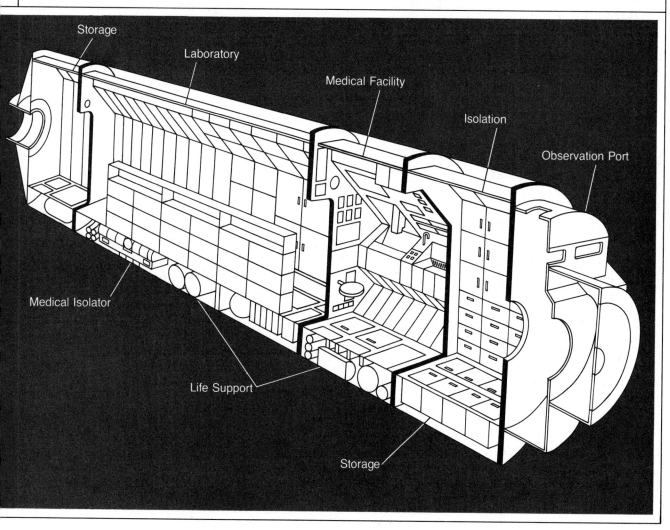

Storage

Laboratory

Medical Facility

Isolation

Observation Port

Medical Isolator

Life Support

Storage

The storage module has the same extension dimensions as the other three modules, but a very different interior design. The module has lines of storage cabinets running down its long axis. There are two widths of cabinet: single width, which is 1 foot (.3 meter) wide with square top and bottom 3 feet by 3 feet (.91 meter by .91 meter), and double width, which is 2 feet wide (.61 meter) and the same length and height.

These cabinets radiate from the center of the module permitting access through the pie-shaped passageways. The core of the module is packed with canisters that can be sequentially unloaded. There is a 3-foot space between the hatchway and the start of the radiating cabinets. Twelve crawlways take up almost half of the module, and six crawlways are available in the remaining half (among the double-wide storage spaces).

The aerocapture ship has six months' worth of emergency supplies, should it be needed. The supplies can be loaded into the empty single-width cabinets in 1-cubic-foot (.028-cubic-meter) boxes.

In emergencies, the storage module can serve as a habitat, but it has few amenities. There are six communications stations and a trash airlock. A connect port for electricity and water would have to be installed using existing hookups to other modules; this installation would require an emergency extravehicular activity (EVA).

Additional outbound supplies are stored in the airlock and crew quarters' section of the Mars Excursion Module, in storage containers throughout the HAB modules, and in a large storage volume in the floors, ceilings, and end cap of the LAB module. Gases are stored in external tanks.

Computerized inventories direct the retrieval robots or the crew to specific cabinets and modules at scheduled times. You may sometimes exceed expected use of certain items. The computer can keep track of these trends and change the schedule accordingly. To reschedule, just select "Inventory" in Main Mission Computer (MMC) software series 900.

Utility Tanks and Connections

A series of pipes and tanks is connected to the outside of the mission modules. The tanks are of a standard size: 12 feet (3.6 meters) long by 5 feet (1.5 meters) in diameter. They contain water, fuel, and waste as generated. There are six tanks attached to the HAB modules and two tanks attached to the LAB and storage modules.

The pipes and tubing system to transfer liquids and slurries between tanks are all controlled by the MMC. Should a pressure sensor or a valve fail, EVA would be necessary to correct the difficulty. Many of the valves and actuators can be either controlled or replaced by hand. The MMC is designed as an "expert" maintenance system and will provide detailed training and reference for such repairs.

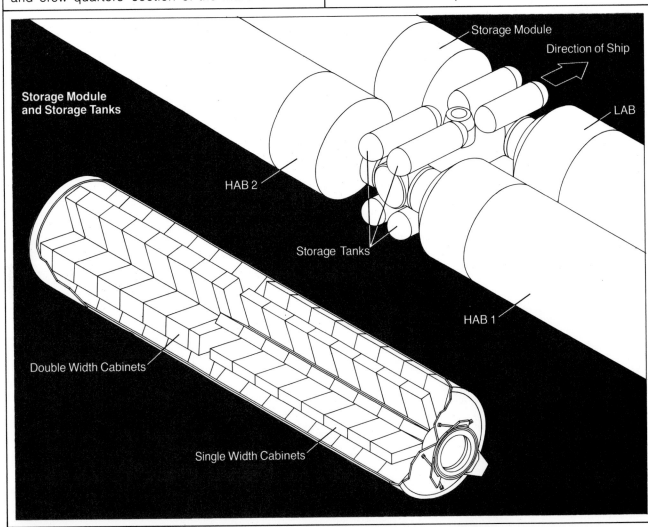

Storage Module
Direction of Ship
LAB

Storage Module and Storage Tanks

HAB 2

Storage Tanks

HAB 1

Double Width Cabinets

Single Width Cabinets

To descend to the surface, the Mars Excursion Module (MEM) is required. Like the Lunar Module of the Apollo program, or the Viking landers, the craft must land softly on the surface of the planet and then provide, like Apollo, life support and ascent from the surface back to an orbital rendezvous.

The MEM has both a descent and an ascent stage. Its overall shape is the familiar gumdrop of the old Apollo spacecraft. This insures a stable entry into the martian atmosphere. Like the Apollo Command Module, the MEM has a lightweight heat shield that protects it from atmospheric heating. The descent engines have a thrust level of 140,000 pounds (635,600 newtons) and are fueled by liquid oxygen and methane. The MEM measures 30 feet (9.1 meters) across the base and 22.9 feet (7 meters) high.

As you leave Mars orbit, the craft has a gross weight of 109,000 pounds (49,400 kilograms), of which 7,400 pounds (3,360 kilograms) is the five solid-fueled deorbit motors, which are jettisoned after the deorbit burn. The MEM carries 30,500 pounds (13,800 kilograms) of propellant for the descent. Your total change in velocity is 4,350 feet (1,325 meters) per second.

During the descent you will be seated on couches in the flight station, two on top, and two below. In the final stages, the two lower crew members stand and land the craft using instrument panels mounted near two side windows. These windows provide visual horizon reference during the final descent phase. Located below the flight station and connected by a tunnel is a 460-cubic-foot (13-cubic-meter) crew compartment shaped like a bite of a doughnut. The crew compartment is 108 inches (2.7 meters) high. The airlock, a small cylindrical chamber off the crew quarters, is your entry and exit port from the module to the surface.

The crew compartment contains life-support equip-

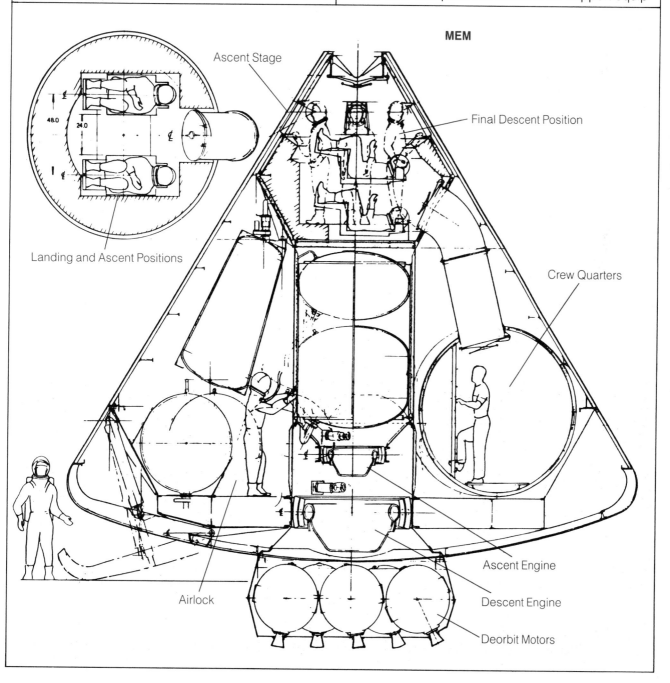

MEM

Ascent Stage

Final Descent Position

48.0   24.0

Landing and Ascent Positions

Crew Quarters

Airlock

Ascent Engine

Descent Engine

Deorbit Motors

ment, a small galley, a small science lab, hammocks for sleeping, and storage room for spacesuits. It is powered by a 2-kilowatt fuel cell, which also produces drinking water as a by-product. The total payload is 4,200 pounds (1,900 kilograms).

The ascent module is nested inside the descent stage. The ascent is accomplished in two stages, each with its own set of tanks and propellant. The total stage weighs 37,200 pounds (16,845 kilograms), with the ac-

tual ascent capsule weighing only 5,260 pounds (2,380 kilograms). Both stages have a total propellant weight of 45,450 pounds (20,585 kilograms), which will produce a velocity change of 20,350 feet per second (6.2 kilometers/second). The ascent engine produces 35,000 pounds (158,900 newtons) of thrust. The ascent capsule is the same compartment in which you made your descent. The docking port at the top of the compartment will be used to reconnect with the main ship.

MEM Tanks and Reaction Control System

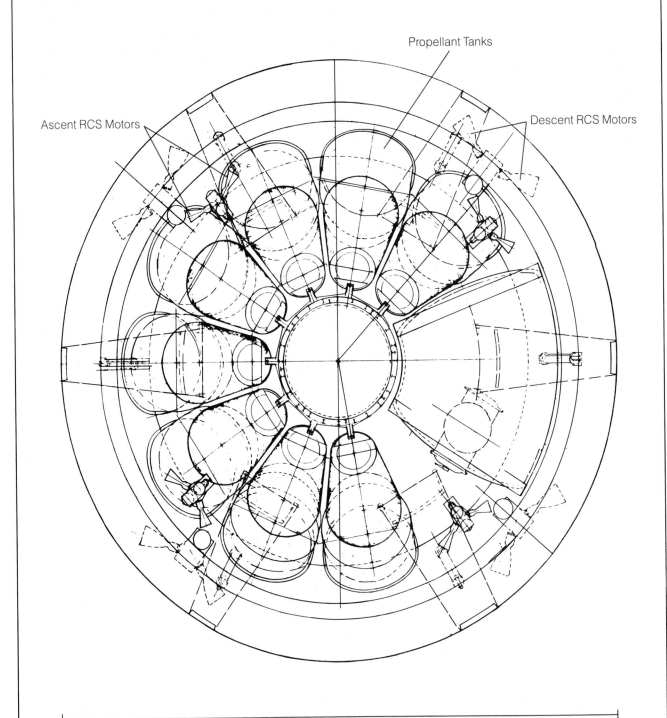

Propellant Tanks

Ascent RCS Motors

Descent RCS Motors

30 ft. Base Diameter

Mars One equipment, including more than 3 million pounds (1.4 million kilograms) of modules, support structures, and fuel, is launched into space using three different vehicles. Most of the payload is delivered to orbit by the Space Shuttle cargo configuration (STS-C or Space Transportation System-Cargo), capable of carrying 82,450 pounds (37,400 kilograms) of payload per launch. This is 17,450 pounds (7,900 kilograms) more than the standard Shuttle configuration and is made possible by using space shuttle uprated engines, which are rated at 450,000 pounds (2,002,500 newtons) of thrust. Special Solid Rocket Boosters (SRB-X) are also used. These generate just over 3 million pounds (13.3 million newtons) of thrust each. The mission has required 28 shuttle launches to place the main modules, the support structure, the fuel tanks and engines, the supplies, and some of the fuel in Earth orbit.

The Soviet Union has contributed five launches of its huge G1 vehicle, which is capable of putting almost 400,000 pounds (181,440 kilograms) into orbit. The G1 is fitted with a large upper-stage fuel tank and has launched 1.2 million pounds (544,000 kilograms) of fuel into orbit in three flights. The fourth flight launched the MEM, while the fifth flight launched the liquid hydrogen load and the Rover.

The Ariane VII vehicles of the ESA have made six launches, delivering the two Mars Airplanes, the three Venus atmospheric probes, the hardlanders and penetrators, and the two comsats. These are mounted on the deployment platforms of the main ship.

Shuttle

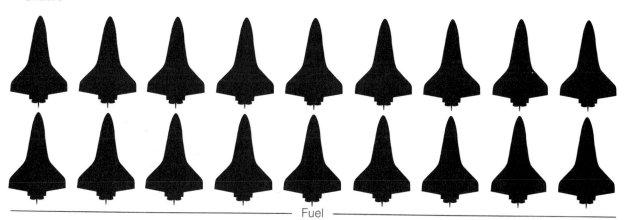

Fuel

Aerocapture Fuel

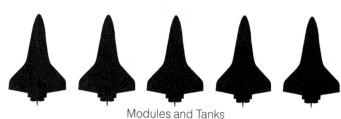

Modules and Tanks

Science Equipment

Ariane

USSR G1

Airplanes, Comsats, Hardlanders, Penetrators and Probes

Fuel and Tankage

Rover Fuel and Tankage

MEM and Fuel

1.6.1

Earth Date	Julian Date	Sol	Mission Phase	Event
Jul 1, 1995	244-9900		0	Report to primary training facility
Same				Ground crew training phase
Feb 18, 1996	245-0132			Report to Kennedy Space Center, Cape Canaveral, Florida
Feb 22, 1996	245-0136		1	STS launch
Same				STS orbital insertion
Same				STS orbital transfer
Feb 22, 1996	245-0136		2*	Arrive at station
Feb 23, 1996	245-0137			Board Mars One—Begin check-out
Mar 2, 1996	245-0145			Final delivery of volatile propellants
Mar 5, 1996	245-0148			Begin TMI burn check
Mar 7, 1996	245-0150		3	TMI
Mar 14, 1996	245-0157			First midcourse correction
Apr 6, 1996	245-0180			Second midcourse correction (if necessary)
May 6, 1996	245-0210.5			Aerocapture vehicle leaves Earth orbit
July 26, 1996	245-0291			Deploy Venus probes
Aug 15, 1996	245-0311.4			Venus swing-by (closest approach)
Aug 18, 1996	245-0314			Begin orbital experiment calibration checks
Aug 18, 1996	245-0314			Begin lander experiment check
Sep 1, 1996	245-0328			Lander battery system check

Earth Date	Julian Date	Sol	Mission Phase	Event
Jan 11, 1997	245-0460			Rover arrival and deorbit
Jan 16, 1997	245-0464			Third course correction (if necessary)
Jan 25, 1997	245-0473			MEM recharge
Feb 14, 1997	245-0494			Separation of hardlanders and penetrators
Feb 18, 1997	245-0498			MOI burn preparation
Feb 20, 1997	245-0500	0	4	MOI
Feb 21, 1997	245-0501	1	5	MOSA begins
Feb 22, 1997	245-0502	2		Deploy comsats
Feb 22, 1997	245-0502	2		Final site analysis
Feb 22, 1997	245-0502	2		Lander final check-out
Feb 24, 1997	245-0504	3		Separation
Same				Entry 800,000 feet altitude
Same				Blackout
Same				Parachute deployed
Same				Descent engine ignition
Same				Landing leg deployment
Feb 24, 1997	245-0504	4		TOUCHDOWN Surface landing/contingency sample
Feb 25, 1997	245-0505	5		Rover rendezvous
Mar 1, 1997	245-0509	9		Begin long traverse

Earth Date	Julian Date	Sol	Mission Phase	Event
Mar 3, 1997	245-0511	11		Deploy Mars Airplanes
Mar 5, 1997	245-0513	13		MEM MOSA first traverse
Mar 7, 1997	245-0515	15		MEM MOSA second traverse
Mar 14, 1997	245-0522	21		MEM MOSA third traverse
Mar 15, 1997	245-0523	22		Begin Phobos/Deimos imaging
Mar 18, 1997	245-0526	25.5		End long traverse
Mar 20, 1997	245-0528	27		Ascend to rendezvous with MEM
Mar 22, 1997	245-0530	29	6	TEI
Mar 23, 1997	245-0531			Debrief day
Mar 25, 1997	245-0533			Begin data reduction
Mar 26, 1997	245-0534			Begin surface sample analysis
Dec 4, 1997	245-0787			EOI burn preparation
Dec 7, 1997	245-0790		7	EOI
Same				Orbital transfer
Dec 8, 1997	245-0791		8	Quarantine facility arrival
Dec 21, 1997	245-0804			Transfer to Shuttle
Same	245-0804		9	STS deorbit and arrival at Kennedy Space Center
Jan 4, 1998	245-0818		10	Leave reconditioning center
Jan 5, 1998	245-0819			Start public relations lecture schedule at UN with shredded computer paper parade

Your flight phase begins with the launch to orbit. You will be launched from the Kennedy Space Center on Feb. 22, 1996 (245-0136 JD). Your destination is the space station and the Mars One main ship, which has been assembled on orbit 1 mile (1.6 kilometers) away. Three members of your crew have already performed all life-support system checks. One other member of the crew is returning by orbital transfer vehicle from the lunar base, where he was completing training for the Mars surface landing.

Your initial job is to activate and check out all other main ship functions. To accomplish this, you split your time between the space station and the main ship. A small transfer vehicle carries you between the two.

During your launch, you sit in the crew transportation module. This module is in the cargo bay and can carry up to ten passengers. A tunnel connects the module with the airlock inside the flight deck of the Shuttle. With the Shuttle in a vertical position on the launch pad, you enter through the crew hatch and walk along the back wall of the flight deck. Place your feet only on the marked areas. You then climb down into the tubular tunnel using the tunnel ribs as steps. In the module, you and the rest of the crew take your places, filling the last seats first. A ground crew member will close the hatch. In an emergency, the hatch can be opened in about one second, but you may have to climb out extremely quickly if there is an on-the-pad launch abort.

Once you are in your seat, please fasten your safety harness. You have a set of headphones that allows you to hear Launch Control, the Shuttle crew, and later, Mission Control. There is also a video monitor that can show you the launch as seen from a window-mounted camera in the cockpit. The module atmosphere, like that of the Shuttle, is an Earth-normal 14.7 pounds per square inch (psi) (100 kilopascals). Should there be a decompression of any kind, an oxygen mask will come out of a compartment at your side. Place the mask over your nose and mouth and breathe normally. You can adjust the mask for proper fit by pulling the two straps on either side of the mask.

You hear several noises and sense several motions during the launch process. Five minutes before lift-off you hear the auxiliary power units (APUs) start up. Three and one-half seconds before lift-off the main engines ignite. At this point you feel a slight rocking motion, first toward your feet, then toward your head. Then the solid rocket boosters are ignited and you feel a push at your back as the Shuttle moves quickly off the pad.

During the launch you also feel an acceleration approaching three g's and you are pressed back in your seat feeling three times heavier. After two minutes, the solid rocket boosters are expended and separated. Six minutes later, the main engines cut off and you get your first taste of zero-g. Two short burns get the ship into orbit and adjusted for space station rendezvous. Once in orbit, you can release your safety harness and exit through the top of the airlock into the space station.

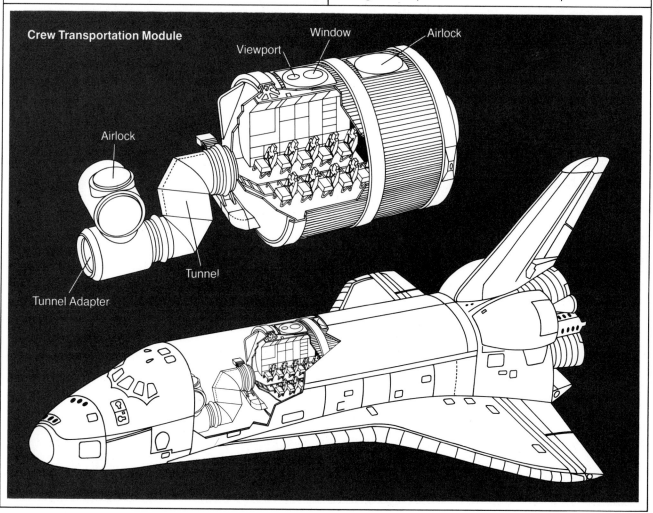

Crew Transportation Module

Viewport • Window • Airlock • Airlock • Tunnel • Tunnel Adapter

While in orbit, you spend some time in the space station. The station is comprised of the same types of modules as the main ship—a satellite-servicing hangar facility, a long extension structure called a tower, and a large solar array which provides the necessary electricity.

The station crew of twelve has been performing orbital check-out of many of the elements on Mars One. The deployable elements—comsats, hardlanders, probes, etc.—were all rechecked and certified in the hangar. Then they were moved to the deployment platforms on the main ship. Using a small transfer vehicle, you now move back and forth between the main ship and the station.

You take your meals and sleep in the station. There are sleep restraints, but there is little privacy. You sleep dormitory-style for several days until the crew moves into the main ship.

The station has an open-ended life-support system. There is a water treatment system, but portable water and air (oxygen and nitrogen) are brought from Earth, while waste water and solid waste are returned to Earth. Food is always brought by shuttle. Crew rotations are typically ninety days, but some of the present crew were specially assigned to Mars One orbital final assembly and have been in orbit for over four months.

Crew operations are very carefully scheduled. Using the Remote Manipulator System (RMS) in the station and the assembly robots telecontrolled from Earth, you assemble the deployment platforms and check out the Mars Rover aerocapture vehicle that will be deployed on Mars. You also perform communications, computer, and telemetry checks between the station and Mars One.

Before leaving the space station, the crew will have a final physical examination. Should anyone fail, another shuttle mission, which will arrive one week after your launch from Earth, can bring a backup crew member.

The Mars One ship is assembled in orbit. The support structures and modules are carefully moved together by assembly crews using Manned Maneuvering Units (MMU). Once the four modules are attached to the cross-shaped transfer tunnel system, the bracings are put in place. Fuel tanks and engines are then mounted in and on the support structure. Finally, the MEM and the deployment platforms are mounted at the forward end and the tanks are fueled from the huge tanks lofted by the G1 boosters.

Most of the equipment and supplies had been launched with the various modules, but a full orbiter-load of supplies now has to be stowed in various storage locations. The most volatile fuels, like liquid hydrogen (LH_2) which had been used during the Earth departure stage, are loaded only a few days before departure. These fuels, even though sealed in containers, leak or "boil off." This means that you need to take as much as 33 percent more of some fuels than you will actually need to compensate for the boil-off.

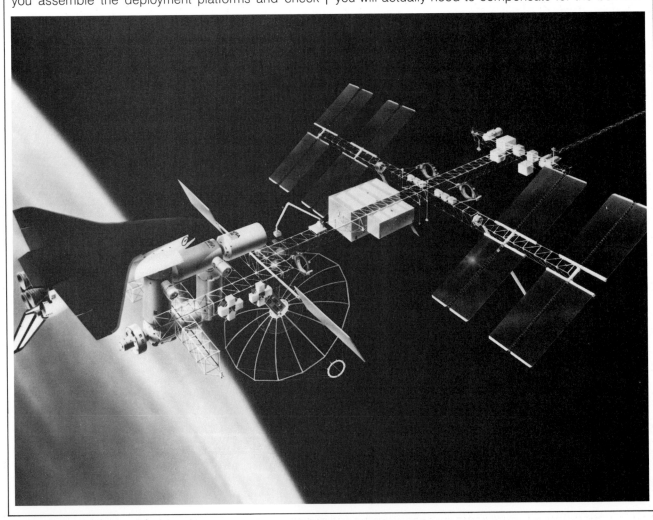

On March 7, 1996 (245-0150 JD), the engines ignite and burn until you have accelerated from 17,500 mph (28,160 kph), your orbital velocity, to 27,900 mph (44,900 kph), your initial interplanetary cruise velocity, and faster than the 25,000 mph (40,200 kph) necessary to escape Earth's gravitational pull. Seven days later, you execute your first midcourse maneuver.

You are settling into your rigorous training schedule, which continues uninterrupted for about 135 days. This schedule consists of special classes, which are loaded into the computers, videodiscs, and onboard hardware. These classes improve your mission and science skills through lessons, simulations, and problem sessions in which you and your team members solve complex mission analysis problems. You also begin your physical conditioning regimen to minimize the deconditioning effects of weightlessness. Thirty days from Venus, your schedule changes to allow the scientific activities at that planet to be carried out.

The training routine then continues in earnest. During the Venus–Mars leg, the preparation, testing, and conditioning of various pieces of equipment, along with many experiments, begin to occupy more of your time.

By thirty days before Mars-arrival, you are operating on an extremely busy work schedule and on sol-length days (one day equals 24.64 Earth hours).

Planetary Positions at TMI

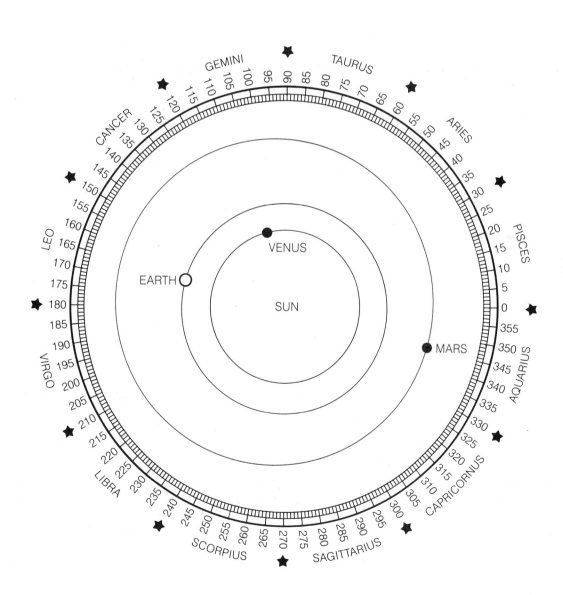

On February 20, 1997 (245-0500 JD) (1 sol), the ship performs a deceleration burn, which establishes orbit around Mars. Three and three-quarter sols later, after a site survey and deployment of the comsats, the MEM is released, deorbits, and lands.

Surface activities last 23.4 sols and include the deployment of the Mars science station, along with a survey of the mesa top in the Candor Chasma (your canyon destination), and a 19.5-sol traverse of the mesa wall and the canyon-floor area.

During the surface activity, one member of the orbital science crew, a mission science specialist, is your primary contact and coordinator. The other science personnel engage in the orbital science activities, which include the deployment and control of two Mars Airplane missions. They also perform surface analysis, studying Mars's two moons, Phobos and Deimos.

The total stay at Mars is a compact 30 days (29.2 sols). This is the busiest and most difficult portion of the mission. Adherence to schedule is essential during this phase. While contingencies always arise, the schedule has been based on experience in lunar survey operations, space station operations, and Apollo lunar exploration activities.

The critical hardware for this phase is the MEM and the Mars Rover (MR). The Rover travels to Mars on a separate vehicle following a faster trajectory and using a specially shaped aerocapture vehicle that takes advantage of the frictional drag of Mars's atmosphere instead of propellant and engines to slow the vehicle into a Mars orbit. The Rover arrives 40 days (39 sols) early, lands on the surface, and is remotely piloted from Earth to the landing zone of the MEM. This early aerobraked arrival provides a very inexpensive way to get the extra weight of the Rover to Mars and a preliminary look at the nature of the landing site, which is valuable for safe MEM operations. The reason so much extra time is needed is that the distance from Mars reduces the effectiveness of the Rover's communication with Earth. It can only move safely perhaps 0.62 miles (1 kilometer) per day. If the landing is over 6.2 miles (10 kilometers) from the expected MEM landing site, it may take over two weeks to get the Rover into place. Then, another week may be needed to evaluate the traverse.

Upon return from the surface, the ascent stage of the MEM, now useless, is deorbited to crash into the martian surface as a calibration explosion for the network of seismometers you have left there to study marsquakes. The transfer operations must be accomplished quickly, because you have only 1 sol left before the main ship engine pushes you out of Mars orbit for your return to Earth.

Planetary Positions at MOSA

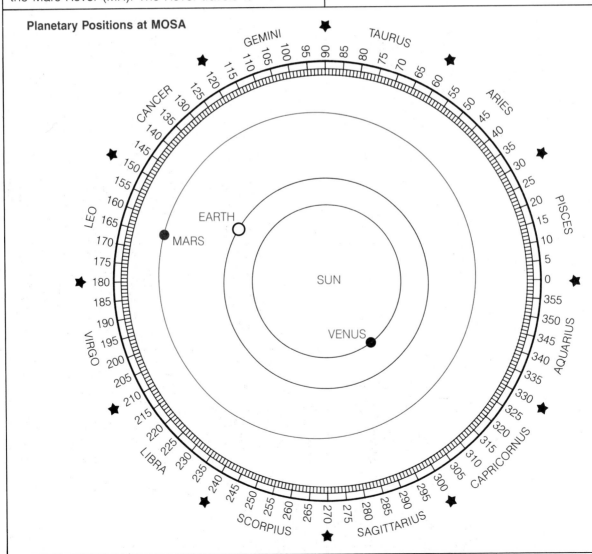

The 260-day return voyage might seem anticlimactic after the intense and exciting period on Mars, but it is a busy and highly important time. You leave Mars orbit on March 22, 1997 (245-0530 JD, 29 sols), and begin the Trans-Earth Coast (TEC).

The first priority is medical checks for the landing crew and safety checks for the samples. You perform a series of tests to be sure the samples are (1) carefully contained in LAB module work areas and (2) not extremely harmful. Should the samples prove highly radioactive, they can be isolated in a shielded compartment in the LAB module.

Should biological or medical problems be detected, the landing crew can be isolated in their HAB module and transferred to the LAB module as necessary. The LAB module has a fairly complete medical facility to handle the most common types of treatment and sim-

ple surgery. Surgery in zero-g can be complicated.

The medical equipment is important even if there are no major health or contamination problems. The crew themselves become laboratory subjects. The length of the voyage, as you remember, has serious physical effects on the human body. Since you are the first crew to be in space for eighteen months, your physiological condition is the subject of great interest and intense study. There are a large number of checks and tests to be made throughout the return leg.

On December 7, 1997 (245-0790 JD), a final burn puts you into a high elliptical Earth orbit. An orbital transfer vehicle then docks, and its engine drops you into a lower circular orbit where you rendezvous with the Quarantine Facility (QF). After the two-week quarantine period and medical evaluation, you return by Shuttle on December 21, 1997 (245-0804 JD).

Planetary Positions at TEC

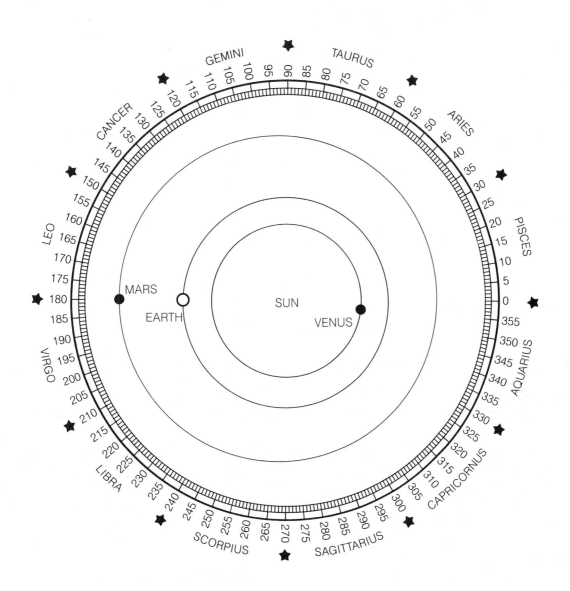

2.0.1

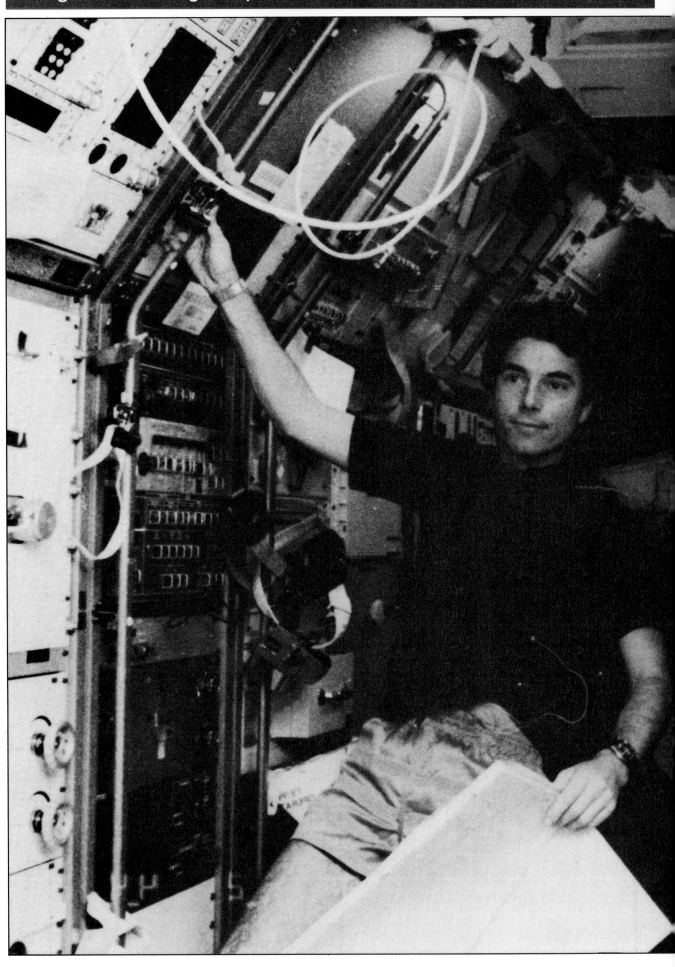

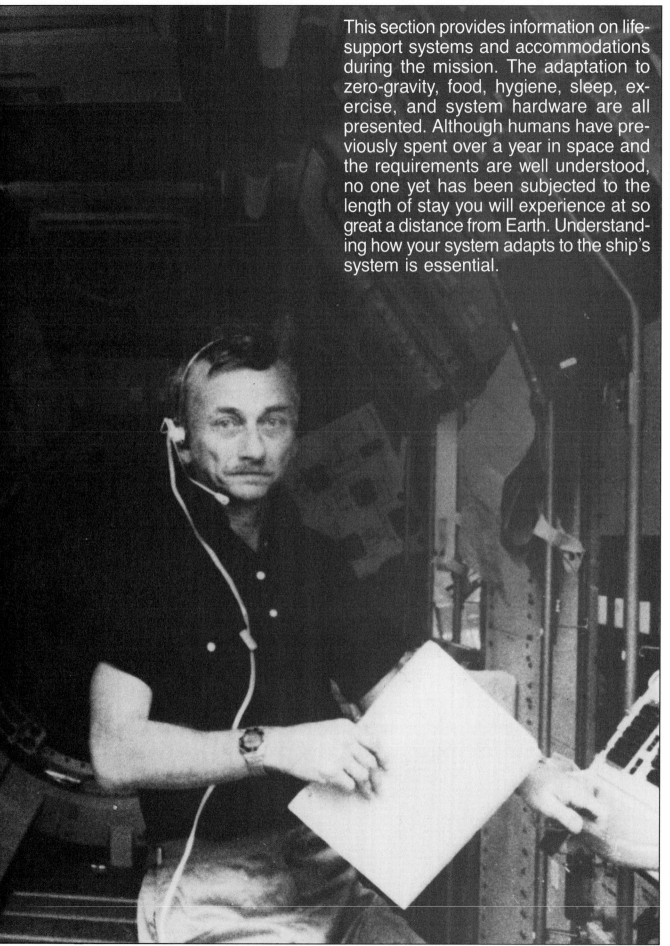

This section provides information on life-support systems and accommodations during the mission. The adaptation to zero-gravity, food, hygiene, sleep, exercise, and system hardware are all presented. Although humans have previously spent over a year in space and the requirements are well understood, no one yet has been subjected to the length of stay you will experience at so great a distance from Earth. Understanding how your system adapts to the ship's system is essential.

2.0.2

The Environmental Control/Life Support System (EC/LSS) keeps the crew alive during the mission. The ship must have the correct pressure, air, water, food, and temperature to sustain life; it must be able to dispose of waste products and contaminants. The complex system for doing all this is outlined in simplifed form in the diagram.

In a closed life-support system, air and water must be reconstituted and recycled while harmful wastes are neutralized and stored.

Waste Products Generated

Source	Description	Basic Rate (lb/man-day)
Crew	Urine solids	0.13
	Fecal	0.38
Food management	Food waste	0.40
	Food packaging	1.18
	Utensils, soap, etc.	0.01
Crew-related	Wipes	0.20
	Hair, nails, skin	0.05
	Toilet tissue	0.014
	Medical supplies	0.02
	Housecleaning supplies	0.02
	Soap, hygiene products	0.033
	Dental	—
	Hair control	—
	Clothing, towels, etc.	0.58

The atmosphere in the HAB modules is an "Earth-normal" 20 percent oxygen and 80 percent nitrogen at a total pressure of 14.7 psi (100 kilopascals). In a closed system, oxygen (O_2) and nitrogen (N_2) need to be generated, humidity and air contamination must be controlled, and carbon dioxide (CO_2) must be reduced. This last process, CO_2 reduction, combines hydrogen (H_2) with carbon dioxide to form water, which is later electrolyzed to produce more oxygen.

$$CO_2 + 2H_2 = C + H_2O + HEAT$$

The hydrogen for this is a by-product of the nitrogen-generation process. Using hydrazine, which is also one of the fuels for propulsion, the required 13.5 pounds (6.1 kilograms) per day of nitrogen needed by the eleven crew members can be produced by the following reactions:

$$N_2H_4 \text{ (hydrazine)} = \tfrac{1}{3} N_2 + \tfrac{4}{3} NH_3$$
$$\tfrac{4}{3} NH_3 = \tfrac{2}{3} N_2 + 2H_2$$

The needed oxygen (20.2 pounds or 9.2 kilograms per day) is generated from water that is electrolyzed —separated electrically by pulling it apart, with hydrogen attracted to the cathode (the minus side) and oxygen to the anode (the plus side). Some electrons ($e-$) remain.

$$2H_2O = 4H^+ + 4e^- + O_2$$
$$4H^+ + 4e^- = H_2$$

About 102.5 pounds (46.6 kilograms) of water is required by the crew each day and is reclaimed by a

Crew Compartment Life Support   All values lb./day for 11-person crew

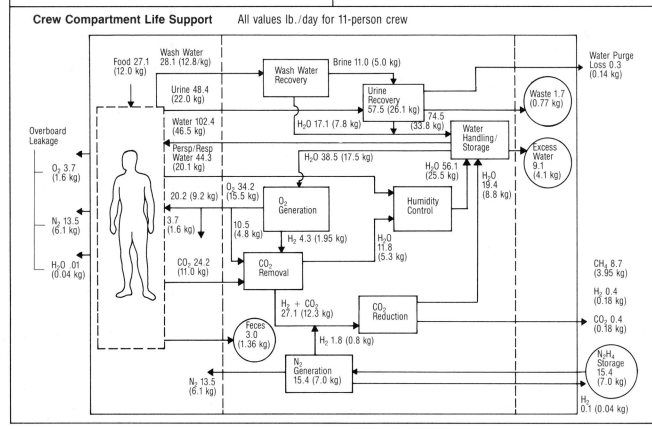

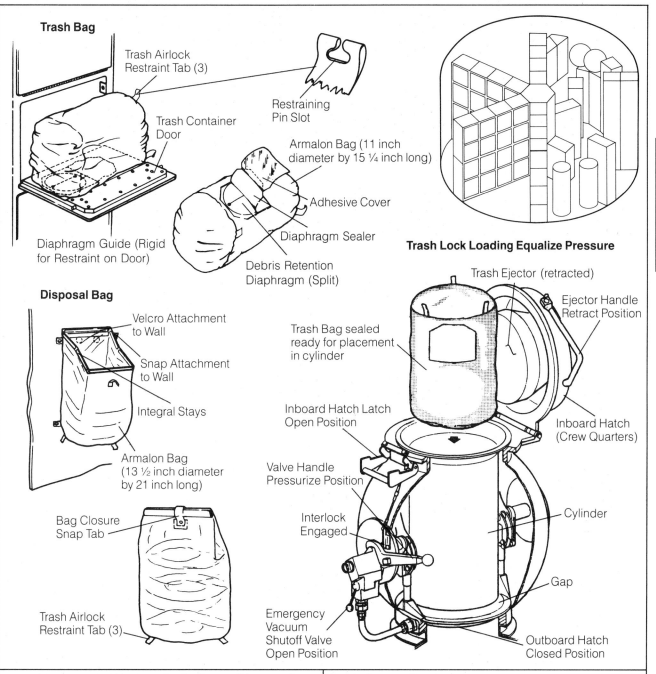

Trash Bag

Trash Airlock Restraint Tab (3)

Trash Container Door

Restraining Pin Slot

Armalon Bag (11 inch diameter by 15 ¼ inch long)

Adhesive Cover

Diaphragm Sealer

Diaphragm Guide (Rigid for Restraint on Door)

Debris Retention Diaphragm (Split)

Trash Lock Loading Equalize Pressure

Disposal Bag

Velcro Attachment to Wall

Snap Attachment to Wall

Integral Stays

Armalon Bag (13 ½ inch diameter by 21 inch long)

Bag Closure Snap Tab

Trash Airlock Restraint Tab (3)

Trash Ejector (retracted)

Ejector Handle Retract Position

Trash Bag sealed ready for placement in cylinder

Inboard Hatch Latch Open Position

Inboard Hatch (Crew Quarters)

Valve Handle Pressurize Position

Interlock Engaged

Cylinder

Gap

Emergency Vacuum Shutoff Valve Open Position

Outboard Hatch Closed Position

complex process. Waste water in the craft comes from several sources. Electricity-generating fuel cells produce water. Humidity in the cabin air comes from perspiration and water vapor that you exhale when you breathe. The whole crew generates a surprising 44 pounds (20 kilograms) per day of water in this way. The crew also generates waste water when they wash (28 pounds or 12.7 kilograms per day) and urinate (49.3 pounds or 22.4 kilograms per day).

All of this can be efficiently recycled through an elaborate system of bacterial, activated-charcoal, and resin filters combined with a distillation process for compressed water vapor. In the water vapor compression process the waste water is evaporated and then compressed. It is then condensed into reclaimed water. The heat given off during the condensation stage in turn evaporates new waste water, completing the recycling process. Finally, a biocide is added to control

bacteria growth.

Solid waste, of course, must also be treated. A trash airlock system with garbage bags is used to store paper, food, and other wastes.

The commode or Waste Collection System (WCS) is equipped to handle excreted wastes. There are three commodes on the ship plus an ample supply of fecal collection bags for both the main ship and the MEM. Operation of the commode is simple. There is an orifice for urinal waste and a seat assembly with a safety belt to hold you in place. Since there is no gravity, a vacuum system is used to draw air through the commode. The airflow moves wastes through the system. This also prevents much of the odor from entering the module. Toilet tissue is in the rack nearby. You should let the fan run for at least one minute after you are finished and the gate valve controlling the airflow is closed. Then simply undo the seat belt and float merrily away.

Fecal containment bags are also necessary for the landing party, since there is no commode in the MEM, and are used as a back-up system should the main craft commodes fail. The bag has a flat top which, when the protective paper is peeled off, is sticky. This as-sures a good seal to your body. You can insert your finger into a small hole and plastic sleeve in the bag to assist the feces. Not a particularly pleasant task, but a necessary one in zero-g. When finished, peel the bag off your body and seal the bag. Inside the bag is a pouch of blue fluid. This fluid is a germicide similar to the fluids used in portable camping toilets on Earth. Squeeze the outer bag until that inner bag breaks, releasing the germicide. Obviously you must do this very carefully. The rolled bag can then be safely disposed of through a trash airlock or in the waste storage compartment in the MEM.

The EC/LSS in each HAB module is normally capable of supporting six people, eight people for extended periods of time, and all eleven people in an emergency. The LAB module can sustain five crew members normally and ten in an emergency. These systems are interconnected and share some supply tanks and components.

Contingency Fecal Bag

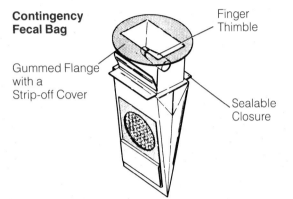

Finger Thimble

Gummed Flange with a Strip-off Cover

Sealable Closure

Waste Management Unit

Fecal Collector Filter

Flush Dispenser

Crewman Restraints

BLOWER/SEPARATOR

1	2	3
ON	ON	ON
OFF	OFF	OFF

Fecal Collector (Exploded View)

Airflow Holes

Hinged Seat

Fecal Collection Receptacle

Fecal Collector

Urine Receptacle Position

Dummy or Female Drawer

Urine Drawer (Exploded View)

Pressure Plate

Urine Bag Box

Facilities for personal hygiene are quite ample in the HAB modules. Each module is equipped with a lavatory sink and a shower facility. The sink is enclosed in a plastic bubble to prevent water from escaping into the module where it might cause short circuits or other damage.

You wash your hands, face, or body by placing a washcloth over your hand, inserting your hand into the sink, and depressing the water dispenser. Hot water is sprayed from three jets onto the washcloth. You then use the cloth to wash. After washing, the cloth should be squeezed to remove the water for recycling. Place the folded washcloth on the base of the squeezing area. Pull the handle firmly until you reach the handrail, then release. It will spring back into position.

A soap dispenser is located next to the sink. Each antibacterial soap bar contains a stainless steel disk, which allows it to be held to the sink wall by a magnetic soap holder. An individual bar can be used no more than two weeks, then discarded.

Lavatory Unit

Contingency Line

Condensate Dump Port

Dump System Hose

Bag Dump Hose

Water Heater

Water Dispenser

Washcloth Squeezer

Squeezer Bag (Enclosed in Cover)

Filter (in Pocket)

Vacuum Dump Valve

H_2O

Handwasher

Water Inlet

H_2O Dispenser Valve

H_2O Heater

Plunger

Hot Water Jets (3)

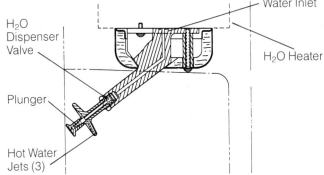

H_2O Dispenser Valve Cutaway

Squeezer

Path of Handle Travel

Piston Return Spring

Flapper Valve (Check Valve)

Operating Handle

Washcloth Squeezing Area

Handrail

Squeezer Bag Inlet

Piston

Water

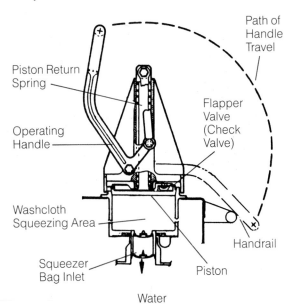

Also attached to the sink is a toothbrush and toothpaste restraint and a tissue and wipe dispenser. The wipes are also antibacterial. Near the sink are towel and washcloth dispensers, drying restraints to hold the washcloths and towels when in use, trash bag containers, and medium-sized trash bags.

Each crew member has a personal-hygiene kit containing necessary personal care items. Each member also has an assigned color code. Towels, cloths, and dispensers all have color bands on them so you can easily identify your own equipment. Since there are six crew members in HAB 1 and only five in HAB 2, six colors are used and repeated in the other module. The colors are red, yellow, orange, green, blue, and purple. Check your color assignment by noting the colored name card on your sleep compartment.

Towel and Washcloth Dispenser

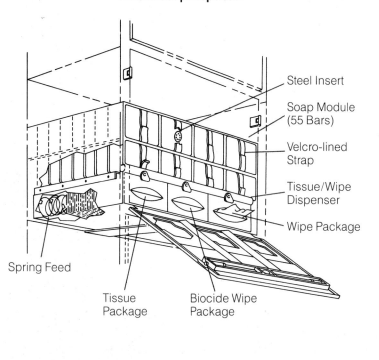

Towel Dispenser
(18 Towels/Dispenser)

Color Code
Decals

Washcloth Module
(28 Washcloths/Module)

Spring Feed
(Integral to Module)

**General Purpose
Tissue/Soap Dispenser**

Steel Insert

Soap Module
(55 Bars)

Velcro-lined
Strap

Tissue/Wipe
Dispenser

Wipe Package

Spring Feed

Tissue
Package

Biocide Wipe
Package

Washcloth/Towel Drying Area

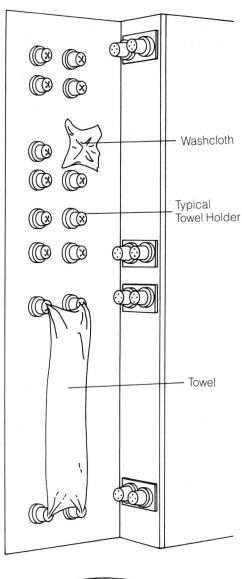

Washcloth

Typical
Towel Holder

Towel

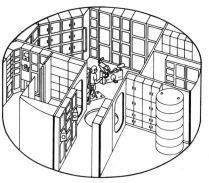

A shower is provided in each HAB module for cleanliness and grooming. You may shower up to three times per week, but two times should suffice. The shower is a collapsible, watertight compartment made of reinforced nylon. This nylon cylinder is attached to the floor and ceiling with ring closures. Air blowing through the shower makes the water flow over you as though there were gravity. Without this system, the water would spray around the chamber. Nitrogen gas pressure and a spray nozzle give a forceful stream of water. A second hose in the shower is a suction head, which you must use to remove all the water before opening the shower compartment. The waste water is drawn through a filter and then channeled to the water revitalization system. Towels, 14 by 32 inches (360 by 810 millimeters), are made of rayon terry cloth. Contamination data collected during the flight will determine how long towels can be used.

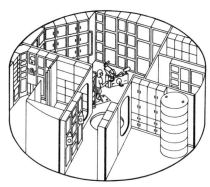

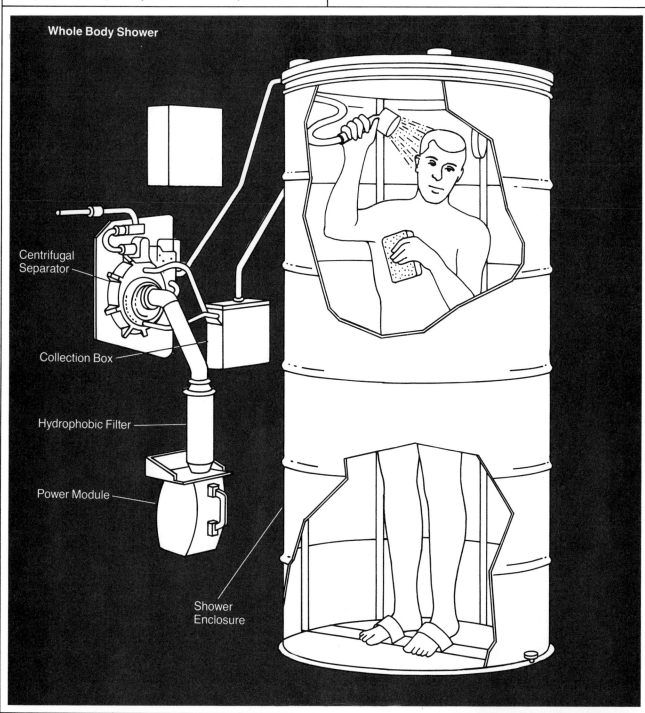

Whole Body Shower

Centrifugal Separator

Collection Box

Hydrophobic Filter

Power Module

Shower Enclosure

During World War II, two important things became part of modern thinking about food during long missions. First, food must be appealing and good tasting; otherwise it may not be eaten. Any child can tell you that about spinach. Second, food must be packaged in attractive, tempting forms. Many soldiers during the war hated the infamous K rations. They often joked that they could survive on K rations a lot longer than they would care to live. For Mars One, every attempt has been made to make food appetizing, nutritious, and practically packaged. Although you won't be having any home cooking for almost two years, you will have a surprisingly good choice of foods.

Eating food serves several functions on a mission of this kind: It provides the necessary source of energy and nutrition; it provides a social occasion during which the group can exchange information and relax; and it provides motivation and morale for the individual (unless he or she is a picky eater).

The menu for the mission is a complex one. Different cultures must be catered to and certain physiological requirements must be met. First, the food must be palatable. This can't be true of everything, but enough desirable food must be available to insure proper intake of sufficient calories and vitamins. Second, the food should be easily digested. Third, the food must

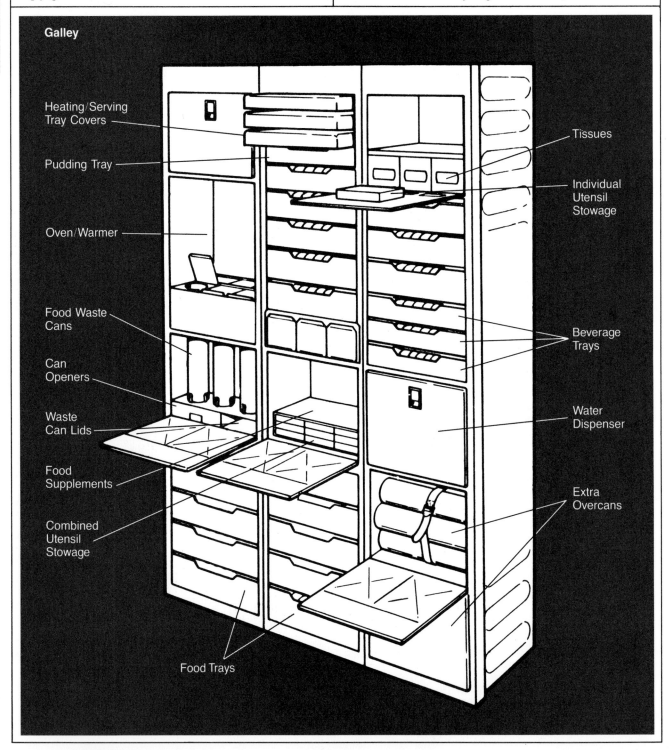

Galley

Heating/Serving Tray Covers

Pudding Tray

Oven/Warmer

Food Waste Cans

Can Openers

Waste Can Lids

Food Supplements

Combined Utensil Stowage

Tissues

Individual Utensil Stowage

Beverage Trays

Water Dispenser

Extra Overcans

Food Trays

Food Storage

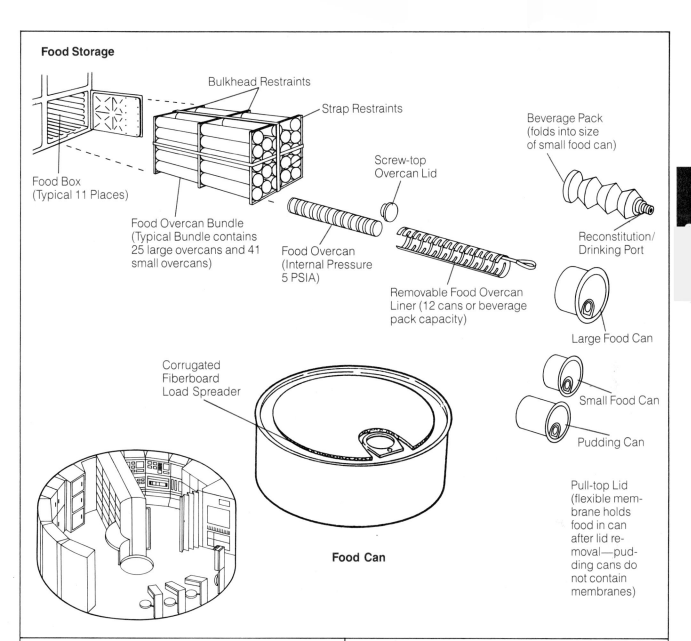

Bulkhead Restraints

Strap Restraints

Food Box (Typical 11 Places)

Food Overcan Bundle (Typical Bundle contains 25 large overcans and 41 small overcans)

Food Overcan (Internal Pressure 5 PSIA)

Screw-top Overcan Lid

Removable Food Overcan Liner (12 cans or beverage pack capacity)

Beverage Pack (folds into size of small food can)

Reconstitution/ Drinking Port

Large Food Can

Small Food Can

Pudding Can

Pull-top Lid (flexible membrane holds food in can after lid removal—pudding cans do not contain membranes)

Corrugated Fiberboard Load Spreader

Food Can

be easy to prepare. Cooking can be a welcome change from heavy work routines, but it can also be a chore. Generally, in the Shuttle and at the space station, cooking is done on a rotating basis. Crew members can determine their own routines.

Finally, the food must be able to withstand spoilage for as long as two years. Bacteria growth is a dangerous condition in the ship and must be continually monitored. Food spoilage could be a serious problem and must be guarded against.

The menus in this section list most of the major foods available to the crew. The foods are prepared in several ways. They can be dehydrated, freeze-dried, or packaged with moisture. The first two processes require the addition of water to reconstitute the food. Some foods or snacks, however, can be eaten dry.

All foods have been specially prepared, though some are versions of food you might take on a camping trip. Special care has been taken to limit certain bacterial formation in the food. Irradiation is used to kill bacteria in some foods, but the old technique used in home canning, heating, is perhaps the most common process.

In space, however, the procedure is called thermostabilization.

Food is stored in on-board lockers and in storage areas. A galley is provided in each HAB module, and an emergency oven is available in the LAB module. Each galley contains an oven, a supply of food trays, about seven days' supply of food, utensils, and a water valve for hot or cold water (measured in one-ounce bursts). Food is packaged in foil pouches, plastic shrink wrap, plastic containers, pop-top cans, tubes, and plastic bottles. Instructions are printed on the ovens, trays, and food. The oven warms to 150°F (66°C) and hot water is dispensed at 130°F (54.4°C).

Cleanup is important from a health and an organizational point of view. After the meal, you must dispose of all containers properly, using the trash disposal system. You must also clean and wipe all surfaces and utensils with germicides.

At mealtimes, HAB groups may wish to visit each other, to exchange members, to eat in shifts, or to stay in teams. Some flexibility in meal schedules is allowable, but only within limits, since the training and operation schedules are demanding.

During the actual stay on the martian surface, your food will be somewhat different. Critical weight and space requirements dictate a diet not unlike that of early Apollo astronauts. Bite-size and rehydratable foods, along with the better-tasting freeze-dried food, will comprise virtually all of your menu. The calorie intake will remain at about 3000 calories per day, but high-energy snacks will be available.

You will probably be too busy and too involved to really mind the drop in food quality. Just think of your surface stay as the ultimate camping trip.

During the final two months of the voyage, your diet is altered slightly to provide high sodium and fluid content. This high-salt, high-fluid regimen increases blood volume, which has been greatly depleted by months of zero-g living.

Food Values for Sample Meals

Constituents	Meal A	Meal B	Meal C	Total
Energy (kcal)	759.0	1123.0	911.0	2793.0
Protein (g)	28.5	45.2	28.7	102.4
Fat (g)	25.4	42.0	32.4	99.8
Carbo-hydrate (g)	106.4	140.0	125.7	372.1
Ash (g)	7.0	6.8	7.3	21.1
Ca (mg)	176.0	505.0	486.0	1168.0
P (mg)	342.0	712.0	592.0	1646.0
Fe (mg)	3.3	4.8	4.9	13.0
Na (mg)	1659.0	1526.0	1916.0	5101.0
K (mg)	818.0	863.0	1047.0	2728.0
Mg (mg)	64.3	89.5	95.3	249.1
Cl as NaCl (g)	4.3	3.1	3.9	11.3

Soft Food Packets

Cheese Spread

Beef Patty

Potato Patty

Crackers

Peaches

Peanut Butter

Mars One Food* List

Applesauce (T)
Apricots, Dried (IM)
Asparagus (R)
Bacon
Bananas (FD)
Beef Almondine (R)
Beef, Barbecue Bits
Beef, Corned (I) (T)
Beef Jerky (IM)
Beef Patty (R)
Beef, Pot Roast
Beef, Slices w/Barbeque Sauce (T)
Beef Steak (I) (T)
Beef Stew
Beef Stroganoff w/Noodles (R)
Bread, Borodino
Bread, Seedless Rye (I) (NF)
Bread, White
Broccoli au Gratin (R)
Breakfast Roll (I) (NF)
Brownies
Candy, Life Savers, Assorted Flavors
  (NF)
Cauliflower w/Cheese (R)
Cereal, Bran Flakes (R)
Cereal, Cornflakes (R)
Cereal, Granola (R)
Cereal, Granola w/Blueberries (R)
Cereal, Granola w/Raisins (R)
Cheddar Cheese Spread (T)

Chicken a la King (T)
Chicken and Noodles (R)
Chicken and Rice (R)
Chicken Salad
Chili Mac w/Beef (R)
Chocolate
Cinnamon Toast Cubes
Cookies, Pecan (NF)
Cookies, Shortbread (NF)
Cottage Cheese
Crackers, Graham (NF)
Eggs, Scrambled (R)
Food Bar, Almond Crunch (NF)
Food Bar, Chocolate Chip (NF)
Food Bar, Granola (NF)
Food Bar, Granola/Raisin (NF)
Food Bar, Peanut Butter/Granola (NF)
Frankfurters (Vienna Sausage) (T)
Fruitcake
Fruit Cocktail (T)
Green Beans, French w/Mushrooms
  (R)
Green Beans and Broccoli (R)
Ham (I) (T)
Honey Cake
Jam/Jelly (T)
Macaroni and Cheese (R)
Meatballs w/Barbecue Sauce (T)
Nuts, Almonds (NF)
Nuts, Cashews (NF)

Nuts, Peanuts (NF)
Peach Ambrosia (R)
Peaches, Dried (IM)
Peaches (T)
Peanut Butter
Pears (FD)
Pears (T)
Peas w/Butter Sauce (R)
Pineapple, Crushed (T)
Pork w/Scalloped Potatoes
Potato Patty (R)
Pudding, Chocolate (R) (T)
Pudding, Lemon (T)
Pudding, Vanilla (R) (T)
Rice
Rice Pilaf (R)
Rice Curry
Salmon (T)
Sausage Patty (R)
Shrimp Creole (R)
Shrimp Cocktail (R)
Soup, Cream of Chicken (R)
Spaghetti w/Meat Sauce (R)
Strawberries (R)
Tomatoes, Stewed (T)
Tuna (T)
Turkey and Gravy (T)
Turkey, Smoked/Sliced (I) (T)
Turkey Tetrazzini (R)
Vegetables, Mixed Italian (R)

Condiments

Pepper
Salt
Barbecue Sauce

Catsup
Hot Mustard
Hot Pepper Sauce

Mustard
Curry Sauce
Soy Sauce

Beverages

Apple Drink
Cocoa
Coffee, Black
Coffee w/Cream
Coffee w/Cream and Sugar
Coffee w/Sugar
Grape Punch

Instant Breakfast, Vanilla
Lemonade
Orange Drink
Orange-grapefruit Drink
Orange-pineapple Drink
Strawberry Drink
Tea

Grapefruit Drink
Instant Breakfast, Chocolate
Instant Breakfast, Strawberry
Tea w/Lemon and Sugar
Tea w/Sugar
Tropical Punch

*Abbreviations in parentheses indicate type of food: T = Thermostabilized, I = Irradiated, IM = Intermediate Moisture, FD = Freeze Dried, R = Rehydratable, and NF = Natural Form.

Sleep

Your personal compartment is your primary sleep location. Occasionally you may sleep in the control center, and the landing party has hammocks for the surface stay. Sleep equipment consists of the sleep restraint assembly, blankets, pillow covers (one per week), body straps, privacy curtains, and light baffles. Earplugs and a sleeping mask are also provided. This equipment is stowed in your wall locker.

Linens

Item	Unit Weight (lb)	Usage Rates (Days)	
		Nominal	Maximum
Sheets	0.37	6	10
Blanket	1.0	(Not applicable)	
Towels	0.75	4	6
Washcloths	0.08	3	6

Shuttle and space station crews often sleep in any position, but the restraint applies pressure to hold you against the padded wall, simulating a mattress. The fasteners for the restraint and the Teflon-coated privacy curtains are edged in Velcro to permit instant breakaway for emergency exit.

On Mars One, the sleep cycle has a special significance. All missions to this point have maintained a 24-hour Earth schedule. For American Shuttle missions, space station missions, and even lunar missions, a 24-hour clock with Central Time Zone reference (mission control) has been used. The martian day (called a "sol") is 24 hours and 39.5 minutes long. As you adjust to martian time, your sleep time adjusts accordingly. By the time you get to Mars it probably increases by about ten to fifteen minutes per day. The extra time may not be physiologically needed, so it can be used as personal time, but with the demanding schedule and the twenty-minute-longer workday, you may find you need the rest.

Noise is harder to control than light in your personal compartment. Some people adjust easily to the constant noise of the ship's various systems, while others require the earplugs mentioned above. Airflow in your compartment can be controlled by adjusting the louvers. Communications headsets can be plugged into the wall connector for communicating instantly with other crew members or for listening to music or audio tapes.

Personal Compartment

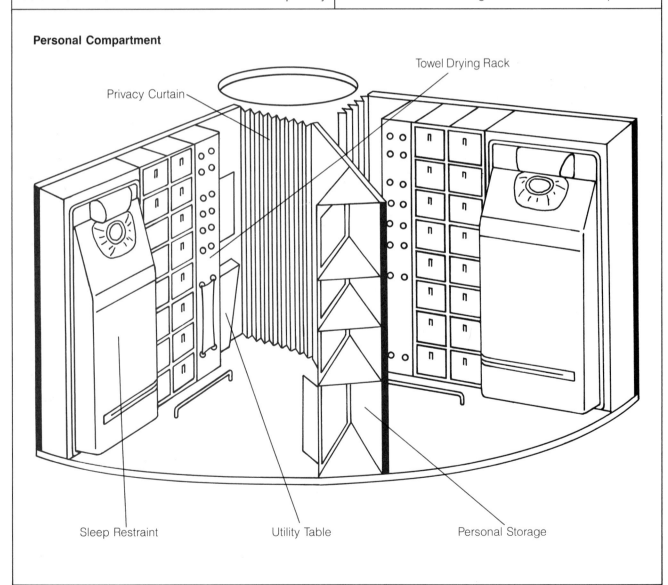

Privacy Curtain

Towel Drying Rack

Sleep Restraint

Utility Table

Personal Storage

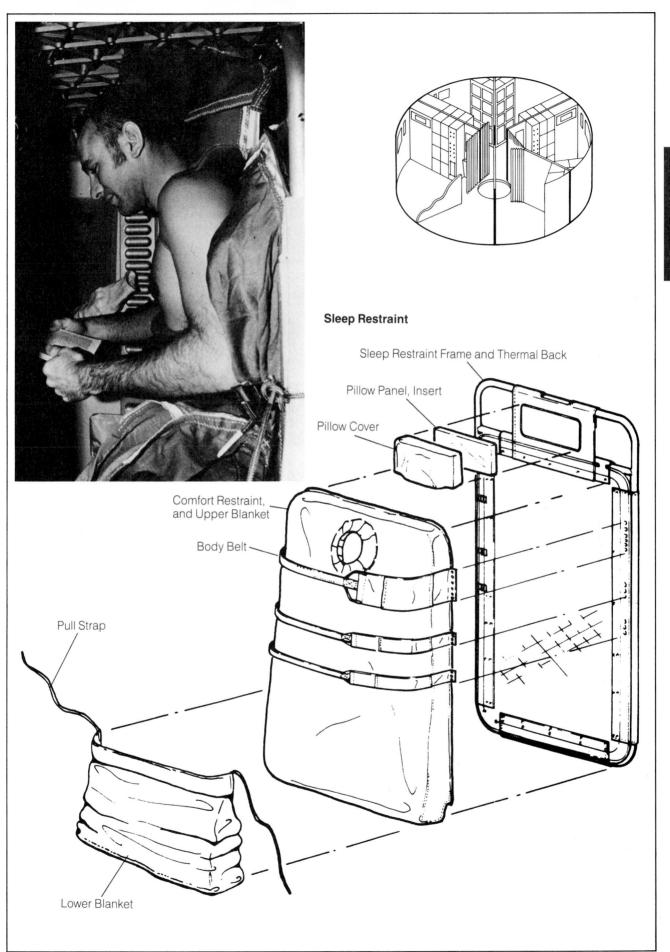

Sleep Restraint

Sleep Restraint Frame and Thermal Back

Pillow Panel, Insert

Pillow Cover

Comfort Restraint,
and Upper Blanket

Body Belt

Pull Strap

Lower Blanket

Communication is one of the most complex and most critical parts of the mission, and several levels of communication are required. They are (1) within module; (2) module to module; (3) main ship to Mars surface; (4) Mars Rover to MEM; (5) to Earth.

Due to the nature of your craft, there is always a certain amount of noise from fans, pumps, and other systems. Although precautions against excessive noise and vibration have been taken, it is still difficult to communicate by shouting from section to section, and impossible to shout from module to module. There are two systems for intramodule and intermodule communi-

announcements. Channels 2 through 5 allow you to talk to any combination of modules through all squawk boxes in that module.

If you wish to talk to a particular box, you can dial that box using the touch panel. Press #, then enter the module number and the box number. For example, #21 gives you the command station (1) in the control center of HAB 2 (2).

To talk over a squawk box, merely set the mode switch to PTT (push to talk) and push the talk button. You can also select the voice-activated microphone (VOX) or the continuously open microphone (HOT). These last

Communication Station

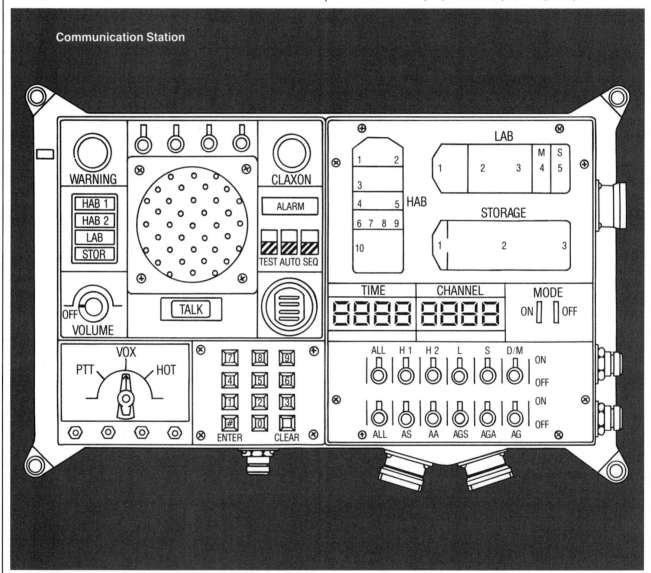

cation. The first system is the communicator's stations or squawk boxes. These boxes are mounted at critical places in each HAB module and the LAB module and supply modules. On each box is a speaker/microphone, a channel selector, buttons and switches, four LED indicators, and a mode selector switch with a talk button. There are ten channel selector switches available, but for now, we will be concerned with only five.

Channel 1 is an all-call override. Anyone using Channel 1 will be heard on all boxes and over any ongoing communication. Obviously, this channel is used in emergencies, by the commander, and for general

two settings are convenient when you are working and need your hands free.

The other five selector switches control settings for communication to Earth (3 channels), and the martian surface (2 channels).

Each crew member is equipped with a portable communicator. This system consists of a headset, cable, and transmitter/battery unit. To use it, just clip the headset/microphone on, clip the unit to your belt, and switch it on. With this apparatus, you can move about the cabin and speak in a normal voice. Your voice will be carried over the nearest squawk box.

Voice Recognition Commands (for hands-free operation)

"COMMO ON"
"COMMO OFF"
"MODULE—(HAB 1, HAB 2, LAB, store, all, MEM, etc.)"
"HELP/MAYDAY"

Each compartment also has a TV switch box. There are two color video cameras in each module, one in the LAB, two on the MEM, and one in the Mars Rover. Each camera weighs six pounds, has low-light and bright-light settings, and an auto-focus feature. A camera cord can stretch up to twenty feet. There are additional plugs in each compartment, and a velcro strap to hold the camera in any position. Two voice channels (6 and 7) are automatically activated when a TV camera is on.

Each day there is one video transmission to Earth and one from Earth. Because the messages travel at the speed of light and take about twenty minutes to get to Mars, two-way conversation is impossible. Just saying "Hello Earth," "Hello Mars," "How are you," "Fine" would take over an hour. Your transmissions are essentially televised reports. A daily video update comes from Earth. It contains technical information and answers to various questions, a brief video newsclip, and two scrambled sections, one with private technical communications and one with private messages for individual crew members.

There are also three data channels (8, 9, and 10). Telemetry, digital information that is transmitted back to Earth, is sent continuously over two of these channels. The system relays life-support and general system conditions to Earth-based flight controllers. Any emergency you have is soon known on Earth, and technical support can be radioed immediately upon receipt.

Transmissions from the martian surface must be relayed to Earth and the main ship. To ensure almost continuous contact, a communications subsatellite system is established around Mars. In this way, the ground party is always able to signal the main ship and/or relay information to Earth.

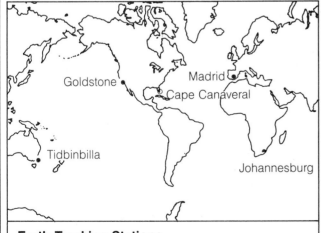

Earth Tracking Stations

• 64- and 26-meter stations
▲ 26-meter station
○ Launch support station

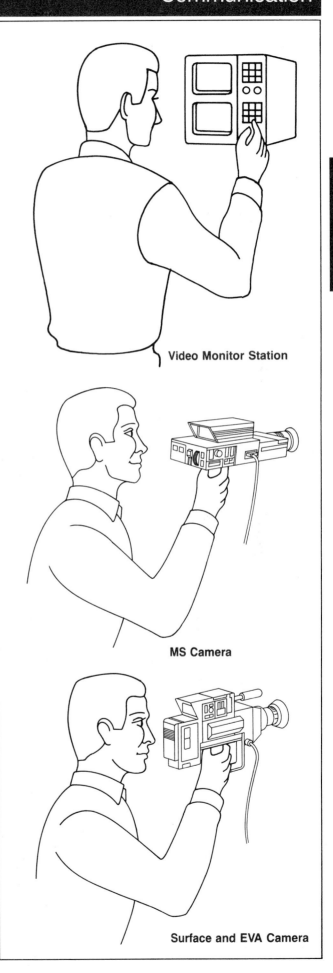

Video Monitor Station

MS Camera

Surface and EVA Camera

Important: Read This Section At Least Once Per Month!

This voyage is one of the most difficult ever attempted. There are many individual and group stresses and strains involved. These problems are not unlike those that have been faced by crews on the Space Shuttle, the Soviet Salyut, nuclear submarines, and remote bases such as Antarctica. If you are carefully self-analytical and highly sensitive to potential problems, you can exercise better self-control and interpersonal skills.

This section will outline potential stress situations, causes, and symptoms, and offer some suggestions for coping with them. Remember—you cannot deal with a problem you are not aware (or won't admit) that you have!

There are many causes for a buildup of behavior-changing stresses that can endanger both the mission and the crew:

Space. You have ample quarters, work areas, and other modules to visit. These are functional, but by no means luxurious. Over the course of the mission, the size and similarity of the modules can lead to boredom, claustrophobia, or irritability. Restlessness and occasionally even dangerous or destructive behavior can be exhibited. Try to clarify for yourself how you feel about where you are and what you are doing.

Noise and vibration. Although the craft is electrically powered, there will always be a background noise level from circulation fans, motors, pumps, and other environmental system components. Subtle vibrations will also be present. It has been found on submarines and on other long space missions that noise and vibration can cause irritability, a tendency to misinterpret communications, and sometimes disorganization or absentmindedness.

Work level. Your training, exercise schedule, in-flight maintenance schedules, simulations, and general zero-g routine will keep you very busy. Daydreaming, hostility, or rebellion have been exhibited in groups that have felt overworked and put upon. You need to constantly examine the importance of your tasks and your motivation. If you are developing a rebellious attitude, a heavy workload could well be the cause.

Interpersonal friction. Even the happiest crews can have differences of opinion or personality traits that are magnified by proximity and duration of contact with others. These can be dealt with individually by using a negotiator or go-between—one of the crew who has an extensive background in psychotherapy—or by crew group sensitivity sessions held on a regular basis during the evenings and on Sundays.

The medical staff is constantly monitoring the crew for signs of stress. This is done by computer analysis of your work performance and exercise performance and by voice stress analysis, which compares voice frequency, speed, and harmonics against "normalized" values. Observations of behavior and a survey of crew log entries also give clues on the crew's well-being. You can, of course, keep a private diary. It can be written, digital, or recorded. Only your duty log entries are read.

Finally, you must attempt to be self-aware. Ask yourself these questions: Am I drowsier than usual? Does a particular person or habit bother me? Would I like to be somewhere else? Have I been making obvious mistakes? Do I feel isolated from others? Do I hate anybody? Am I participating fully in my activities?

Occasional recreation and frequent periods of personal time will go a long way toward providing the social interaction or privacy you feel you need. Occasional treats or surprises will also occur during the mission. Remember: your survival depends upon understanding, creativity, dedication, and, when required, obedience to command.

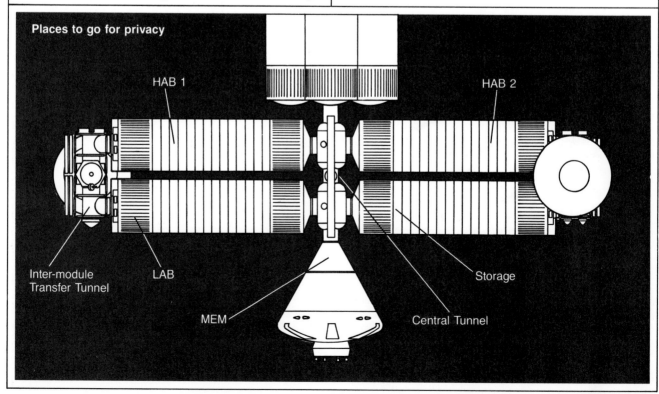

Places to go for privacy

HAB 1

HAB 2

Inter-module Transfer Tunnel

LAB

Storage

MEM

Central Tunnel

This mission subjects you to about eighteen months of weightlessness. This absence of gravity has a significant effect on your body, and therefore requires extensive measures to maintain top condition. On the planet, the constant pull of the Earth is something you hardly notice, but it is very important. Everything we do is affected by gravity. Our sense of balance, the way our body moves, even our basic skeletal structure is a product of the gravity in our environment. We even measure ourselves against gravity: how high we jump; how much we lift; how far we throw. This means our body is constantly using the pull of gravity as a conditioning element.

Away from the gravitational pull of the Earth, your body loses several things. With no force to work against, muscles weaken, body fluids redistribute themselves, bones begin to decalcify, the cardiovascular system weakens, and other chemical and physical changes take place. Experience in space stations and on the lunar surface, however, have taught us how to handle these conditions.

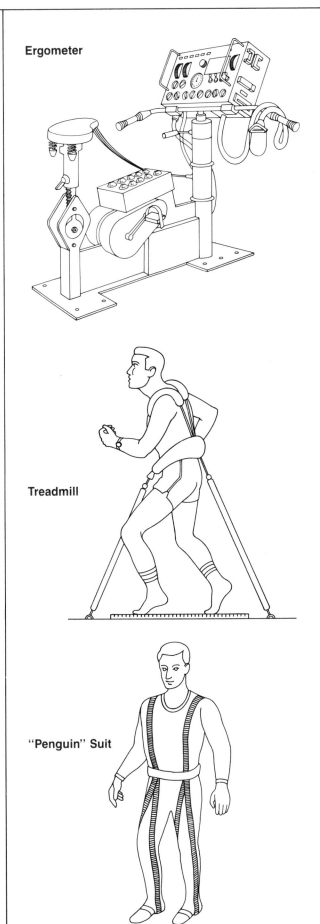

Ergometer

Treadmill

"Penguin" Suit

Exercise Time Required to Maintain One-Gravity (normal) Capacities

Physical Parameter	Exercise Modality	
	Walk	*Jog*
Leg Strength	15–20 min/day	5 min/day
Leg Endurance	25–30 min/day	15–20 min/day
Cardiorespiratory Endurance	30 min/day	15–20 min/day
Bone Strength	1–2 hrs/day	30–90 min/day
Coordination	10 min/day	5 min/day
	1-g Equivalent Forces on Leg Vessels	
Blood and Fluid Redistribution and Loss	1–3 hrs/day in addition to above exercises. This should be a static exercise which would not interfere with other duties.	

The principal techniques for coping with weightlessness, also called zero-gravity or zero-g, are diet and exercise. During the flight you will have several adjustments in your diet. Early in the flight, during Earth orbital check-out, you need to modify your diet to help the body cope with the zero-g adjustment. Your caloric intake is reduced slightly. During the mission your diet is kept fairly constant; the surface party's food style, however, changes during Mars activities.

Exercise is critical. You must spend a significant part of every day maintaining a regular exercise routine.

There are numerous exercise devices on board ship. Some devices allow you to do work or recreation activities while using them. The health facility in your HAB module is equipped with a variety of these devices. Remember that your workout schedule requires a minimum of two hours each day.

Each HAB module has a bicycle ergometer, a treadmill, and several loading devices for active exercise. The ergometer is a variable-effort bicycle. Pedaling gives your legs and cardiovascular system a healthy workout. To use the ergometer, pull yourself onto the seat and fasten the waist strap. Then pull the foot restraints over your shoes and place the air regulator hose in your mouth. Finally, strap the biosensor harness around your chest, adjust the torque, and begin pedaling. If you do not use the treadmill during the day, you will need to pedal for at least thirty minutes. Your oxygen intake and carbon dioxide output are measured during the exercise to monitor your overall condition and provide information about your metabolic rate. The blood pressure measuring apparatus should also be used at least twice a week.

The treadmill is an old device. It was used in Skylab in the early 1970s and is still used on space station and Shuttle missions. Its operation is simple. Put on your walking booties or just a pair of socks. Strap on the body harness and connect the bungee cords from the anchors on the treadmill to the grommets on the harness. This provides a "downward pull" for your body to work against. You may walk briskly or jog on the treadmill. Minimum daily walking time is one hour, so you might want to listen to some music or watch a movie while exercising. There is a video monitor in the health facility for this purpose. Jogging requires a minimum daily workout of thirty minutes, but, if your condition warrants, perhaps as long as ninety minutes will be required. (A walking exercise could require as long as two hours.) This conditioning is for leg strength and endurance, cardiorespiratory endurance, bone strength, and coordination. Loading devices like rope stretches and spring devices can also be used to supplement your treadmill/ergometer program.

During prolonged weightlessness, there is a certain amount of blood and body fluid loss. Another one to three hours per day of static exercise can help to stabilize that loss. There are several devices that can be worn during other activities. One of these clothing items is called a "penguin" suit. It was developed for the Soviet cosmonauts and has come into wide use for space station dwellers. One was issued to you as part of your clothing allotment; it can be worn all day. The suit has elastic bands woven through it to provide constant pulling on your legs and midsection. It works against your muscles by opposing movements and is an effective toning device.

A bit more clumsy, the "Chibis" suit can give your cardiovascular system an excellent reconditioning. You climb into a Chibis for at least thirty minutes per week on the outbound leg, forty minutes per week on the inbound leg, and almost one hour per day during the last four weeks of the mission and the quarantine period.

The Chibis looks like a costume for a 1950s science fiction movie, but once you put it on and start the micropump, a negative pressure is put on your lower body producing a good workout for your heart. During the final month of the mission, you will drink about 300 milliliters of water during your daily stint in the Chibis suit to replenish your depleted body fluid level.

The total exercise program is so important that you must devote about two to four hours per day to it. Remember, it is absolutely necessary and can be a welcome change from the demanding training schedules you are following.

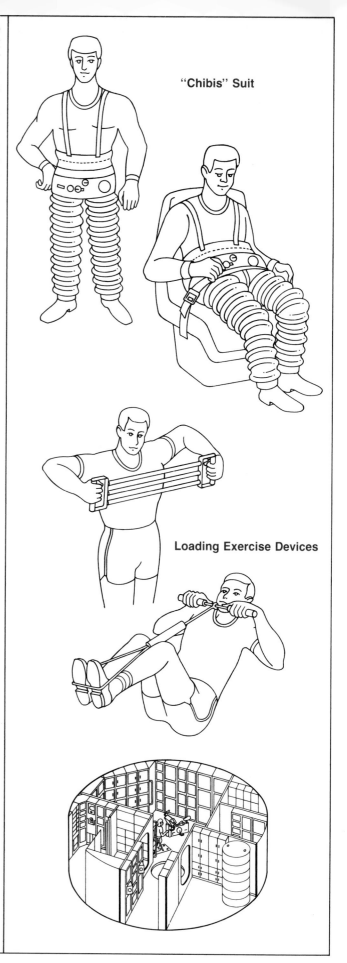

"Chibis" Suit

Loading Exercise Devices

Capabilities of the Mars One Medical Facility		
Group	Type	Tests
I	Clinical Evaluation	Patient history Physical examination
II	Cardiovascular	Electrocardiogram Vectorcardiogram Cardiac output Arterial blood pressure Venous pressure Phonocardiogram Heart rate
III	Metabolism	Energy metabolism Balance studies Body mass Temperatures (core and skin)

IV	Clinical Laboratory	Complete blood count
		Urinalysis
		Plasma volume
		Electrolytes
		  (blood and urine)
		Total protein count
		Blood glucose
		Blood pH; pO_2; pCO_2
		Reticulocyte count
		Red blood cell fragility
		Red blood cell mass
		  and survival

V	Behavioral Effects	Vision Audiometric

There are medical kits located in each HAB module, and a complete medical facility is located in the LAB module. This facility includes an examination table, a sterilizer, a refrigerator/freezer, an X-ray machine, a sink, a work surface, and diagnostic equipment.

All of the crew has had first-aid training consisting of vital signs analysis (pulse, blood pressure, temperature, pupil size); eye, ear, nose, and throat examinations; basic emergency procedures (CPR, Heimlich maneuver); bleeding control; bandaging and splinting; basic dental procedures; and electrocardiogram (EKG) reading. All have been trained in using the medical kit.

Two crew members have medical degrees. They are capable of most surgical procedures that might arise during the mission. They are also responsible for conducting periodic physical checkups and for maintaining medical records. One has a background in surgery, the other in bacteriology. Both have extensive general practice experience.

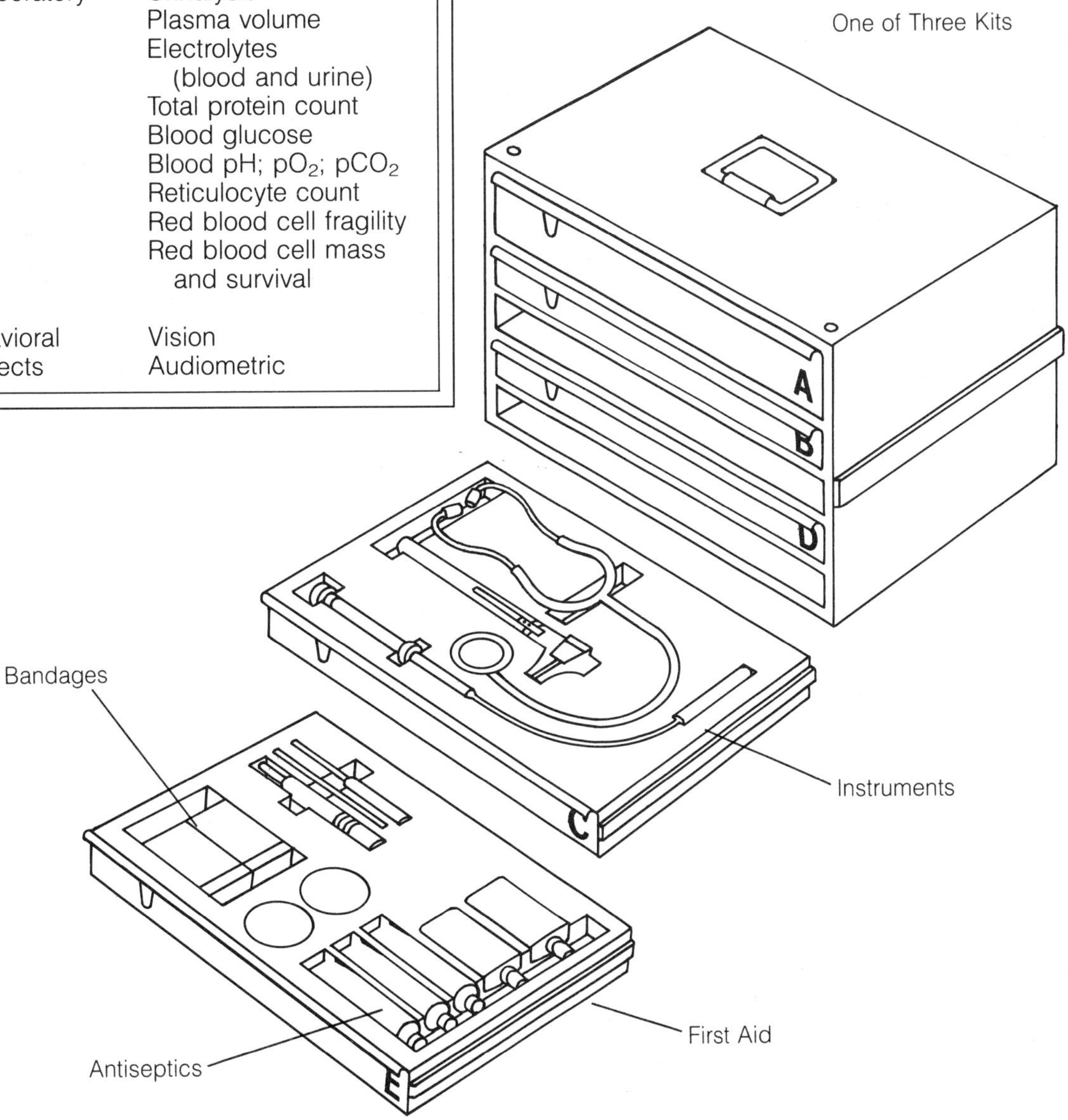

2.8.1

One of Three Kits

A
B
D

Bandages

Instruments

Antiseptics

First Aid

C

E

2.8.2

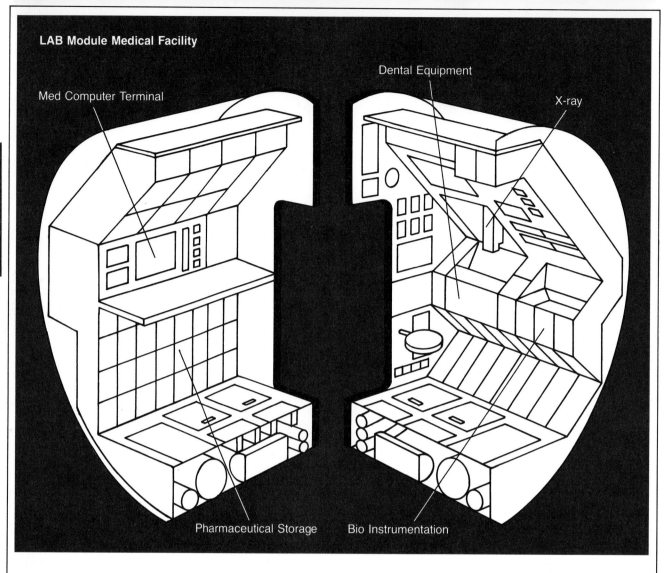

LAB Module Medical Facility

Med Computer Terminal

Dental Equipment

X-ray

Pharmaceutical Storage

Bio Instrumentation

Medical Isolator

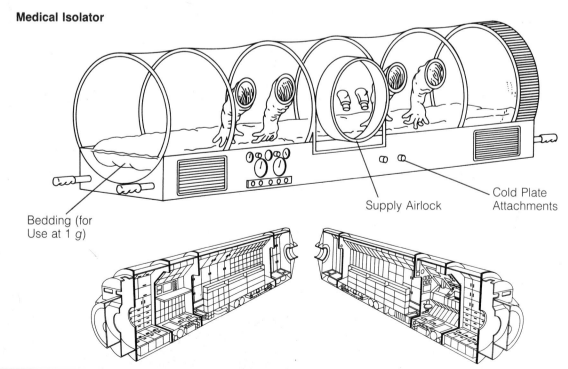

Bedding (for Use at 1 *g*)

Supply Airlock

Cold Plate Attachments

On a mission of this type, comfortable and functional clothing is essential. Your clothing requirements are relatively simple. The modules are kept at a temperature between 65° and 75° F (18° to 24° C). In this "shirt-sleeve" environment, all you really need are trousers, shirts, underwear, and socks. The clothing is made of fire-retardant cotton. Velcro-lined or zippered pockets are provided in the outerwear. Footwear and a lightweight jacket complete your ensemble.

Crew Apparel

Item	Unit Weight (lb)	Usage Rates (Days)	
		Nominal	Maximum
Shirt (short sleeve)	0.27	3	6
Trousers	0.77	6	12
Jacket	0.62	(As required)	
Undershirt	0.17	2	3
Undershorts	0.17	2	3
Socks (pair)	0.04	2	3
Shoes (pair)	0.55	(Not applicable)	
Brassiere	0.17	2	3

Total clothing weight for the entire crew runs just under 1,500 pounds (680 kilograms). In addition, personal effects for the crew are limited to 500 pounds (227 kilograms). Personal effects include toilet articles, grooming equipment, cleansers, and miscellaneous articles such as pens, pencils, watches, etc.

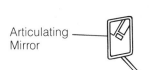

Articulating Mirror

Personal Effects

Item	Per Crew Member/Month Weight (lb)
Toilet articles (toothbrush, toothpaste, etc.)	0.12
Grooming equipment (shaving equipment, combs, hair and nail trimmers, etc.)	0.34
Cleansers (soap, antiseptics, deodorants, shampoo, etc.)	0.62
Personal equipment (items of crew's choice)	1.00

Although there is a selection of computerized literature, games, and music available on board, you may wish to use some of your approximately 5 pounds (2.3 kilograms) of discretionary items for cassettes and travel sets of games, books, etc.

Typical Hygiene Kit Contents

Shaving Cream	6 oz. (180 ml)
Razor	1
Styptic Pencil	1
Toothpaste	3 oz. (90 ml)
Toothbrush	1
Dental floss	80 in. (2 m)
Soap	4 oz. (120 ml)
Emolient	6 oz. (180 ml)
Safety Swabs	30
Hair Brush	1
Hair Cream	3 oz. (90 ml)
Nail Clippers	1
Deodorant	1.5 oz. (45 ml)
Expectorant Collector	15

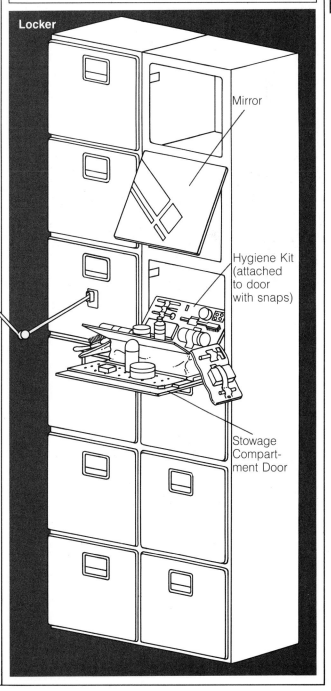

Locker

Mirror

Hygiene Kit (attached to door with snaps)

Stowage Compartment Door

Standard In-flight Coveralls

Standard In-flight Coveralls

Dirt, debris, and droplets of water can be extremely bothersome and possibly hazardous in a spacecraft. As part of the crew's cleanup routine, a customized vacuum cleaner is used to capture such particles.

The vacuum consists of a high-powered blower unit, a debris bag, and hose connections in a portable unit. A handle and strap help maneuver the vacuum. The vacuum's 15-foot (4.6 meters) power cable and 4-foot (1.2 meters) flex hose allow you to work at a distance of 20 feet (6.1 meters) from the power outlet. A surface tool, a crevice tool, and a brush attachment are available. To replace the bag, merely open the hinged bag access door. The bag should be replaced either when full or at weekly intervals. Each bag has an air inlet and a vapor port for airflow exit. A small plunger is located in the bag compartment to keep the unit from starting if no bag is present.

The vacuum's blower circuit is identical to the blower unit in the fecal and urine collection assemblies. These units may be interchanged in the event of a system breakdown. Check the manual for repair and service of the vacuum.

Vacuum Cleaner and Accessories

Attachment Stowage

Hose Stowage

Waist Tether

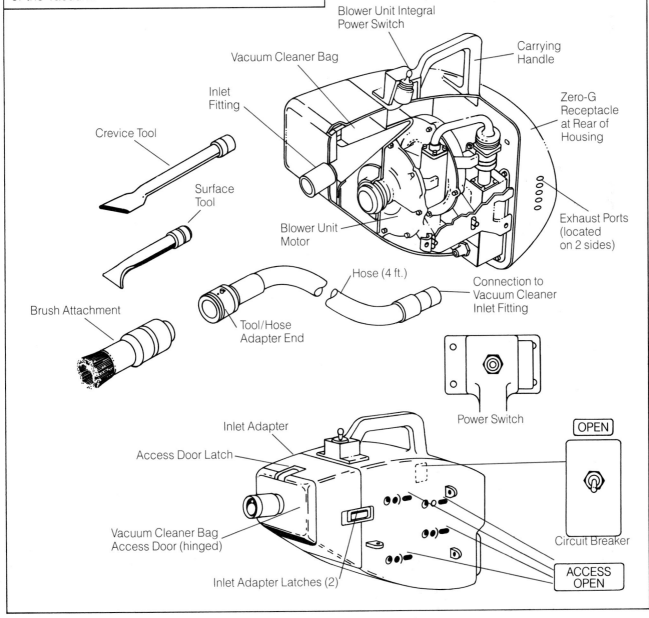

Blower Unit Integral Power Switch

Vacuum Cleaner Bag

Carrying Handle

Inlet Fitting

Crevice Tool

Zero-G Receptacle at Rear of Housing

Surface Tool

Blower Unit Motor

Exhaust Ports (located on 2 sides)

Brush Attachment

Hose (4 ft.)

Tool/Hose Adapter End

Connection to Vacuum Cleaner Inlet Fitting

Power Switch

Inlet Adapter

Access Door Latch

OPEN

Vacuum Cleaner Bag Access Door (hinged)

Circuit Breaker

Inlet Adapter Latches (2)

ACCESS OPEN

All tools considered necessary for known maintenance tasks are provided in two Master Tool Kits (MTK). An MTK is located in the control center of each module near the exit hatch. Each kit contains a number of all-purpose tools that were found to be useful on earlier Skylab, Salyut, Shuttle, and space station missions. These tools are adaptable to virtually any repair task you may face.

The LAB module has a special tool kit that relates to LAB equipment and general servicing in that area. Likewise, the MEM and the Mars Rover each have specialized tool kits that duplicate some of the components of the MTK.

In the airlock, there is a small docking module repair kit and extravehicular activity tool kit for outside repairs, airlock repairs, and suit repairs. There is also a small tool kit in the supply module to facilitate repair of storage containers, latches, etc. Tools are placed in soft pouches and secured by Velcro strips. The pouches are placed in a sectioned tool caddy and stowed in floor lockers. The tools are used for maintenance, periodic cleaning, electrical servicing, component replacement, and emergency repairs. Tools are magnetized when appropriate, or have Velcro spots.

Master Tool Kit

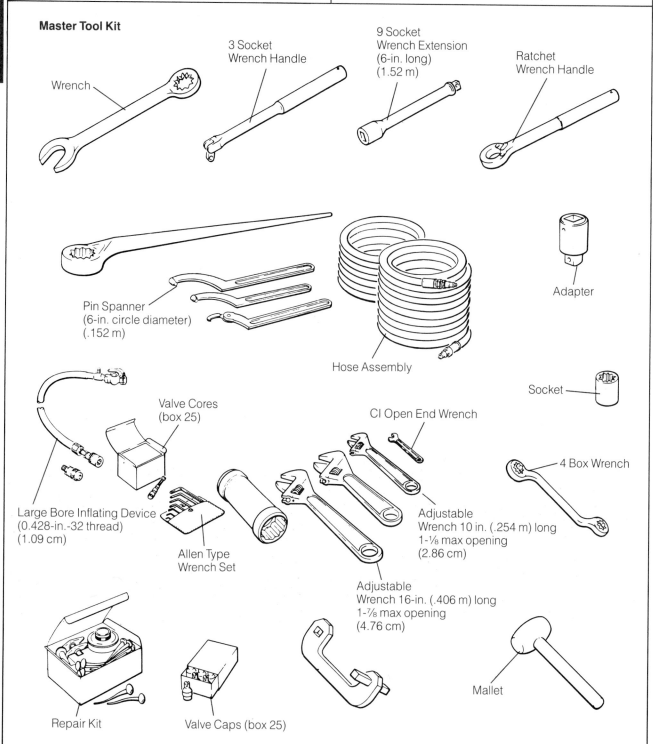

Wrench

3 Socket Wrench Handle

9 Socket Wrench Extension (6-in. long) (1.52 m)

Ratchet Wrench Handle

Adapter

Pin Spanner (6-in. circle diameter) (.152 m)

Hose Assembly

Socket

Valve Cores (box 25)

CI Open End Wrench

4 Box Wrench

Large Bore Inflating Device (0.428-in.-32 thread) (1.09 cm)

Allen Type Wrench Set

Adjustable Wrench 10 in. (.254 m) long 1-1/8 max opening (2.86 cm)

Adjustable Wrench 16-in. (.406 m) long 1-7/8 max opening (4.76 cm)

Mallet

Repair Kit

Valve Caps (box 25)

Contents of Tool Kits

General

Torque Handle	7/16 Wrench
Torque Wrench	1/2 Wrench
Spin Handle	9/16 Wrench
Ratchet Handle	11/16 Wrench
Speeder Handle	3/4 Wrench
Experiment Handle	13/16 Flarenut Wrench
4-inch Extension	Adjustable Wrench
8-inch Extension	3/64 Allen Wrench
12-inch Extension	5/64 Allen Wrench
1/4 8-point STD Socket	3/32 Allen Wrench
1/4 STD Socket	Slip Joint Pliers
5/16 STD Socket	Channel Lock Pliers
3/8 STD Socket	Needle Nose Pliers
7/16 STD Socket	Vise Grip Pliers
5/16 Deepwell Socket	Cutter Pliers
3/8 Deepwell Socket	Connector Pliers
7/16 Deepwell Socket	Pin Straightener Pliers
1/2 Deepwell Socket	3/32 Blade Driver
9/16 Deepwell Socket	3/16 Blade Driver
3/8 Blade Driver Bit	Phillips Driver 1
Hi-torque Driver Bit 1	Phillips Driver 2
Hi-torque Driver Bit 2	Phillips Offset Driver
Hi-torque Driver Bit 3	Hammer
1/16 Allen Bit	1/16 Punch
3/32 Allen Bit	3/32 Punch
7/64 Allen Bit	3/16 Punch
1/8 Allen Bit	O-ring Extractor
5/32 SQ Allen Bit	Knife
5/32 Allen Bit	Tweezer
5/32 Allen Bit-moded	Retrieval Mirror
3/16 Allen Bit	Retrieval Hook
3/16 Allen Bit-moded	Mechanical Fingers
3/16 × 3½ Allen Bit	Pinch Bar
3/16 Long Allen Bit	Vise
3/16 Long Allen Bit-moded	C Clamp
3/16 90° Allen Bit	Velcro-pile
1/4 Allen Bit	Velcro-hook
Universal Joint	3/4-inch Neutral Tape
11/16 Crowfoot Wrench	1-inch Red Tape
3/4 Crowfoot Wrench	2-inch Neutral Tape
1 Crowfoot Wrench	Safety Wipe
1 1/8 Crowfoot Wrench	Lacing Twine
1 3/8 Crowfoot Wrench	Lubricant
5/16 Wrench	H₂O System Lubricant
11/32 Wrench	Scissors
3/8 Wrench	

Miscellaneous Tools and Equipment

Vacuum Cleaner	Wet Wipes
Docking-latch Tool	Electrode Kit Wet Wipes
Latch-release Tool	Tissues
Seal Assembly	MEMU Maint Kit
Orifice-cleaning Tool	Tool Caddy
Biocide Wipes	Utility Belt
Utility Wipes	Mechanical Fingers

Contingency Tool Kit

Spin Handle	7/16 Wrench
Ratchet Handle	Connector Pliers
4-inch Extension	Phillips Driver 2
1/4 Deepwell Socket	1/8 Blade Driver
5/16 STD Socket	3-inch Flat Patch
3/8 Deepwell Socket	5 3/4 Blister Patch
7/16 Deepwell Socket	7 1/4-inch Blister Patch
Hi-torque Driver Bit 3	8½-inch Blister Patch
3/64 Allen Wrench	Universal Sealant
1/4 Wrench	1-inch Red Tape
1/8 Allen Bit	2-inch Neutral Tape
5/32 SQ Allen Bit	Scissors
3/16 90° Allen Bit	Pinch Bar
3/16 Long Allen Bit	Tool Caddy
Accutron Timer Key	Utility Belt
1/16 Allen Wrench	

Repair Kit

Duct Tape	Polybutene Sealant
Repair Patch, Flat	Plumbers Tape
Repair Patch, Dome, 5-inch	Velcro (Hook and Pile)
Repair Patch, Dome, 7-inch	Snap Assembly
Repair Patch, Dome, 8-inch	

Hatch Tool Kit

Snap-ring Removal Tool	Mallet
Punch	Seal-loosening Tool

MEM Tool Kit

Tool B (Ratchet)	Tool 1 (Socket)
Tool E (Handle)	Tool 2 (Screwdriver)
Tool F (End Wrench)	Tool 3 (Torque Tip 8)
Tool L (CDC Driver)	Tool 4 (Torque Tip 10)
Tool R (Driver)	Tool 5 (Torque Tip 12)
Tool V (U-joint Driver)	Tool 6 (Torque Tip 6)
Tool W (Ratchet)	

Water System Servicing Equipment

Hose Assembly	Adapter Assembly
Jumper Hose Assembly	Deionizer Assembly

Spare Tools

7/16 STD Socket (1)	3/4 Wrench (1)
7/64 Allen Bit (1)	3/64 Allen Wrench (3)
5/32 Allen Bit (3)	3/32 Allen Wrench (1)
3/16 Allen Bit (1)	3/32 Blade Driver (1)
3/16 Long Allen Bit (1)	3/16 Blade Driver (1)
1/4 Allen Bit (2)	Swiss Army Knife (1)

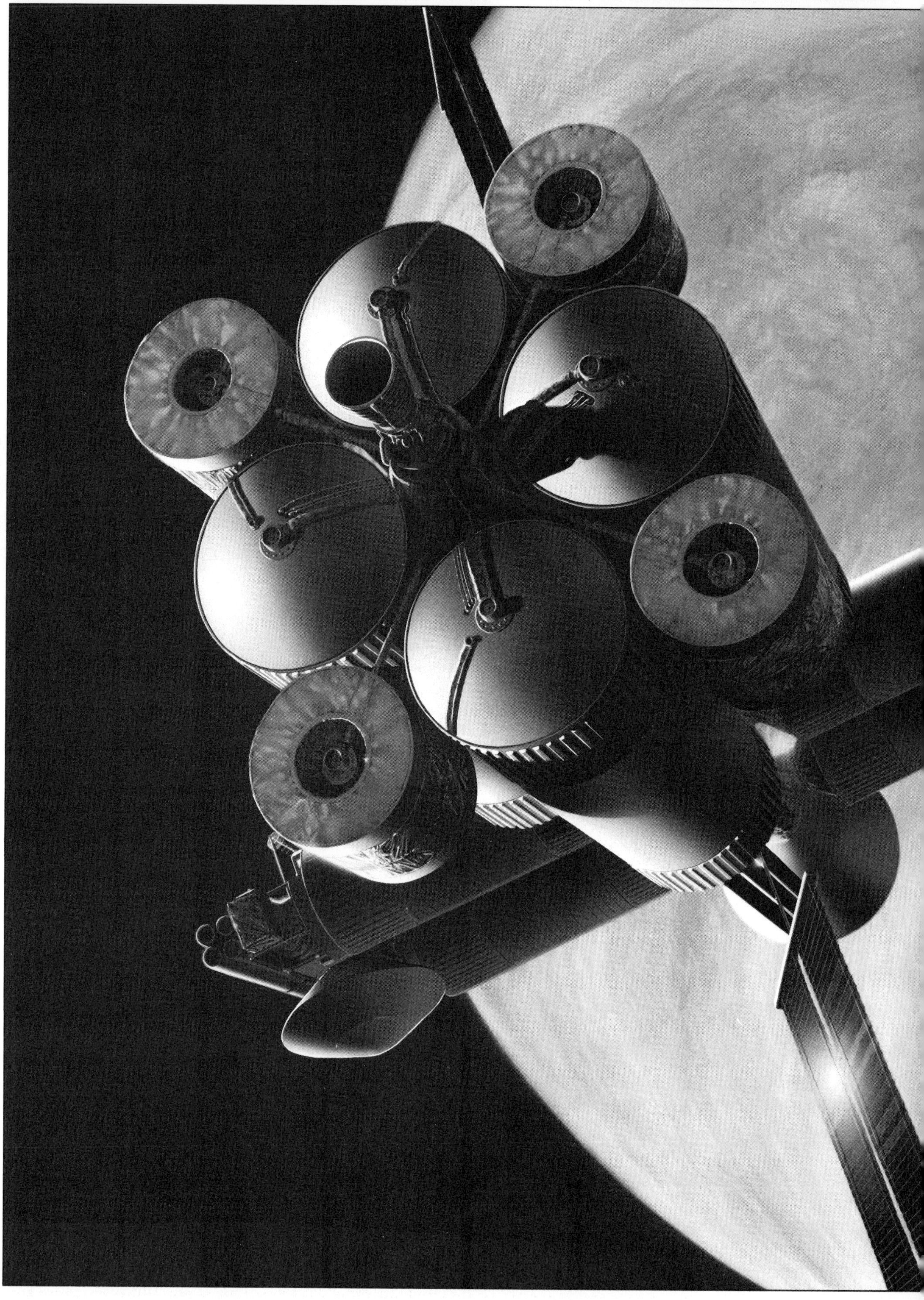

This section covers the period from Trans-Mars Injection to your arrival in the Mars vicinity. Included are schedules and details of your outbound activities and training, and a description of the Venus swing-by.

3.0.2

March 7, 1996 (245-0150 JD). The TMI checklist and heliocentric diagram indicate operational activity and planetary configuration during the Trans-Mars Injection burn.

Prior to the burn, complete the fuel and engine condition checklists, the system condition checklist, and the computer and time synchronization checks.
This is the official beginning of the mission clock.

TMI Checklist

Time to Ignition	Hrs:Min:Sec	Event
TIG	−01:00:00	Store loose items Prepare for burn
TIG	−00:30:00	Check tank pressures Cycle MMC to 100 series
TIG	−00:25:00	Check Reaction Control System (RCS) Check backup computers
TIG	−00:15:00	Trim orientation for burn
TIG	−00:03:00	Check crew condition
TIG	−00:02:00	Arm engine ignition
TIG	−00:00:15	Execute burn command AUTO
TIG	−00:00:00	Burn ignition

Planetary Positions at TMI

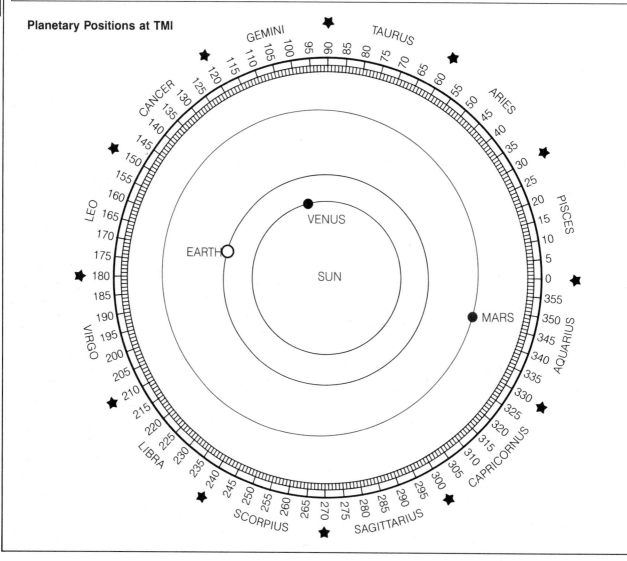

All space missions record events using at least three clocks. The time at Mission Control, Houston, Texas, Central Standard Time (CST), is generally the standard operating clock time. Mission events are also recorded using Greenwich Mean Time (GMT), also called Zulu time. The total amount of time used during the mission is referred to as Ground Elapsed Time (GET). This third clock is often used for total mission planning. Unfortunately, Mars does not rotate at the same speed as Earth. The martian day, called the "sol," is 24 hours 39.5 minutes in length.

Once you have left the Earth, you switch to the martian sol. The change cannot be immediate, however. Your biological clock is still on Earth time. To help the crew adjust gradually to martian time, seven seconds are added to every day. By the time the ship is about two Earth months from Mars, the crew is operating on the sol cycle. The reverse process is used on the inbound leg.

Three calendars are also used—the conventional calendar, the Julian calendar, used in astronomy and space science, and the martian calendar. A short computer program can tell you what day it is for any of the three at any time. You will find it most helpful to think in terms of sols on the outbound leg. The Julian calendar measures days consecutively, not in months; so does the martian calendar. Thus the conventional date of departure from Earth orbit is March 7, 1996, the Julian date is 245-0150, and the martian date is sol −340.77 (sol 0 is your arrival at Mars). This manual gives all operational dates in modern and Julian notation; only events on Mars are recorded in sols.

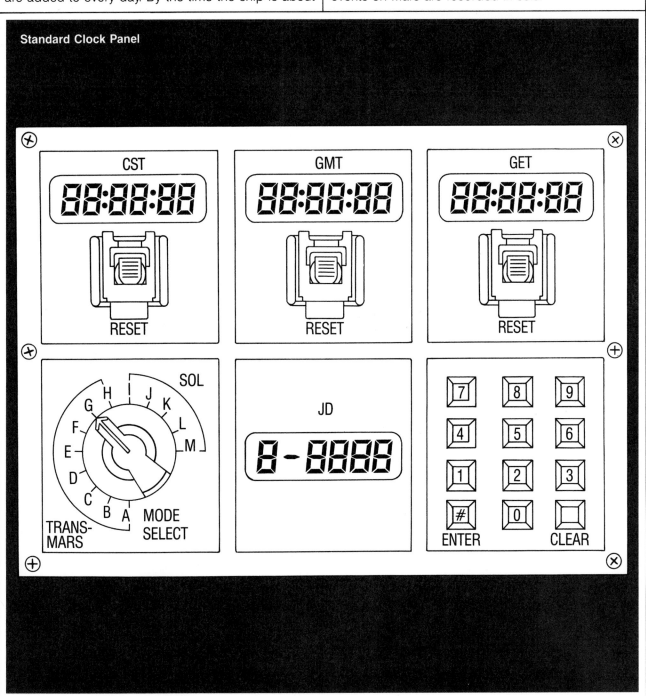

Standard Clock Panel

Training Tasks

Outbound Daily Schedule

3.2.1

*Communication to/from Earth is accomplished during personal time

*Wednesday PM—Crew planning and assessment meetings

*Sunday schedule—free AM until exercise session PM— weekly physical, report/ problem analysis, and intergroup meeting

Time (hrs.)	Length of Activity (hrs.)	HAB 1 — Commander / Pilot / Chief Science Officer / Science Specialist #1 / Science Specialist #2 / Science Specialist #3
1–8	8	Sleep
8	:30	Personal time
9	:45	Breakfast
10		System maint
10–12	3	Training
13	1	Exercise A
14	1	Exercise B
15	:45	Lunch
16–18	3:30	Training
19	1	Exercise and personal time
20	1	Exercise and personal time
21–22	1:15	Dinner
23	1:30	Maintenance and housekeeping
24	:45	Personal time

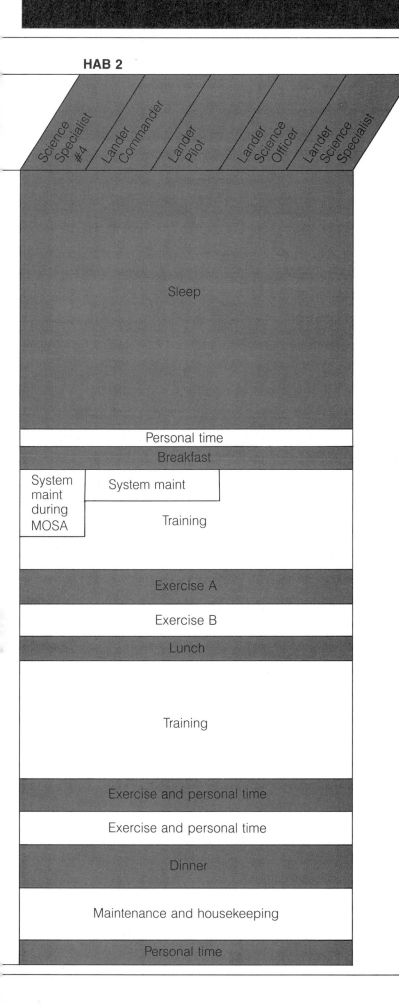

HAB 2

Science Specialist #4 / Lander Commander / Lander Pilot / Lander Science Officer / Lander Science Specialist

Sleep

Personal time

Breakfast

System maint during MOSA | System maint

Training

Exercise A

Exercise B

Lunch

Training

Exercise and personal time

Exercise and personal time

Dinner

Maintenance and housekeeping

Personal time

The length of this mission permits time for outbound training. Because of the complexity of the systems and procedures involved and the difficulty in maintaining your skills over a long period such as this, a rigorous training review and simulation schedule is essential.

There are several areas for training activities: general systems, medical and first-aid procedures, abort procedures, systems simulations, and science series studies. General systems studies deal with ship systems—life support, basic procedures, repair, etc. Medical and first-aid procedures deal with diagnosis and treatment. Abort procedures cover all abort situations from TMI to EOI and include Mars landing aborts and special emergency procedures. Systems simulations are full-scale dry runs of all major events and involve either the entire crew or specific groups. Science series studies involve a review of all scientific activities, including geological and biomedical functions. The geology series covers orbital sensing, atmosphere, geophysics, and surface tasks. The biomedical series covers hygiene and physiology.

Sequences and schedules are supervised by the chief science officer and are assigned by mission responsibility. The mission commander and pilot spend most of their time reviewing general systems, abort modes, and systems simulations. The lander commander and pilot spend their time reviewing landing procedures and aborts, portions of the geology series, medical procedures, and systems simulations. The lander science crew and their orbital counterpart, Science Specialist 4, review the complete geology series, lander systems, general systems, general simulations, medical procedures, and lander/Rover aborts. The other science specialists go through the general systems and systems simulation programs, along with the orbital geology series, the biomedical series, and special deployment procedures training.

Training activities are varied, with certain groups of simulations scheduled in advance. There are also problem simulations to be solved in group meetings, and a series of emergency simulations and drills, some without notice. These are all considered part of your training program. They keep you in a high state of readiness with a high degree of confidence.

3.2.2

Venus Swing-by

The Mars One craft swings by Venus on August 15, 1996 (245-0311.4 JD). This provides the crew with an opportunity to practice some tasks that will be useful at Mars and to add to the general knowledge of Venus.

The planet Venus has been more difficult to study than Mars. Like Mars, it has a thick atmosphere formed mostly of carbon dioxide. But on this Earth-sized planet, that atmosphere has produced a "greenhouse" effect. Venus is only 70 million miles (112 million kilometers) from the Sun, the Earth is 93 million miles (150 million kilometers). The intense solar radiation penetrates Venus's carbon atmosphere and is trapped. This causes a surface temperature of 981°F (527°C), a temperature prohibiting human exploration. In addition, the opaque atmosphere denies access to the planet by telescopes. To operate spacecraft and equipment in such an environment is extremely difficult.

The Soviet Union has been somewhat successful in sending back a few precious photographs from the planet by way of unmanned landers. The United States' Mariner 10 (1973), Pioneer Venus (1978), and Venus Radar Mapper (1989) also studied the clouds, the atmosphere, and the surface of Venus. These missions mapped the planet and found volcanoes and large upland regions on the scalding surface. But there is still a great need for further atmospheric research.

Your mission is to deploy three atmospheric probes that will measure trace elements and compounds in the atmosphere. It is hoped that these tests will also give important clues about the environment of the inner solar system during the formation of the planets. The tasks for launching these probes are similar to those for deploying penetrators and hardlanders at Mars, so the experience is also a valuable training exercise.

The probes you deploy are similar to those of Pioneer Venus in shape and size, but carry different and better instrumentation. There are one large probe and two smaller ones. The largest probe is 5 feet (1.5 meters) in diameter and weighs 645 pounds (315 kilograms). It contains a titanium pressure vessel that includes a nephelometer to study the clouds, a series of temperature and pressure sensors, a gas chromatograph, a mass spectrometer, and accelerometers to measure atmospheric turbulence. The probe is protected by an aeroshell to provide stable aerodynamic braking.

The smaller probes are 30 inches (0.8 meters) in diameter and weigh 200 pounds (90 kilograms). Each has a gas chromatograph and a mass spectrometer, as well as temperature and pressure sensors and accelerometers. The magnetometers on the main ship are able to study the magnetic interaction around Venus and the flow of solar particles in the venusian atmosphere.

The three probes are deployed on July 26, 1996 (245-0291 JD), twenty days before the closest approach to Venus. They enter the atmosphere of Venus at about 26,000 mph (42,000 kph). Communications from the probes begin about 22 minutes before atmospheric entry. The g-forces vary from 220 to 450 g. Forty-two miles (67 kilometers) above the surface, the aeroshell is jettisoned. At 30 miles (47 kilometers) the parachutes are jettisoned and the probes free-fall to the surface. The total time from atmospheric entry to surface landing is 55 minutes. The three probes are targeted as

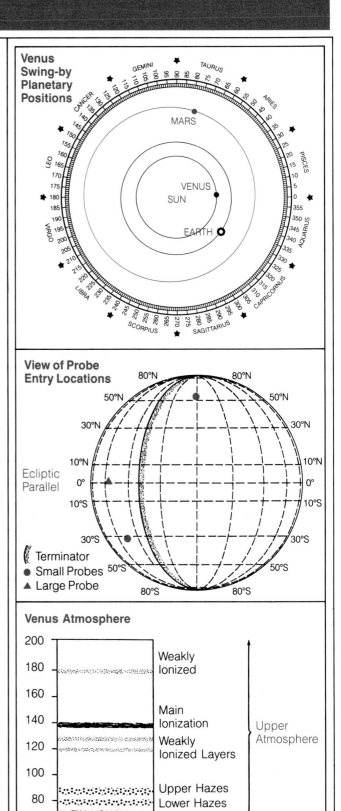

Venus Swing-by Planetary Positions

View of Probe Entry Locations

(Terminator
● Small Probes
▲ Large Probe

Ecliptic Parallel

Venus Atmosphere

Weakly Ionized

Main Ionization

Weakly Ionized Layers

Upper Hazes
Lower Hazes

Tropopause Clouds

Wind Shear

Low Hazes
Aerosols Dust

Clear Atmosphere Surface

Crust

Upper Atmosphere

Clouds

Lower Atmosphere

Height km

Wind Speed m/s

follows: the large probe near the equator, the first small probe in the north latitudes (45°N), and the second small probe at 30°S on the day side of Venus.

During the swing-by, you come within 5,756.9 miles (9,264.5 kilometers) of the planet's surface, a distance of 1.531 Venus radii. Your path bends the spacecraft course by 44.7° and heads you toward Mars. As you approach Venus, you are at an angle of about 80° to its equator, so you swing over both the northern and southern hemispheres. At the closest approach, you are just southeast of the huge upland region Aphrodite Terra and over a point at 158.2°E, 36°S. As you leave the planet's range, you are treated to a sunrise and a view of Venus as a magnificent, receding crescent.

Now you return to your regular training routine. Mars is still 188.6 days (183.6 sols) ahead.

Venus's Surface — Because of Greenland Effect, Ishtar looks larger than Aphrodite

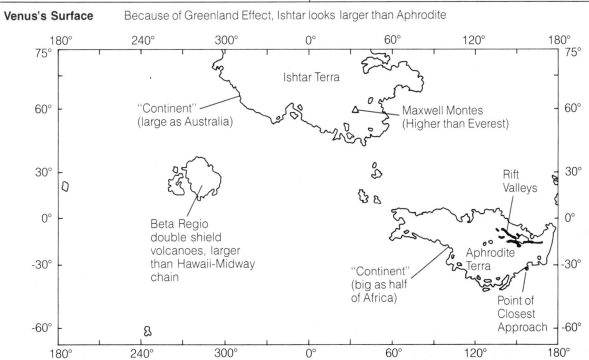

Balloon Drop and Separation Sequence

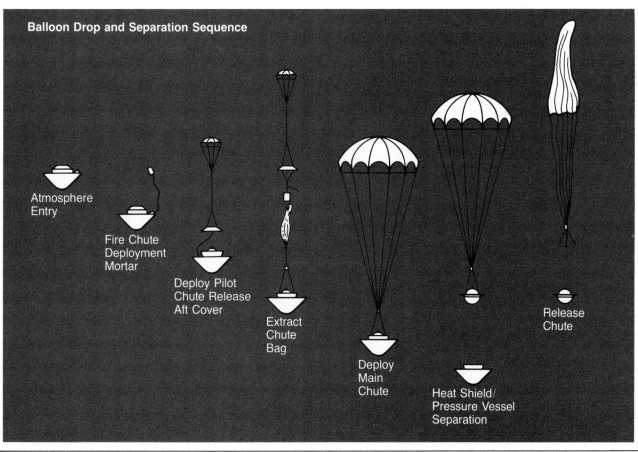

Small Probe

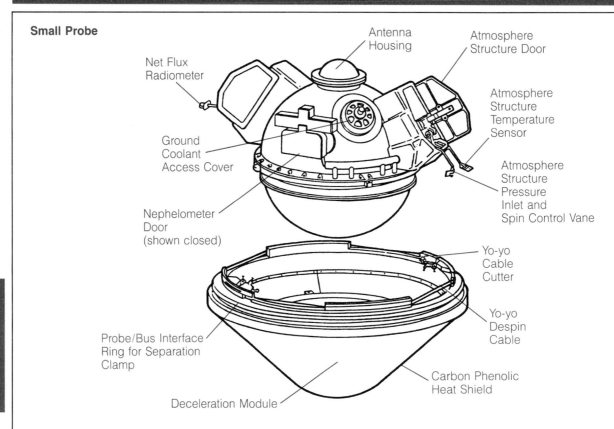

Antenna Housing

Atmosphere Structure Door

Net Flux Radiometer

Atmosphere Structure Temperature Sensor

Ground Coolant Access Cover

Atmosphere Structure Pressure Inlet and Spin Control Vane

Nephelometer Door (shown closed)

Yo-yo Cable Cutter

Yo-yo Despin Cable

Probe/Bus Interface Ring for Separation Clamp

Carbon Phenolic Heat Shield

Deceleration Module

Large Probe

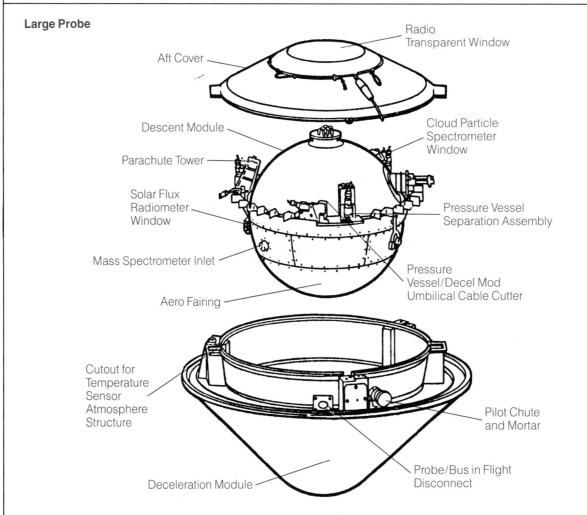

Radio Transparent Window

Aft Cover

Descent Module

Cloud Particle Spectrometer Window

Parachute Tower

Solar Flux Radiometer Window

Pressure Vessel Separation Assembly

Mass Spectrometer Inlet

Aero Fairing

Pressure Vessel/Decel Mod Umbilical Cable Cutter

Cutout for Temperature Sensor Atmosphere Structure

Pilot Chute and Mortar

Deceleration Module

Probe/Bus in Flight Disconnect

Large Probe Experiments

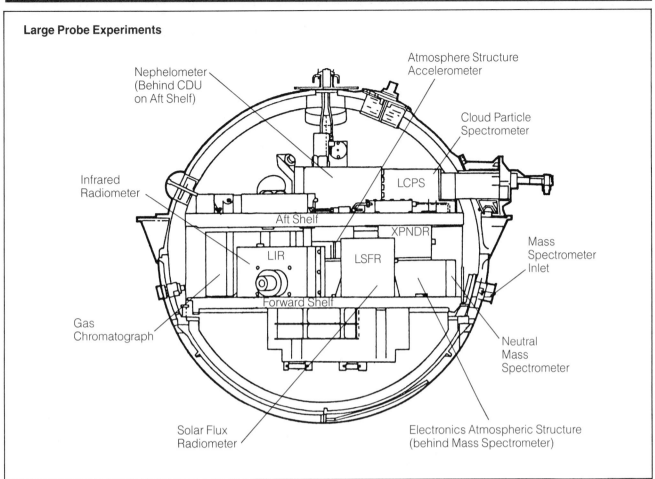

Large Probe Pressure Vessel

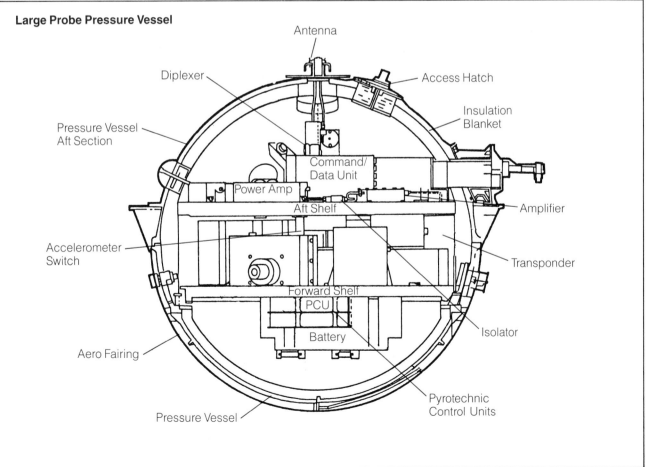

3.3.4

Navigation

In space, there is a multitude of stars to navigate by. Of course, light in the craft may make it hard to see them, so you need some navigation instrumentation. While your basic course is that of a bullet moving under the influence of various gravitational fields, you still need to know where you are, in what direction you are headed, and in what orientation your craft is. This knowledge is necessary in order to make small adjustments, called midcourse corrections, to the trajectory (flight path). The orientation of the craft is also important for communication, since some antennas must be precisely aimed for good results.

There are a number of ways of knowing your position along the flight path. The ship is equipped with several navigation sensors. One type of sensor can lock in on the Sun, another on a star. Each sun sensor, really five separate sensors, keeps you from wobbling up/down or left/right. A star sensor keeps the craft from rolling.

An automated attitude control system responds to any change by the sensors. If the ship position drifts in relation to the Sun or Canopus, the reference star, signals are sent to the Reaction Control System (RCS), correcting the ship's orientation.

The radio signals you send and receive also carry navigational information. The slight shift of signals as you move away from or toward the Earth, like the increase or decrease in the whistle pitch of a train, will indicate your velocity. Passing behind a planet cuts off the signal and also permits use of radio waves to precisely fix your position at both Venus and Mars, and to provide additional information about the atmospheres of both planets.

3.4.1

Digital Standard Star Tracker System

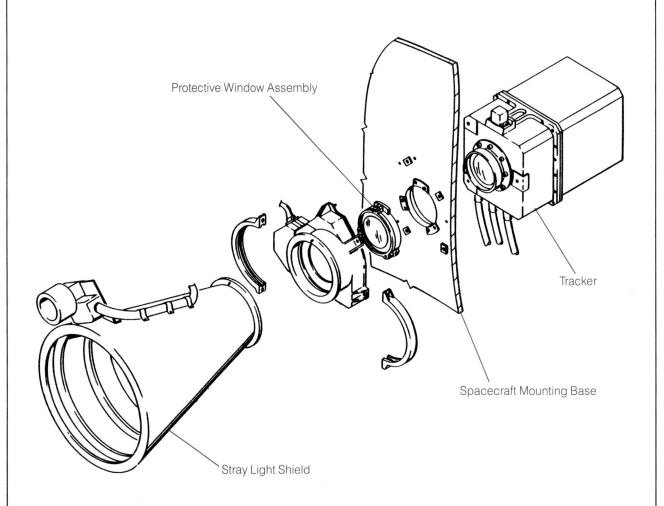

Protective Window Assembly

Tracker

Spacecraft Mounting Base

Stray Light Shield

No matter how precise an engine burn is, there is always the chance of a slight deviation. The engine may shut off a little before or after the planned time. The thrust may be slightly more or less than expected. One of these conditions may cause slight or even significant variance from the ideal trajectory. Normally, these variations are not serious, but do need to be corrected. A slight deviation at one end of a voyage of tens of millions of miles can produce a deviation of thousands of miles from the expected arrival point. Great precision can be achieved, however. Pioneer 10, for example, arrived only eleven seconds late after a voyage of 1.5 billion miles.

To smooth these differences, small engine burns, called midcourse maneuvers, are used. These burns compensate for whatever irregularities have occurred in the ideal flight path. They are usually short in duration (a few seconds), but they can be critical on a mission like Mars One.

The ship has the capability of performing four midcourse maneuvers during the outbound leg, if they are required. One burn at seven days out and a second one twenty-three days later may be all that is required.

Prior to the midcourse maneuver, the crew receives telemetry updates from Mission Control on velocity and trajectory. This data is compared to the ship's own inertial guidance information, and the MMC then provides the direction and length of the midcourse correctional burns.

Expect minor correctional burns in Mars's orbit and at least four more midcourse corrections during the return leg.

Planetary Positions at Mars Arrival

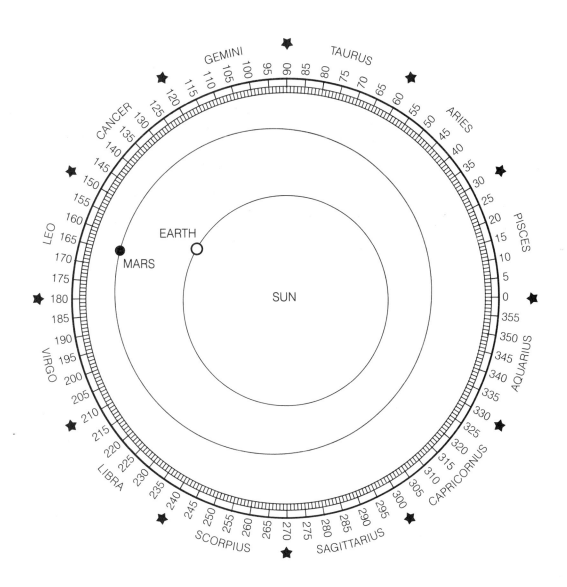

3.4.2

4.0.1

This section outlines your activities at Mars. It should be studied thoroughly prior to arrival since these activities are intense. Maneuvers and orbital and surface activities are described, along with necessary equipment and procedures for your research.

4.0.2

Aerocapture Operations

The value of your short stay at Mars is maximized by some advance knowledge of the landing site. It has been decided to put the Rover on the planet's surface in advance of the landing and explore the site remotely. To do this, the Rover has to be delivered to Mars first. The fastest and cheapest way to accomplish this is with a separate vehicle flying a faster trajectory and not requiring a load of fuel to slow into martian orbit. This saves weight and, therefore, money. With no fuel to stop

the vehicle, however, the only way to brake it is to fly it through the drag of the martian atmosphere. This must be done carefully, since too much of a dip would destroy the vehicle and too little would send it skipping off into space.

To accomplish this task, a specially designed aerodynamic shell is used. The shell, shaped like a flattened cone, enters the martian atmosphere, dips into it until enough energy is lost to atmospheric drag, then

Planetary Positions and Aerocapture Trajectory

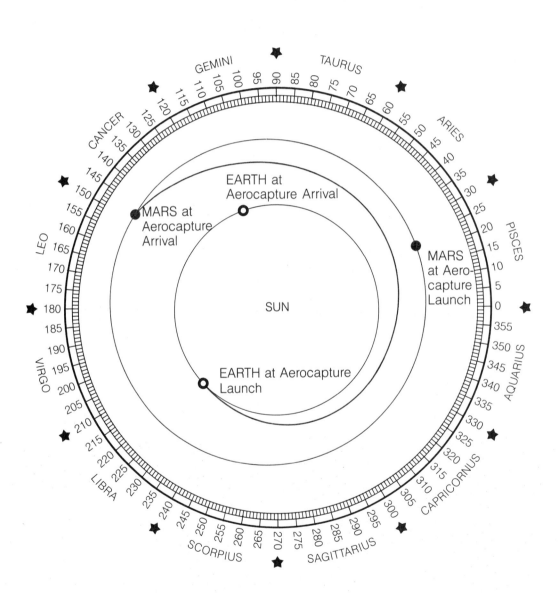

4.1.1

pulls out, performs a small burn, and is captured in an orbit. This procedure is known as aerocapture. The orbiting aerobraked ship has a load of consumables and emergency spares for the main ship when you arrive.

The Mars Rover is ejected inside an aeroshell, and small deorbit motors fire. The Rover descends, deploys three parachutes, and fires a small burst just above the surface. Its aeroshell has been jettisoned during parachute descent, so the Rover is ready to go on arrival. It is then maneuvered remotely to the expected MEM landing site.

The aerocapture ship consists of a TMI stage and the aerocapture vehicle containing the Rover. The ship requires a velocity change of 10,500 mph (16,900 kph) to leave Earth orbit, and departs on Monday, May 6, 1996 (245-0210.50). The aerocapture vehicle is 14.1 feet (4.3 meters) across its base and 33.8 feet (10.3 meters) long. It is covered with a thermal protection

Aerocapture Sequence of Events

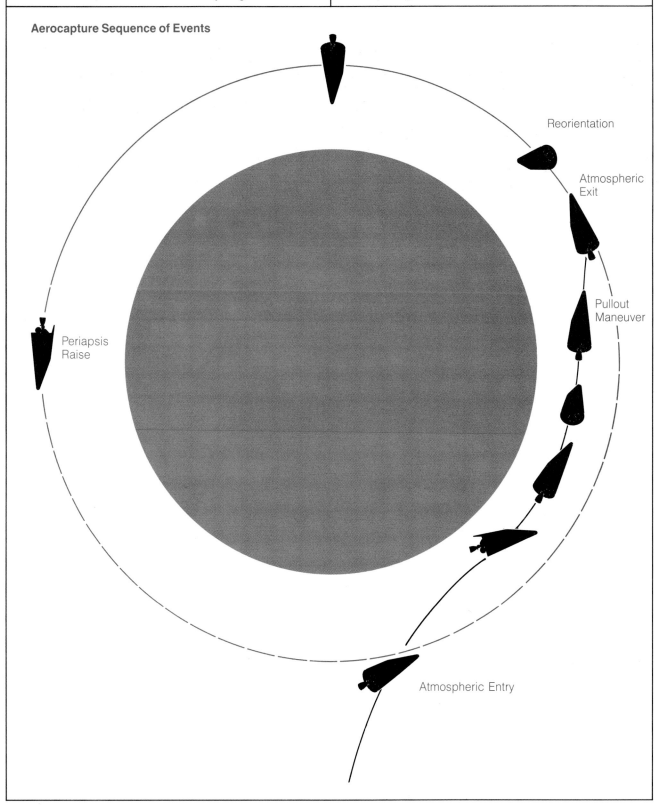

Reorientation

Atmospheric Exit

Pullout Maneuver

Periapsis Raise

4.1.2

Atmospheric Entry

Aerocapture Operations

system (TPS) made of Nomex blanketing similar to the low heat Nomex of the Shuttle orbiters, and with a silicone ablative material (SAM) of a type used in special applications on the highly heated bottom side.

During the voyage, the ship flies with its side toward the Sun and its nose pointing at right angles to the Sun/planets' plane—the ecliptic. Because the nose points toward the Sun's, Earth's, and Mars's northern hemispheres, it is called a "nose North" position. The

vehicle has Sun and star sensors and a reaction control system to maintain its attitude. On Thursday, December 12, 1996 (245-0430 JD), thirty days from atmospheric entry, a trajectory correction maneuver (TCM) is done. Precise navigational data is collected from the first TCM until just 12 hours before entry. Then a final TCM is performed to adjust the vehicle attitude and make certain that it is reoriented to the correct entry position.

Rover Landing Sequence

1. Orbit

2. Deorbit Burn

3. Deorbit and Coast

4. Deploy Parachutes

5. Jettison Aeroshell

6. Deploy Parachutes

7. Fire Detachable Engines and Release Parachutes

8. Landing and Release Engines

The vehicle arrives at Mars on Saturday, January 11, 1997 (245-0460 JD). After entry, the RCS holds the vehicle in the proper orientation. This should produce only 1.5 g of force (one and one-half times the force of Earth's gravity). The Rover computer is continually predicting the velocity of the vehicle and the velocity required to exit the atmosphere. At the right velocity the vehicle then orients itself for the maximum lift and exits the atmosphere. Its new velocity assures capture by Mars's gravity. The Rover deorbits four days later—26 days (25.2 sols) before you arrive. In a complex procedure, the Rover's systems are activated by remote commands from Earth. Two television cameras are deployed, and a traverse begins. Because of the distance from Earth, the Rover cannot move continuously. A certain distance is scouted and the Rover is directed to move a safe fraction of that distance. It is never allowed to go over its visual horizon.

Aerocapture Shell

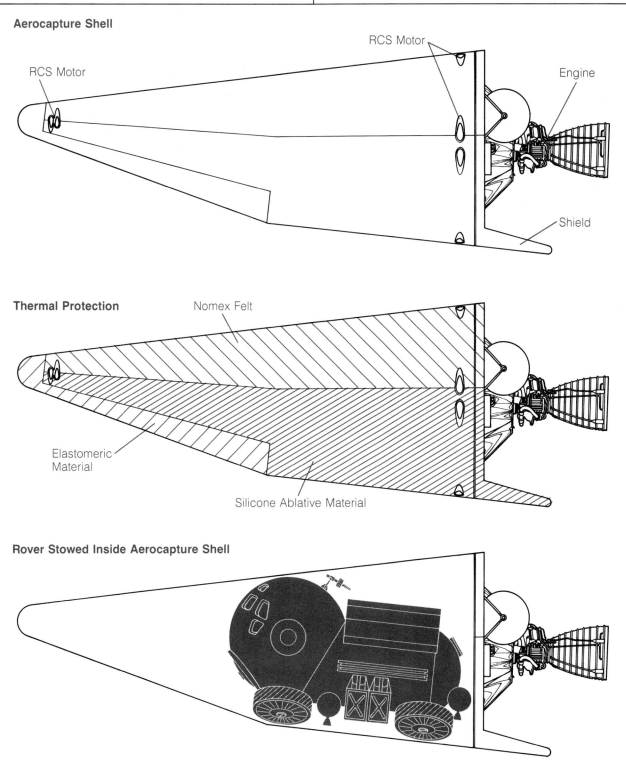

RCS Motor

RCS Motor

Engine

RCS Motor

Shield

Thermal Protection

Nomex Felt

Elastomeric Material

Silicone Ablative Material

Rover Stowed Inside Aerocapture Shell

4.1.4

Hardlander and Penetrator Deployment

Obviously, the Mars One landing crew can explore only a small fraction of the martian surface. While the landing site was selected to provide the greatest possible information, there are other regions that must be explored. To do this, hardlanders and penetrators are stowed aboard on the same pallet as the Venus probes. They are released on approach to Mars with a procedure similar to that used to deploy the atmospheric entry probes on Venus. These devices deorbit and, targeted at deployment, essentially crash-land at different sites around the planet. This procedure creates a global network of stations to study surface weather data and global seismic data (marsquakes).

The hardlander is a small spherical spacecraft. It has three legs, upward-protruding antennas and weather sensors, and an arm that extends away from the spacecraft. The end of the arm has an auger to drill into the surface. Inside the auger is a small seismometer, a radioisotope heater, and an electric heater. The arm drops onto the surface and the auger rotates at about one revolution per minute for about fifteen minutes. This action buries the seismometer at an appropriate depth. This procedure minimizes wind noise, which affects the instrument.

The penetrators are tube-like structures that slam into the martian surface at almost 20,000 g. (If you were driving at 60 mph and stopped in one one-hundredth of a second by crashing into a wall, you would hit that wall at about 275 g.) A penetrator is divided into two parts: a forebody, which will penetrate the surface to a

4.2.1

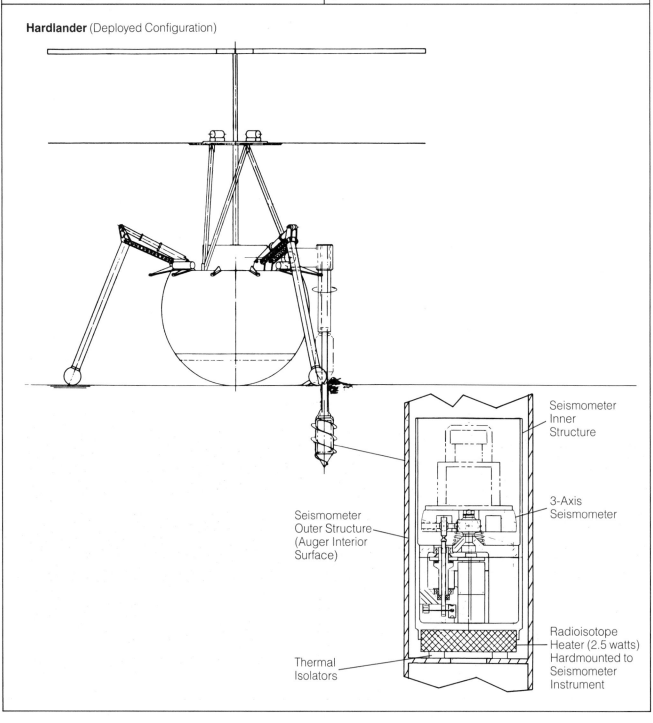

Hardlander (Deployed Configuration)

Seismometer Inner Structure

3-Axis Seismometer

Seismometer Outer Structure (Auger Interior Surface)

Radioisotope Heater (2.5 watts) Hardmounted to Seismometer Instrument

Thermal Isolators

Penetrator

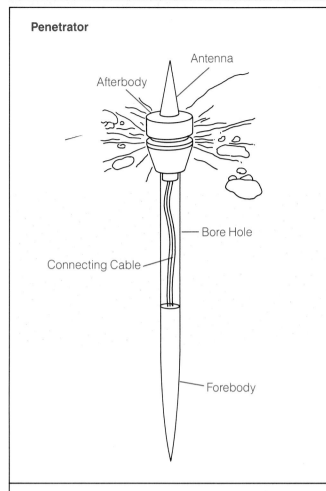

- Antenna
- Afterbody
- Bore Hole
- Connecting Cable
- Forebody

Penetrator Forebody

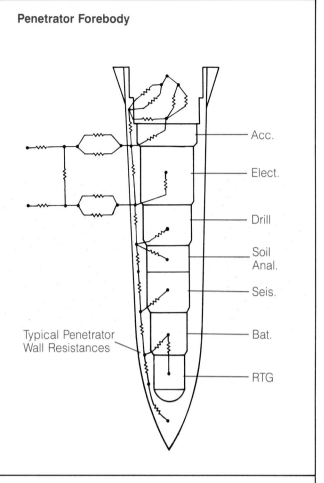

- Acc.
- Elect.
- Drill
- Soil Anal.
- Seis.
- Bat.
- RTG
- Typical Penetrator Wall Resistances

4.2.2

Mars Penetrator Afterbody Deployment

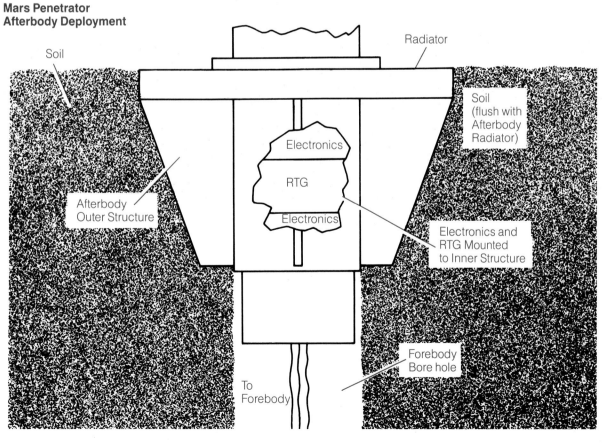

- Soil
- Radiator
- Soil (flush with Afterbody Radiator)
- Afterbody Outer Structure
- Electronics
- RTG
- Electronics
- Electronics and RTG Mounted to Inner Structure
- To Forebody
- Forebody Bore hole

depth of about 47 feet (15 meters), and an afterbody, which embeds itself above the forebody hole, but protrudes above the surface.

The forebody contains a 10-watt radioisotope thermoelectric generator (RTG), a battery, a seismometer, and a soil analysis unit. Studying the subsurface soil, the Mars One crew can learn a great deal about the permafrost and thus more about the total water situation on the planet. The afterbody is about 12.9 inches (.32 meter) long and contains two temperature detectors, a humidity sensor, a wind speed/direction instrument, and an antenna. After impact, a dust cover is released and explosive bolts are fired, which deploy the temperature detectors at heights of 19 inches (.5 meter) and 60 inches (1.5 meters). The wind speed instrument and antenna are on the higher mast, while the lower temperature sensor shares its mast with the humidity sensor. The dust cover is then thrown off, and the top surface of the afterbody acts as a heat radiator.

The temperature sensors are each housed in such a way that the atmosphere can flow freely past three thermocouples, which respond to heat. The housing for the temperature sensors is designed so that the thermocouples are not exposed to the Sun, the sky, or the rest of the penetrator, sources which could ruin the accuracy of the measurements. The thermocouples are compared to determine the actual surface temperature. The ability to take three separate measurements provides a backup if any individual thermocouple should fail.

The hardlanders and penetrators are deployed approximately 48 hours before Mars Orbit Injection (MOI). They must be deployed at precise angles with only a 5-degree margin for error. If the penetrators' entry angle into the atmosphere is too high, they will skip off into space. If the entry angle is too low, they will overheat and be useless. The pattern of impact is a ring around the martian surface. The precise location of the ring is determined by controlling the time of arrival. The maxi-

4.2.3

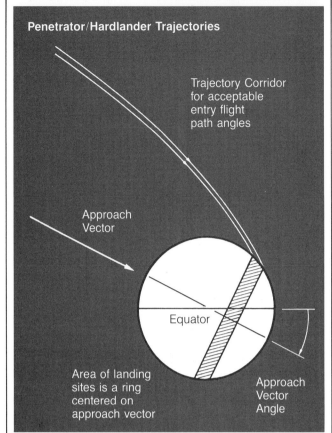

Penetrator/Hardlander Trajectories

Trajectory Corridor for acceptable entry flight path angles

Approach Vector

Equator

Area of landing sites is a ring centered on approach vector

Approach Vector Angle

mum northern martian latitude reachable would be 38° N. The southernmost latitude would be 75° S.

Prior to separation of the hardlanders and penetrators, you perform preflight checks. These include charging batteries, checking the voltage and thermal output of batteries and RTGs, checking transmitters and sensors, and checking navigation information for final computations of separation times.

Penetrator/Hardlander Landing Zone

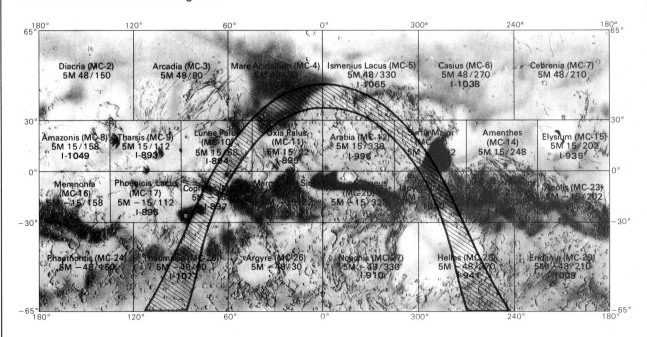

Feb. 20, 1997 (245-0500 JD) (sol 0). The MOI checklist and heliocentric chart indicate planetary position and activities during your Mars orbit injection burn.

Prior to this activity, complete the engine and fuel condition checklists. Should there be a misfire or abort, reset the computer and call up the MOI abort mode checklist sequence.

MOI Checklist

Time to ignition	Hrs:Min:Sec	Event
TIG	−00:20:00	Load 200 series into MMC
TIG	−00:16:00	Check fuel tank pressurization
TIG	−00:15:00	Abort check
TIG	−00:02:00	Arm engine ignition
TIG	−00:00:10	Execute burn command
TIG	−00:00:00	Burn ignition

Planetary Positions at Mars Arrival

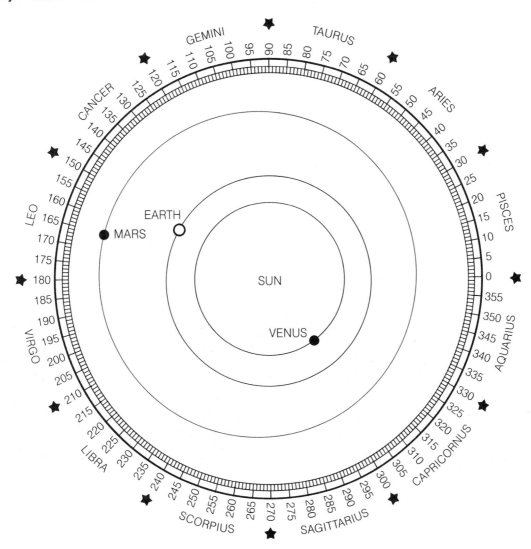

Comsat Deployment

Mars Rover mobile operations, data collection from the network of penetrators and hardlanders, Mars Airplane operations, MEM communication operations, and surface navigation all require almost continual contact between the surface and the main ship and/or Earth. To ensure the availability of these links and to permit the main ship to do some orbital modification to study Phobos and Deimos, two communications subsatellites are deployed and placed in stationary orbits.

Each satellite has four channels called transponders: one to carry video, one to carry audio and telemetry, and two spares. The satellites are placed 120° apart at an altitude of 10,612 miles (17,075 kilometers). Comsat 1 is located at 0° N, 60° W. Comsat 2 is located 0° N, 300° W. They both have an orbital period of 1 sol (24 hours, 39 minutes) and therefore appear motionless in the sky from the ground. Ground coverage will be sufficient to reach all operational areas.

Deployment is accomplished by a spring-loaded system, which separates the satellites from the main ship at apoapsis. When the comsats are several hundred meters away, the first burn occurs.

Deployment of the satellites requires two firings of the small "kick motor" on the comsats. The first burn reduces the apoapsis distance from 20,200 miles (32,600 kilometers) to 10,612 miles (17,075 kilometers). The second burn is the "kick" necessary to circularize the orbit, which has its period equal to Mars's rotation rate—1 sol.

Each satellite has three antennas with a power output of 30 watts. Each is powered by two 8-by-4-foot (2.4-by-1.2-meters) solar arrays, which generate 245 watts. Nickel-cadmium batteries supply electrical power when the craft is behind Mars.

Each comsat also has a beacon. By locking in on this radio beacon, transmissions from Earth, and the beacon on the main ship, the surface party can accurately determine its position.

4.3.1

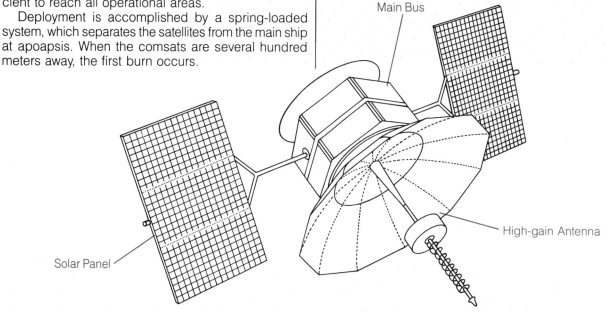

Main Bus

High-gain Antenna

Solar Panel

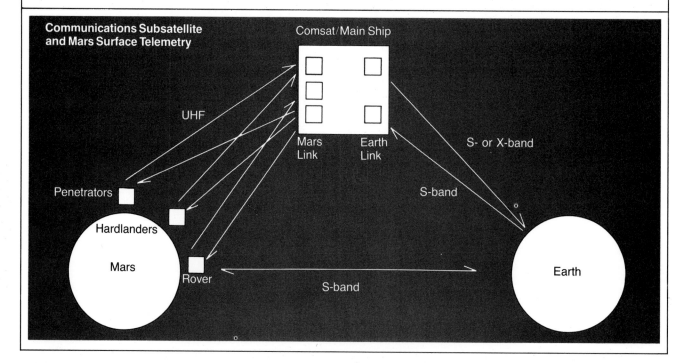

Communications Subsatellite and Mars Surface Telemetry

Comsat/Main Ship

UHF

Mars Link

Earth Link

S- or X-band

S-band

Penetrators

Hardlanders

Mars

Rover

S-band

Earth

Even with your Mars Rover mobile laboratory you can only explore a relatively few miles of surface at the bottom of only one canyon. The network of penetrators and hardlanders generates data from other regions, but doesn't permit gathering information about the atmosphere above several feet and from regions inaccessible to easy exploration.

Because Mars has an atmosphere, wide-ranging, safe exploration can be accomplished with a remotely piloted (unmanned) airplane. Such an aircraft can be controlled to explore a good cross section of the lower atmosphere and to visit a wide variety of regions, providing extremely close-range images of the surface. With the airplane the Mars One team can sample the surface at widely distant spots and with great speed.

You will deploy two airplanes from orbit. Each airplane is folded and housed in a protective aeroshell. After atmospheric entry, a mortar deploys a parachute that slows the assembly to under Mach 1. After the aeroshell is jettisoned, the airplane begins to unfold. The tail booms extend and lock, followed by the wings and the tail. Finally the propeller unfolds. While the craft is still in a nearly vertical dive, the parachute is jettisoned and the propeller moves like a windmill until the engine starts, pulling the aircraft out of the dive and leveling it at cruising altitude.

Since the horsepower required for flight on Mars is only 23.2 percent of that required on Earth, the possible range of each aircraft is 2.65 times that on Earth.

The engine weighs 7 pounds and produces 7 horsepower. The wingspan of each aircraft is 22 feet (6.7 meters). Overall weight on Earth is 200 pounds (91 kilograms). The 50-pound scientific payload consists of atmospheric temperature and pressure sensors, a mini-high-resolution camera, and solar cells and batteries for power generating 130 watts. Each airplane has a range of 3,000 miles (4,800 kilometers) and can stay in the air for about 16.5 hours.

The airplane's camera is cycled to transmit one frame every 10 seconds at an altitude of 5,000 feet (1,524 meters). This produces a 20 percent overlap from image to image. The telemetry is transmitted at a rate of 520 kilobits per second using a 53-watt transmitter to the orbiting comsats. The transmission frequency is 1.62 gigahertz.

After deployment, you guide the aircraft on predetermined flight paths. One flies from Tharsis, over your landing site and into the southern hemisphere. The second overflies the north pole and dune areas. They are on a preprogrammed course, but can be remotely controlled manually by the orbiting crew to permit flexibility and to take advantage of any unexpected research opportunity.

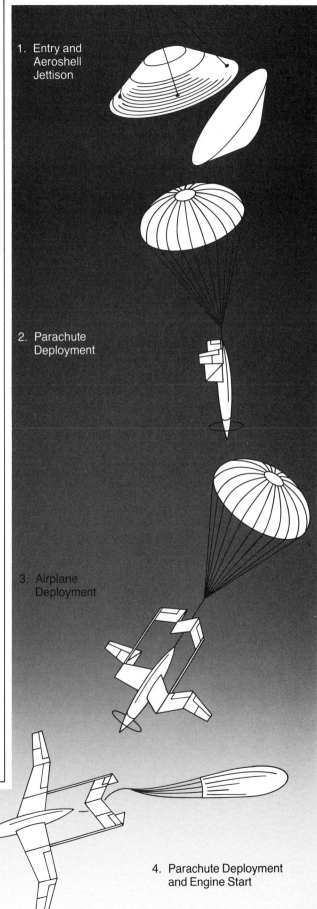

1. Entry and Aeroshell Jettison

2. Parachute Deployment

3. Airplane Deployment

4. Parachute Deployment and Engine Start

4.3.2

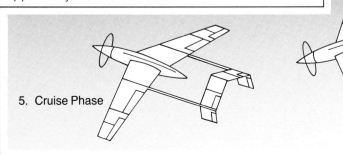

5. Cruise Phase

Mars Airplane Deployment

Mars Airplane

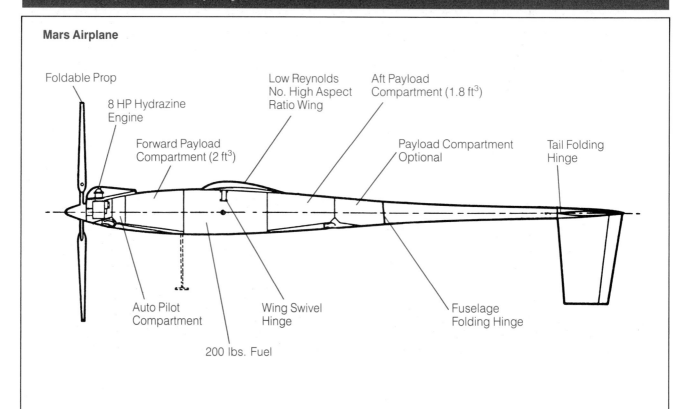

Foldable Prop

8 HP Hydrazine Engine

Low Reynolds No. High Aspect Ratio Wing

Aft Payload Compartment (1.8 ft^3)

Forward Payload Compartment (2 ft^3)

Payload Compartment Optional

Tail Folding Hinge

Auto Pilot Compartment

Wing Swivel Hinge

Fuselage Folding Hinge

200 lbs. Fuel

Propulsion System   Hydrazine Powered Engine

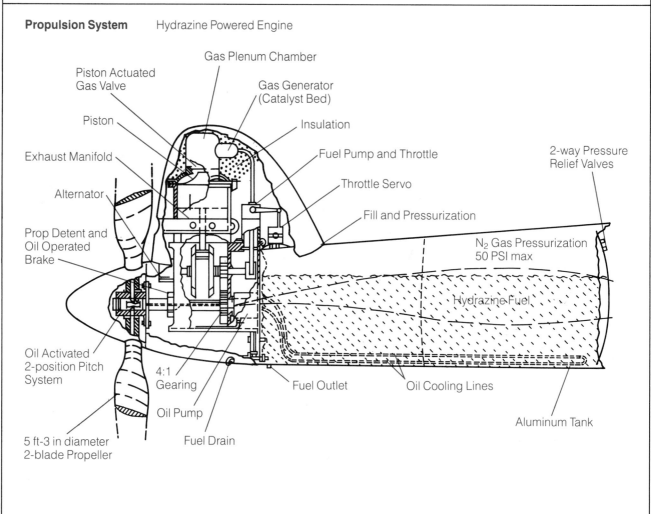

Piston Actuated Gas Valve

Gas Plenum Chamber

Gas Generator (Catalyst Bed)

Piston

Insulation

Exhaust Manifold

Fuel Pump and Throttle

Alternator

Throttle Servo

Prop Detent and Oil Operated Brake

Fill and Pressurization

2-way Pressure Relief Valves

N$_2$ Gas Pressurization 50 PSI max

Hydrazine Fuel

Oil Activated 2-position Pitch System

4:1 Gearing

Fuel Outlet

Oil Cooling Lines

Oil Pump

Aluminum Tank

5 ft-3 in diameter 2-blade Propeller

Fuel Drain

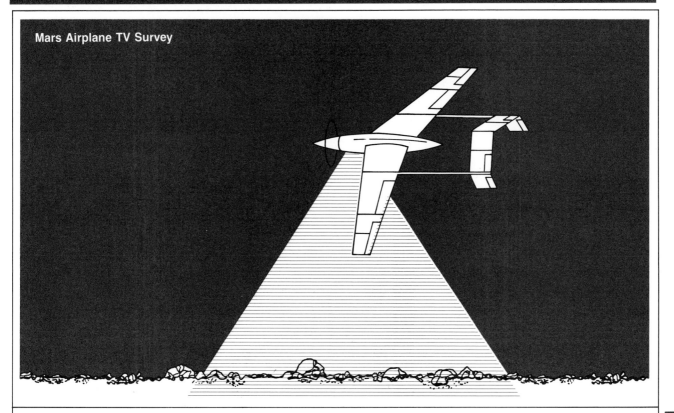

Mars Airplane TV Survey

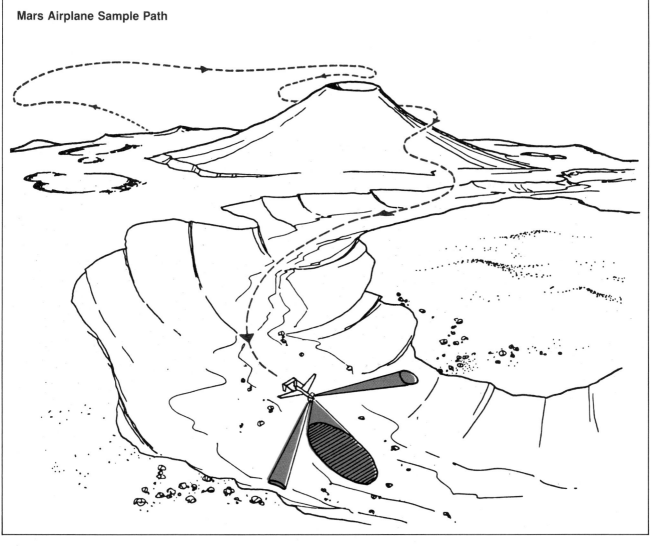

Mars Airplane Sample Path

4.3.4

Mars Airplane Deployment

**Mars Airplane
Range Position
Determination**

Comsat
at
Time t_2

Comsat
at
Time t_1

B

A

Plane is located at point A or B.
the intersection of the constant
range loci on the surface

4.3.5

**Mars Airplane
Telecommunications**

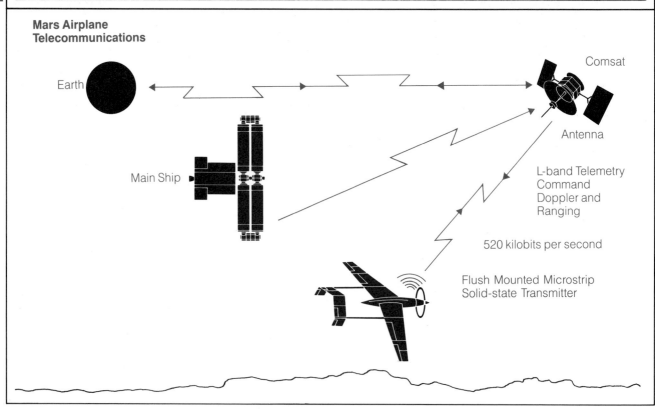

Earth

Comsat

Antenna

Main Ship

L-band Telemetry
Command
Doppler and
Ranging

520 kilobits per second

Flush Mounted Microstrip
Solid-state Transmitter

The orbital science team changes the orbit of the main ship to permit imaging of the two moons, Phobos and Deimos. This can be done relatively easily by adjusting the orbit of the main ship so that the orbit of the moon and the orbit of the ship coincide. For example, Phobos would orbit three times for every one orbit of the main ship; then they would have a close encounter. Deimos, with its slower orbital speed, would orbit five times for every four revolutions of the main ship, producing quite a few encounters.

Your ship approaches as close as 54.7 miles (88 kilometers) to Phobos and within 17.4 miles (28 kilometers) of Deimos. At these distances the crew can get spectacular images and excellent measurements of these puzzling bodies.

The low albedo (reflectivity) of these dark gray bodies, and their interesting orbital paths and surface markings can be better studied now than on any prior mission. Using an ultraviolet spectrometer and other instruments, a careful analysis of the surface of the moons can be performed. The crew studies the moons' mineral contents and surface histories. A gamma-ray spectrometer provides information on nuclear composition.

In addition to size, Phobos and Deimos have some other striking differences. Phobos has a density of crater impact and extensive cracks and grooves that resemble our own airless Moon, while Deimos is far smoother, and the few large craters that do exist there have flat floors and are very eroded.

Because of their appearances and odd orbital paths,

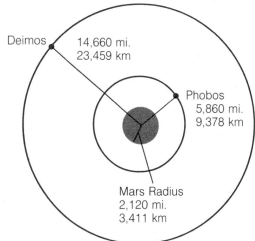

Phobos and Deimos are thought by many scientists to be asteroids trapped by the martian pull. One of the hypotheses explaining how asteroids could have been captured by Mars is that eons ago, Mars had a much thicker atmosphere. Theoretically, asteroids might have entered that atmosphere and been slowed down enough to be captured by the planet's gravitational force. (This is the same type of aerocapture used by the Mars Rover.) The data your crew collects can help resolve this problem. For a further discussion of Phobos and Deimos, see Section 7.3.6.

4.3.6

The highly cratered Deimos.

Phobos and Deimos

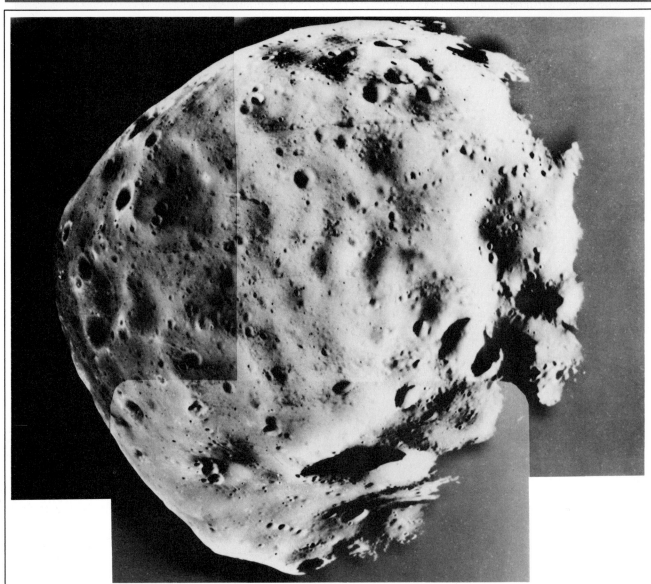

Phobos with its interesting linear features.

Orbital Visual Imaging Subsystem

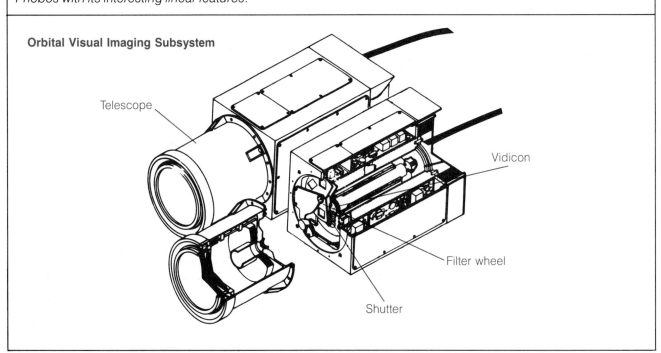

4.3.7

Read This Before MEM Separation.
Note: All Time in Sols, Mars Hours, Mars Minutes.
Preparation for your descent to the surface begins only 1.45 sols (1.5 days) after MOI. Approximately 60 Mars hours (M hours) prior to separation of the (MEM) from the main ship the pre-separation phase begins. During this period you recheck all components of the MEM, update the main landing computer, check the agreement between this computer and the MMC, and recheck all supplies and consumables. There is also a final physical evaluation.

Thirty M hours before separation (S − 30, read S "minus" 30) you begin a power systems check and battery charge. Batteries are charged and tested sequentially. At S − 24 M hours you begin the final MEM systems check. This gives you time to change out or evaluate any component performing below minimum safety or operational levels. At S − 18.5 M hours you go to sleep to be awakened at S − 10.5 for a long and busy day.

At S − 9.5 M hours, you begin an update of the descent software. The crew boards the MEM for the actual descent at this time. You stay in the MEM for another 14.5 to 15 hours before you reach the surface. The in-tervening period before separation is comprised of a final systems check and a series of navigation and guidance updates.

Two seconds before separation, the computer generates the "separation go" command and the automatic sequence takes over. Four minutes after separation the MEM is reoriented using the MEM's Reaction Control System (RCS) for the deorbit burn. You are now five hours from the martian surface.

Twenty-five minutes later the solid deorbit motors fire and take the module out of orbit on its pre-entry coast.

One hour before entry into the atmosphere you activate the Upper Atmosphere Mass Spectrometer (UAMS), which gives an analysis of the atmospheric elements through entry interface.

Atmospheric entry is defined as passing through 800,000 feet (244 kilometers) altitude, but the greatest deceleration occurs at between 19 and 15 miles (30.5 and 24.5 kilometers). During this period, altitude is judged by the inertial guidance system and the radar altimeter.

Parachute deployment occurs at an altitude of 19,250 feet (5.8 kilometers); chutes reduce speed from 770 to

4.4.1

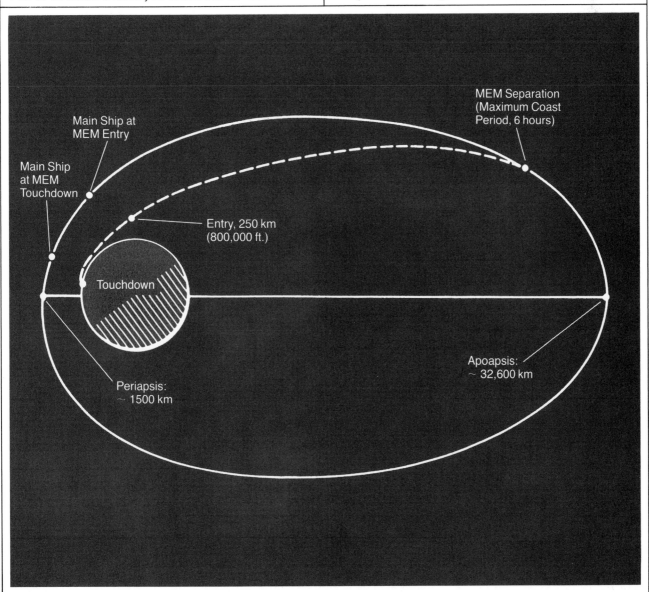

Main Ship at MEM Entry

Main Ship at MEM Touchdown

MEM Separation (Maximum Coast Period, 6 hours)

Entry, 250 km (800,000 ft.)

Touchdown

Apoapsis: ~ 32,600 km

Periapsis: ~ 1500 km

Upper Atmospheric Mass Spectrometer

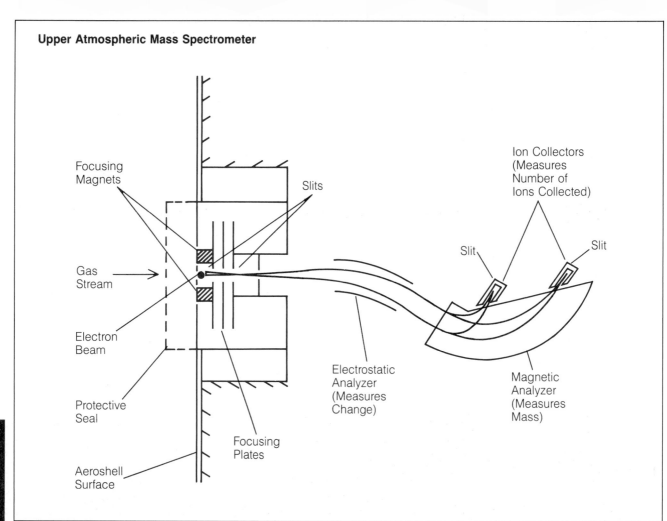

Focusing Magnets

Gas Stream

Electron Beam

Protective Seal

Aeroshell Surface

Focusing Plates

Slits

Ion Collectors (Measures Number of Ions Collected)

Slit

Slit

Electrostatic Analyzer (Measures Change)

Magnetic Analyzer (Measures Mass)

170 feet/second (844 to 187 kph). These three main chutes separate at 4,700 feet (1.4 kilometers) altitude about one minute later. At this point, the module's landing legs deploy into position for touchdown.

The descent engines are fired simultaneously with parachute jettison forty seconds before touchdown. At this point, you perform a maneuver called a "tip up," which brings the MEM to a vertical position for the landing. The engines reduce velocity to a point about 55 feet (16.8 meters) above the surface, at a speed of only 8 mph (12.9 kph), and a constant velocity descent to the surface takes place. During this final phase, you should make any necessary adjustments for boulders or other small obstacles apparent at the chosen landing site. (See Section 4.5.1 regarding possible landing areas.) (Note: The velocity radar can sense dust kicked up by the engine during the final seconds and give an incorrect reading. Check the engine throttle setting and hold it constant for the last two seconds despite any sudden change in altitude reading.)

Count down your final descent, indicating downward motion and translation (forward movement to adjust the precise landing spot). After landing, you must shut down the descent engines, make an emergency check of the ascent engine, shut down landing systems, and prepare for EVA-1.

This first extravehicular activity is designed to collect a contingency sample should you have to leave Mars quickly. First, complete a landing site navigation orientation and take a short 15-minute break for eating. EVA preparation begins 1.5 M hours after touchdown. Begin by stowing loose items and moving into the lower compartment where suits and the airlock are located. You and another crew member don the suits (see description of suits in Section 4.5.10) and one hour later, you become the first humans to set foot on Mars. In a televised ceremony, you plant a flagpole that has a United Nations flag, small flags from those nations directly participating, and a microdot on a plaque with the flags and signatures of the leaders of every nation on Earth. Don't be nervous, but your television audience is expected to be 3 billion people. The Earth date is February 20, 1997.

You then have one hour to fill the contingency sample box with a suite of rocks from the site and to take one core sample. While you are on the surface, the remaining two crew members are checking the location of the Mars Rover with respect to the landing site. If it is within 6 miles (9.6 kilometers), they will go out and retrieve it the following morning. If it is over 6 miles (9.6 kilometers) away, the orbital crew will begin a rapid process of remotely bringing it as close as possible as quickly as possible, since the MR will be needed for the long traverse which must start within the next three sols. On returning, the EVA crew doffs suits, stows equipment, transfers the sample box to the ascent module, and takes a well-deserved sleep period. It will have been a long sol.

Descent Checklist

Time	Activity	Velocity	Altitude
Separation			
S – 60:00:00	Begin descent preparation/validation tests		Orbit
S – 30:00:00	MEM electrical check/battery charge		Orbit
S – 24:00:00	Begin MEM systems check		Orbit
S – 18:30:00	Sleep period		Orbit
S – 10:30:00	Wakeup call		Orbit
S – 09:30:00	Update descent software		Orbit
S – 03:30:00	Update guidance and navigation computer		Orbit
S – 01:00:00	Navigation check/don spacesuits		Orbit
S – 00:20:00	Propulsion check		Orbit
S – 00:00:02	SEPARATION GO command		Orbit
S – 00:00:00 (L – 05:00:00)	Separation		Orbit
S + 00:03:00	Separate UAMS cover		Orbit
S + 00:04:00	MEM reorientation maneuver		Orbit
S + 00:29:12	Deorbit burn start		Orbit
S + 00:30:00	Deorbit engine shutdown		Orbit
Entry			
E – 01:00:00	Start UAMS		
E – 00:12:00	Tape recorders power on		
E – 00:10:00	Pressure sensors on		
E – 00:00:00 (L – 00:08:55)	Entry angle = 14.1° 0.05g	10,294 mph (16,566 kph)	800,000 ft. (244 km)

4.4.3

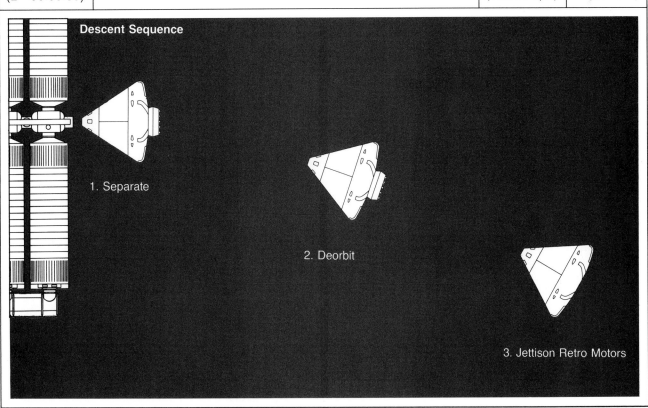

Descent Sequence

1. Separate

2. Deorbit

3. Jettison Retro Motors

Descent and Landing

Descent Checklist

Time	Activity	Velocity	Altitude
Landing			
L − 00:06:00	UAMS off		
L − 00:04:32	Stagnation temperature instrument deployed	1.1 km/sec	
L − 00:01:37	Main parachutes deployed	770 ft/sec	19,200 ft. (5.8 km)
L − 00:00:40	Descent engine ignition	128 mph (207 kph)	4,700 ft. (1.4 km)
L − 00:00:38	Deploy landing gear/jettison parachute		
L − 00:00:30	Tip-up maneuver		
L − 00:00:05	Begin descent	8 mph (12.8 km/hr)	55 ft. (16.8 km)
L − 00:00:00	Touchdown	0	0
L + 00:00:05	Engine stop/Engine arm off		
L + 00:00:15	STAY/NO STAY		
L + 00:10:00	Align guidance system		
L + 00:15:00	Vent descent propulsion system as required Tape recorder power off Batteries off/reset		
L + 00:30:00	Doff helmets and gloves worn in case of depressurization during landing		
L + 00:45:00	Landing site orientation; antenna (HGA) deployment; check BUS voltages		
L + 01:15:00	Eat period		
L + 01:30:00	EVA-1 prep (see EVA checklist); stow loose items.		

4.4.4

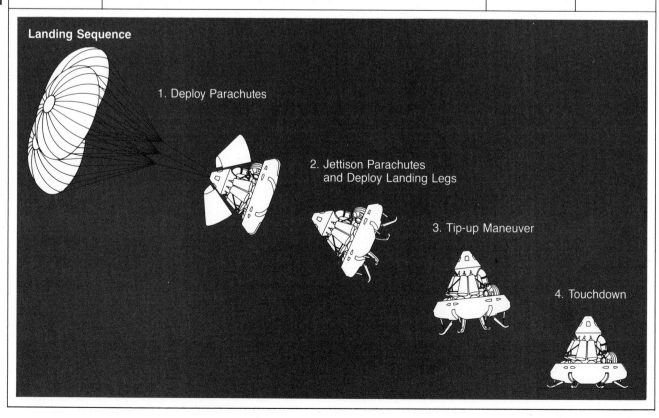

Landing Sequence

1. Deploy Parachutes
2. Jettison Parachutes and Deploy Landing Legs
3. Tip-up Maneuver
4. Touchdown

Your primary landing site is on a mesa on the western side of Candor Chasma (Shining Canyon). Candor Chasma is located around 6°S, 73°W, and is part of the Valles Marineris. Candor is the middle trough of three parallel canyons. Ophir Chasma is to the north of it and Melas Chasma is to the south.

All of these canyons are thought to have been formed as the plateau they are in, part of the highest region on the planet, cracked (faulted) and subsided. The canyons appear to be grabens, a depressed area between major parallel faults. After the slump, erosion, caused by wind or permafrost melt, or a combination of the two, ate out the canyon material, forming the canyons. In Candor, fault systems and broken canyon walls have exposed martian rock down to a depth of 2.5 miles

(4 kilometers).

The rim of the canyon, the caprock, is composed of basalt flows that must have formed during the earliest periods of volcanic activity at the nearby Tharsis Bulge. Before that, the region was probably part of the heavily cratered terrain typical of the martian southern hemisphere. This was then covered by a series of layers of volcanic flows mixed with volcanic debris. Finally, windblown deposits cover the surface.

The walls of the canyon are composed of parallel layers. Following normal geologic theory, this would represent a layered history of events similar to the evolution of the Grand Canyon on Earth. The lower part of the canyon has thin layers on the canyon floor that could be eolian (windblown) deposits or tectonically broken

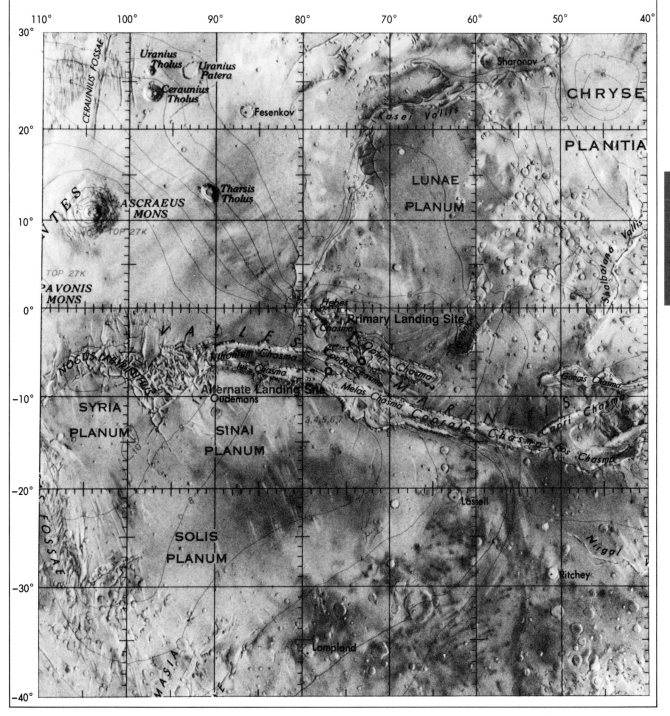

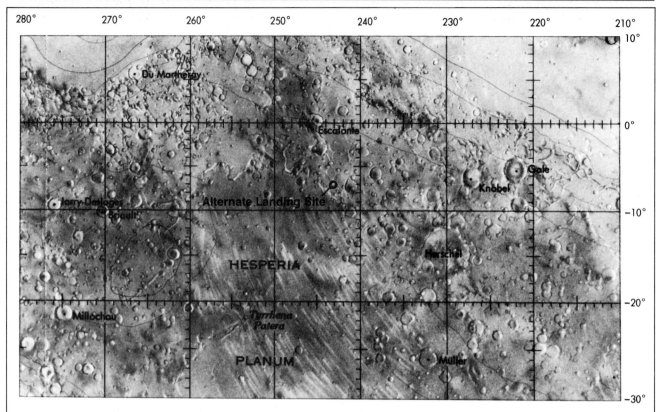

rocks. The upper layers are thicker and more rugged and might be the expected lava flows. Gravity slides all along the walls have piled up high heaps of rock and debris called talus.

The canyon floor has been heavily eroded and huge areas of bedrock have been exposed. High temperatures on the valley floor during the martian night suggest a rocky terrain, probably with many boulders. Near the west end of the canyon, the floor is only about 1.25 miles (2 kilometers) deep at the center. Here, the walls have collapsed, and the canyon opens into Ophir and Melas Chasmas. The canyon floor is fairly flat in this area with sand and perhaps only a 2° slope. You may therefore encounter some sand and small dunes along the floor.

There is a mesa in Candor that stands about 0.8 miles (1.3 kilometers) above the canyon floor The temperatures on the top of the mesa indicate a smooth surface that might be fine grained and have few rocks. This may be similar to the caprock and surrounding plateaus. The mesa walls slope downward, revealing light and dark layers that should tell the story of what went on during the history of the valley formation. Studies of these layers will allow you to detect whether any water events occurred, and if any organics ever existed.

There are two major theories about how the mesa formed. The first theory suggests that the mesa might be just a remnant of the original bedrock in the valley. As the valley eroded away, these older rocks were exposed; therefore, the mesa should correspond to the older layers of rock in the canyon wall. A second theory holds that the mesa might be composed of deposits that filled the canyon after it formed. A layer of canyon wall deposits covered the valley floor. The next layer could have been a thick layer, perhaps of volcanic origin, which actually formed the mesa. On top of this are more

layers of material, then layers of landslides from the canyon walls. Finally, a layer of wind-deposited dark debris covers the whole area.

Only careful sampling, analysis, and dating of these layers can finally answer the question of martian valley formation. But these findings will have far greater meaning. By traversing the canyon you can later actually date, using radioactivity, sequences of volcanic rocks to give a volcanic history of the region. This chemical analysis will give a history of rock formation under the martian crust over time and an idea of the eruption sequences in martian history. You may also find clues to the events that formed the martian channel system in the soils of the valley, and the chemical changes caused by water and climate. You may even find traces of solar activity embedded in the rocks. Coupled with lunar data, this will give more information on the past behavior of the Sun, its variation and its effects on Mars.

To accomplish the landing, you have to navigate precisely. The mesa is a relatively small target, but if you are able to land there, the traverses can yield an exceptionally rich volume of data.

Should you not be able to land at Candor, two backup sites have been chosen. One is at Hebes Chasma to the northwest of Candor. Hebes is at 7°S, 77°W, and also has a mesa structure. The mesa, at 1°S, 73°W, is lower, and the whole canyon is much shallower. The mesa layering is not as well defined. The site should still provide a record, however, of the episodes on Mars between the ancient cratered terrain and the formation of lava layers from the Tharsis region.

A final backup site is at Tyrrhena Terra in the channeled, heavily cratered terrain located at 7°S, 243°W. If landing occurs here a different type of mission would result, involving a sampling of the earliest crustal rocks on Mars and a study of the possible stages of crustal

Candor Chasma—Two Views

Geologic Cross Section Sketches Showing
Two Rationales for the Present Position of
the Candor Chasma Mesa Layered Deposits

Theory 1: Old Sequence

Theory 2: Valley Fill—Young Sequence

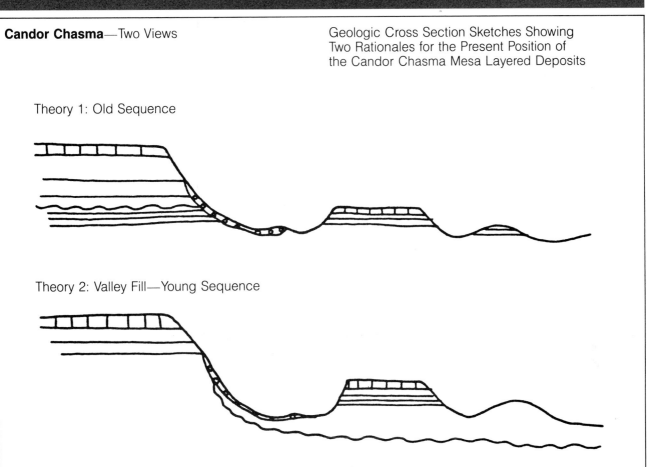

Candor Terrain

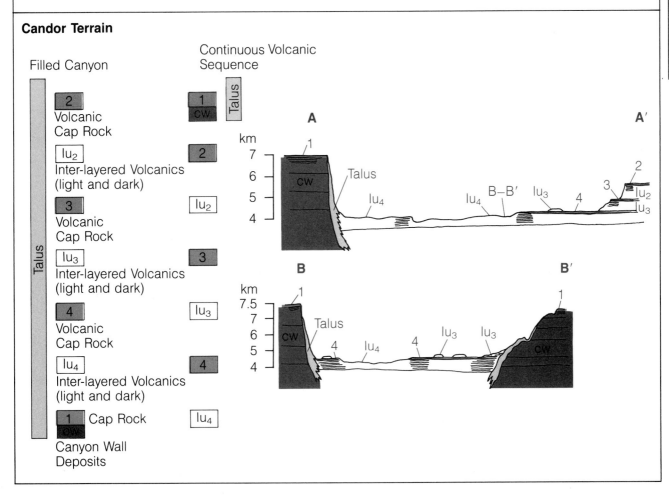

Filled Canyon

Continuous Volcanic Sequence

2 Volcanic Cap Rock	**1** CW
lu₂ Inter-layered Volcanics (light and dark)	**2**
3 Volcanic Cap Rock	lu₂
lu₃ Inter-layered Volcanics (light and dark)	**3**
4 Volcanic Cap Rock	lu₃
lu₄ Inter-layered Volcanics (light and dark)	**4**
1 CW Cap Rock	lu₄

Talus

Canyon Wall Deposits

rock formation. Such information on early cratering would help fix the rate of cratering on Mars and make the geologic time scale based on crater rate more accurate. Since much of Mars's surface is similar to this area, such a mission would make possible very accurate orbital geologic maps for much of the planet, and would also provide clues as to the formation of the martian channels. Although this is a third choice, it is a site of high interest and of great value. It will almost certainly be visited on one of the next missions.

The Traverses

Having landed first, the Mars Rover is steered by remote control to within one mile (1.6 kilometers) of your landing site. This should take it on a journey of no more than 4 miles (6.4 kilometers), given the navigational accuracy we can achieve. During the drive, its cameras will give you your first look at the terrain on the mesa. You will also be able to evaluate the condition and performance of your Rover vehicle. Based on that remotely piloted performance, you will have a fairly good idea of whether you can accomplish the ambitious research schedule planned, or if you must fall back on one of two other plans.

MEM Crew Surface Time Allocation

Activity	Time	Cum. Time
Sleep	8:00	8:00
Eat	1:45	9:45
Personal hygiene	1:00	10:45
Don suit	:20	11:05
EVA	8:00	19:05
Doff suit and maint.	:30	19:35
Debrief	1:10	20:45
Uncommitted (recreation, travel, etc.)	3:15	24:00

EVA	Time	EVA Time Remaining
Seal suit		8:00
Check out suit	:30	7:30
Outside airlock activities	7:00	:30
Ingress/clean suit	:30	0:00
Vent suit	—	—

Minimum Plan (no Rover contingency)

If the Rover should not be available, your landing site can be moved to come as close as possible to the mesa rim (1.5 miles or 2.5 kilometers). This permits a long traverse to the edge on foot with a mobile scientific cart. You can carry enough supplies to reach the mesa rim and sample some of the layered rock below the rim. You can also carry out the extensive mesa-top

science program. This traverse can be done at least three times.

Moderate Plan (Rover performance minimal, velocity = 1 mph or 1.6 kph)

If the Rover is available, but its performance proves less than expected, you have to scale down your traverses. This plan allows you to accomplish two traverses of about 60 kilometers each. By moving the landing site to within 3 miles (5 kilometers) of the mesa rim, the maximum amount of terrain could still be explored.

Nominal Plan (full-Rover performance, velocity = 3–7 mph (5–11 kph))

This plan calls for an extremely ambitious traverse, with optional branches, of about 100 miles (160 kilometers). This plan is not without risks—if your vehicle were to break down on this traverse, you would not be able to walk back to the module. The Mars Rover, however, was designed to provide at least triple-redundant systems for virtually every major component, and can be fairly easily repaired. The Mars Rover can also be used as an automated explorer to sample other terrain after you leave.

The long traverse is designed to take 19.5 sols. You must average 7.5 miles (12 km) per day. This traverse permits a detailed sampling of the various layers in the mesa walls, some canyon floor areas, a dark deposit region, and a visit to the talus of canyon wall deposits. Optional branches can include a longer traverse westward across the canyon floor. Decisions on precise routing are a function of actual terrain conditions, preliminary analysis of early findings, and continual evaluation of Rover performance.

One of the most important elements of the traverse is knowing where you are. This is not only necessary to finding your way, but also to accurately fixing the locations of samples. The terrain may be such that hills, craters, or canyon wall structures may hide landmarks, making navigation fixes difficult. At night, if there are no dust storms, a theodolite and a tilt sensor can be used. Homing radio signals from the MEM and navigational signals from the communications satellites can also provide location and direction information.

Finally, a dead-reckoning system is included. It consists of a directional gyro that senses motion disturbance and computes deviations, and therefore the amount of motion. An odometer displays distance traveled. Gyro and odometer data are then fed into the Rover's navigation computer. A time reference signal is added, and the readouts tell you where you are, and how far off the preprogrammed course you are. It will even tell you, as you turn the steering, whether you are heading in the best direction for staying on track, or if you are straying. It will also give you the rate at which you are approaching or moving away from the preprogrammed track.

The following map and table describe the long traverse, the important stops along the route, and the types of samples you should obtain at different points in your journey.

4.5.4

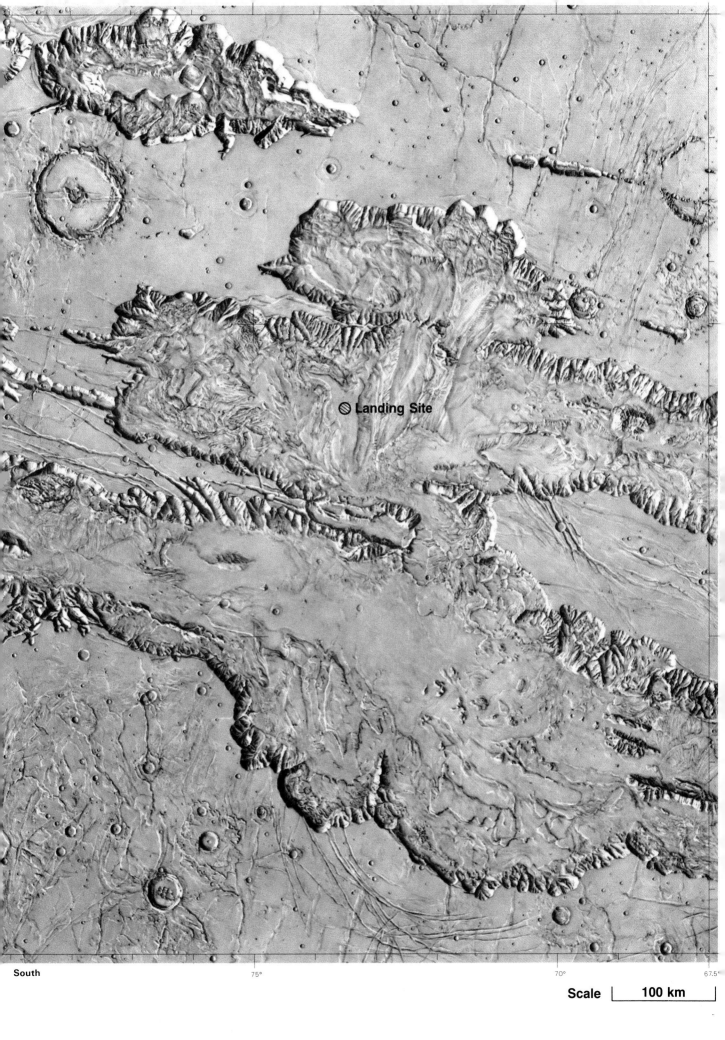

⊚ Landing Site

Scale | 100 km

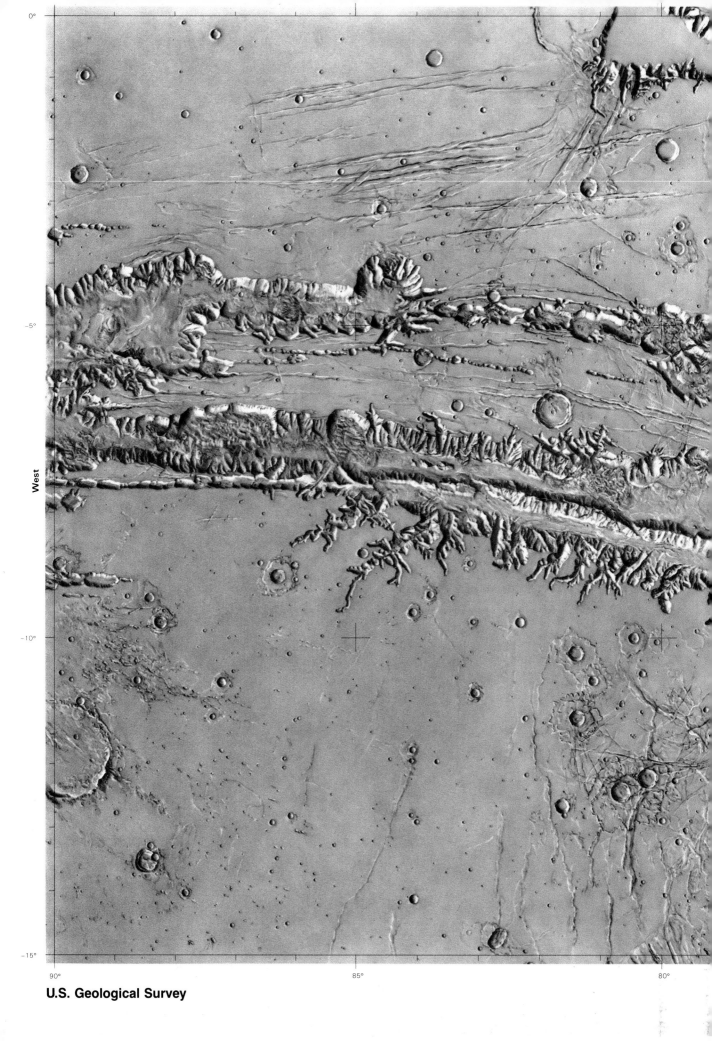

0°

-5°

West

-10°

-15°

90° 85° 80°

U.S. Geological Survey

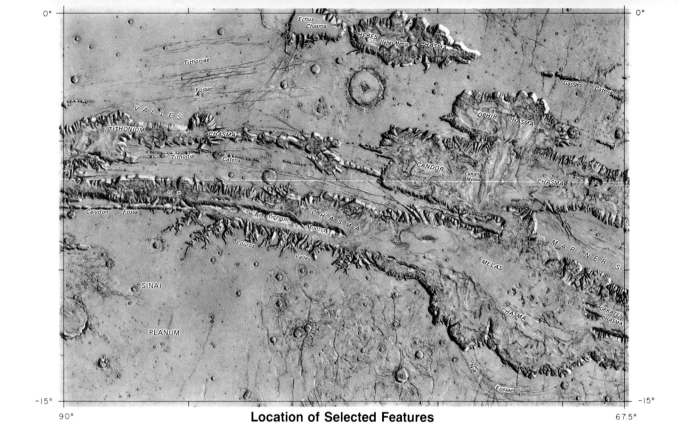

Location of Selected Features

Map of Candor Chasma Region

The Landing Site

Long Traverse Stops

Station	Terrain Member	Material to be Sampled	Rock Type(s)	Distance from Landing Site
1 (landing site), 2	lc_1	caprock material of landing-site mesa; regolith	possible volcanic flows, clastic volcanics, and eolian debris. Regolith should be present	
3	$2/lc_1$	outcrop of plains forming unit #2 and possible regolith	volcanic flow	
4	lu_2; lc_1	upper part of section lu_2 at contact with unit $\#2/lc_1$	Interlayered light and dark pyroclastic material; individual layers ~ 300 m thick	
5	lu_2	lower section lu_2	" "	
6	lu_3	upper lu_3 section	" "	
7	lu_3	mid-section lu_3	" "	
8	lu_3; cf	lu_3 and #4 at contact	" "	40.0 km
9	lu_2	lower section of lu_2 below NW tip of landing-site mesa	" " (possibly same horizon as station 5)	
10,11	lu_2	lu_2 lower in sequence than station 9, below NW tip of landing-site mesa	probably same horizon as station 6 and 7	
12	(not mapped)	plains forming unit #3	volcanic flow	80.0 km
13	lu_3	layered terrain of lu_3	smooth volcanic flow	
14, 15	dd	dark deposits	dark, low albedo eolian material	

4.5.6

Route A

Geologic Map of Candor Site on Mars

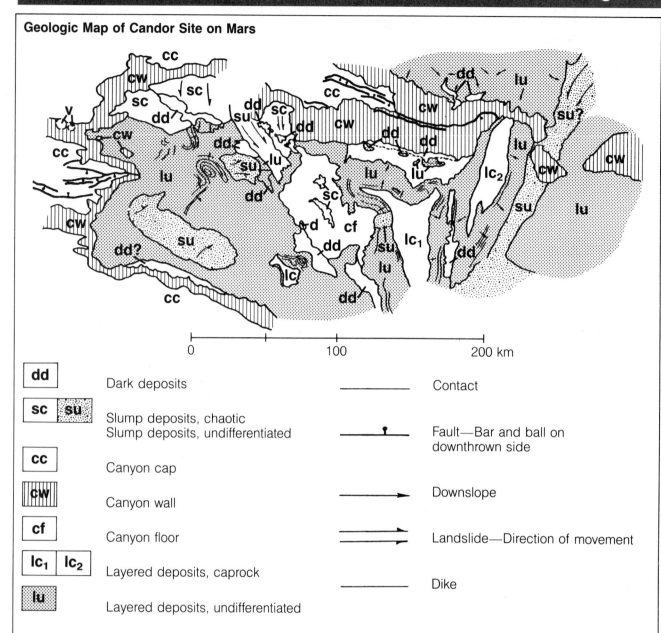

dd	Dark deposits	————— Contact
sc **su**	Slump deposits, chaotic Slump deposits, undifferentiated	————•— Fault—Bar and ball on downthrown side
cc	Canyon cap	—————→ Downslope
cw	Canyon wall		
cf	Canyon floor	—————⇒ Landslide—Direction of movement
lc₁ **lc₂**	Layered deposits, caprock	————— Dike
lu	Layered deposits, undifferentiated	

Scale: 0 — 100 km — 200 km

Explanation

Dd   Dark deposits
Materials with low albedo that transect and overlie all other units. Deposits here irregular, diffuse outlines. Occur mostly in low areas. Mapped only where extensive deposits exists. *Interpretation:* Probably eolian debris of relatively recent origin.

Sc   Slump deposits, chaotic
Masses of chaotic materials at the base of canyon walls. *Interpretation:* Landslide deposits incorporating mostly Canyon Wall material (cw).

Su   Slump deposits, undifferentiated
Fan-shaped or tongue-shaped deposits of materials commonly with a marked linear surface texture. *Interpretation:* Landslide deposits incorporating mostly layered materials of unit Lu.

Lc   Layered deposits, caprock
Forms upper layer of stratified deposits which form "mesa"-like features within the canyon. Upper surface flat and featureless except for space craters. *Interpretation:* More resistant layer at the top of or within a layered sequence that post-dates the canyon and partially fills it. Layers may be volcanic (interbedded tuffs and flows) or lake sediments.

Lu   Layered deposits, undifferential
Same as Lc, but excludes caprock.

Cc   Canyon caprock
Forms flat, sparsely cratered, faulted surface into which canyon is cut. *Interpretation:* Old lava plain.

Cw   Canyon wall deposits
Materials that form the walls of the canyon. Layers visible at top of section. Forms bifurcating spurs in canyon walls and intervening talus. *Interpretation:* Succession of volcanic deposits, may include ancient cratered megaregolith low in section.

Cf   Canyon floor deposits
Forms flat floor of canyon where sediments are absent. *Interpretation:* Exhumed lava plain on ancient cratered megaregolith.

Long Traverse Stops

Station	Terrain Member	Material to be Sampled	Rock Type(s)	Distance from Landing Site
16–19	cw talus	#1/cc (high mesa) wall and talus deposits in deep canyon	fragmental volcanic debris from canyon wall	100.0 km
20	dd	dark deposits at contact of canyon wall	dark, low albedo eolian material?	
21	lu$_3$	basal layered deposit of lu$_3$	volcanic flow or pyroclastic material	
22, 23	lu$_3$	outcrop of light albedo layer on surface #4	pyroclastics or volcanic flow	
24	cf	smooth surface flow; possible regolith, eolian veneer	volcanic flow	150.0 km
25	sc/lower lu$_3$	outlier of light, layered terrain on top of #4	light pyroclastic	170.0 km
26	cf	dark plains forming unit #4/cf	volcanic flow	
27–31	lu$_2$;lu$_3$	layered deposits between plains units #2 and #4	dark and light volcanic flows and pyroclastics	
32	lu$_2$	layered deposits; similar to those at stations 9 and 10 except lower in section	light and dark volcanic flows and pyroclastics	194.0 km
ROUTE A 33	lc$_1$	mesa caprock, rim	volcanic	
34–36	lc$_1$	mesa caprock, rim	volcanic with eolian debris	236.0 km
ROUTE B same as stops 9-1				244.0 km

4.5.7

Route B

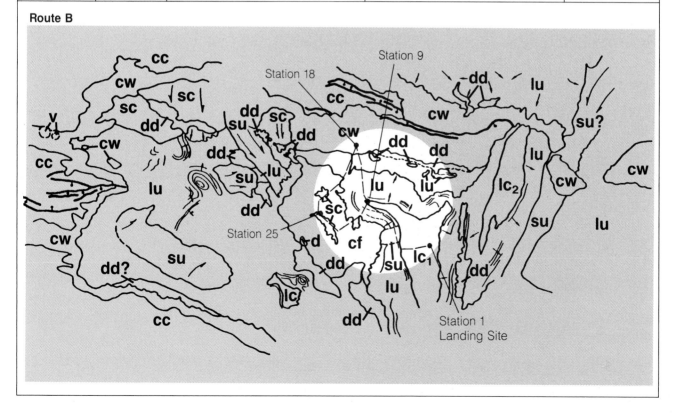

Mars Rover was launched in its aerocapture vehicle on May 6, 1996 (245-0210 JD), swung by Venus on June 14, 1996 (245-0249.2 JD), and arrived at Mars January 11, 1997 (245-0460 JD), 40 days (39 sols) ahead of you. After descent and landing, the Mars Rover (MR, or Rover) was remotely guided on a traverse to within one-half kilometer of your expected landing site. The 7,300-pound (3,330-kilogram) Rover, which will be used for the long traverse (19.5 sols), is made of two basic modules. The forward module is a sphere with a diameter of 10 feet (3 meters). The second module is a tanklike affair 84 inches (2.1 meters) in diameter. These modules are nested together and sit on four 60-inch (1.53-meter) diameter wheels. The wheelbase is 147 inches (3.7 meters) and tool and sample boxes are mounted between the wheels on both sides. Overall length is 20 feet (6.1 meters). Ground clearance is 25 inches (.65 meters) which should permit safe passage over much of the rock-strewn terrain.

Rover has four electric motors. Electric power is provided by a fuel cell which also produces fresh water, and by a series of silver-zinc 36 volt batteries. The Rover has a range of 30 miles (48 kilometers) per battery charge. The fuel cell trickle charges the batteries at night.

Rover is capable of about 10 mph (16 kph) maximum and 7 mph (11.2 kph) cruise. It can negotiate slopes of up to 25 degrees.

The top of the second module is surrounded by 95-inch (2.4-meter) long radiators for the fuel cell. On top there is a low-gain antenna and mounting brackets for portable video cameras. Two intelligent robot arms are attached to the sides of the spherical module. These arms are integrated with the main landing computer and can be used for contingency sample gathering, general sample gathering, and trenching for manual sample gathering. The arms, coupled with the computer, will have their own active collection program, and can be controlled remotely from orbit as well.

Voice Recognition Commands	
You say:	Rover responds:
"ROVER"	"ROVER"
"AHEAD"	
"BACK"	repeats
"LEFT"	command
"RIGHT"	
"ONE" (1 = .25 mph)	
"TWO" (2 = .50 mph)	repeats
"THREE" (3 = 1 mph)	rate
"FOUR" (4 = 2 mph)	
"STOP"	"STOPPING"
"LIGHT ON"	"LIGHT ON"
"LIGHT OFF"	"LIGHT OFF"
"CAM ON" (TV)	"CAM ON"
"CAM OFF" (TV)	"CAM OFF"
"MIKE HOT" (ground to air)	"MIKE HOT"
"MIKE HOT OFF"	"MIKE HOT OFF"
"MAYDAY" (turns on cam and mike)	"MAYDAY"

4.5.8

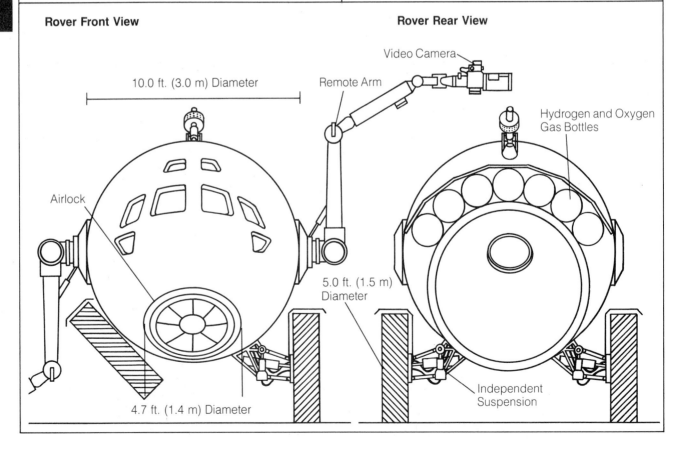

Rover Front View

10.0 ft. (3.0 m) Diameter

Airlock

4.7 ft. (1.4 m) Diameter

Rover Rear View

Video Camera

Remote Arm

Hydrogen and Oxygen Gas Bottles

5.0 ft. (1.5 m) Diameter

Independent Suspension

Rover Side View

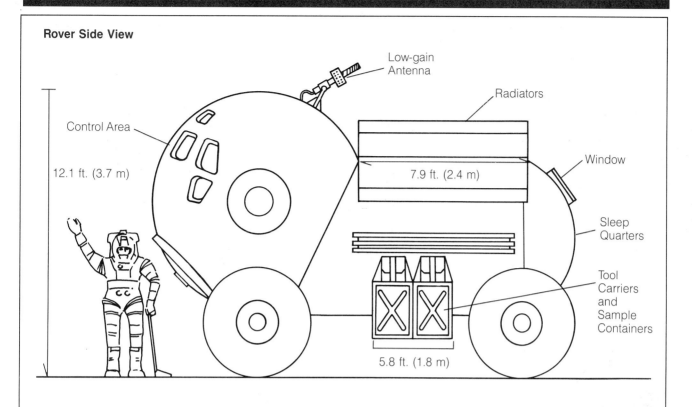

Low-gain Antenna

Control Area

12.1 ft. (3.7 m)

Radiators

Window

7.9 ft. (2.4 m)

Sleep Quarters

Tool Carriers and Sample Containers

5.8 ft. (1.8 m)

Rover Top View

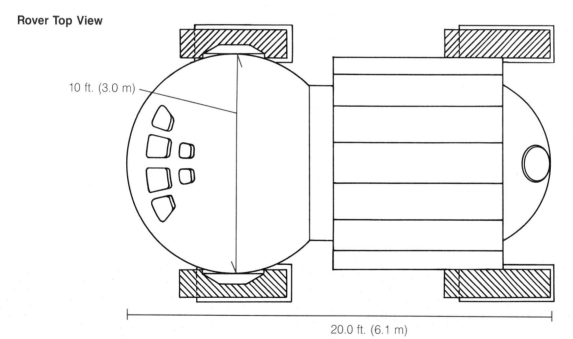

10 ft. (3.0 m)

20.0 ft. (6.1 m)

Lithium hydroxide (LiOH) canisters are used to remove carbon dioxide from the air, and a portable water purification unit will allow you to recycle liquid waste. Solid wastes will be stored in an airtight compartment. Fecal collection bags will be used for solid waste and a urine collection device for liquids. Biocide wipes will be used for cleanliness. There will be no showers until you are back at the main ship.

The suits, portable life-support system backpacks (PLSS), and an umbilical arrangement are stored inside. The Rover has no airlock. When you open the hatch for EVAs, both crewmen must be suited up, even if only one is working outside. The 58-inch (1.5-meter) diameter hatch is the only way in and out of the Rover. An umbilical can be fed out the open hatch and permits a 20-foot (6.1-meter) radius of movement without needing a PLSS backpack. This will permit very short stops to pick up special samples or make quick observations.

Inside Rover is a driving station, a large storage closet section (on the starboard side), a narrow 18-inch (.45-meter) aisle in the second module with storage compartments, and above them, two narrow berths with hammocks. Suits may be hung near the hatch or placed in the berths, depending on your activities. The inside is fairly cramped, but you will be spending about six hours per day outside and eight hours sleeping.

On the outbound and inbound legs of the mission, a spacesuit is only worn for extravehicular activity, and then mostly while doing emergency repairs. On the surface of Mars, however, it is critical. The suit is different from the Shuttle Extravehicular Mobility Unit (EMU). The EMU has a hard upper torso, like a hard vest, but has soft legs and arms. That suit is pressurized with pure oxygen at 4.1 psi (28 kilopascals). In order to use the EMU you have to pre-breathe oxygen for about two and one-half hours. This is to purge your system of blood nitrogen, which would bubble in your bloodstream in the lower pressure of the suit and cause the bends.

Remember, the Shuttle, like the main ship, has an oxygen/nitrogen atmosphere at 14.7 psi (100 kilopascals) pressure.

Obviously, for the continual exit and entrance into the MEM and the Rover, you don't want to have to pre-breathe all the time, so you will use the Mars Extravehicular Mobility Unit (MEMU). The MEMU is a hard-suit; this means that almost all major components of the suit are not made of layers of thin fabric, but of solid tubes connected by a series of joints designed to permit nearly normal motion. The joints are called "constant volume joints" because no matter what position they are in, the

4.5.10

Cooling Garment, front

Cooling Garment, back

volume of air in them is the same. If this were not true, changes in air pressure would mean that, in certain positions, the suit would be harder to move in. These joints are more commonly referred to as "stovepipe joints."

The MEMU has a pressure of 9 pounds psi (62 kilopascals). This is an oxygen/nitrogen mix and is only 1 psi (6.9 kilopascals) lower than that of the MEM and the same as that of the Rover. This means you can don and doff your suit without pre-breathing and as often as you need to without fearing the bends.

The stovepipe joints have a unique seal and bear-ing system with Teflon lining for smooth operation and a tight fit. The suit provides nearly normal shoulder/arm movement with the exception of the side-to-side arm swing. Without the suit, your arm can swing back and across your chest through an angle of 137°. The suit allows only 113° movement in this direction. Total hip-leg extension (swinging your leg forward and back like a pendulum) is 103°, whereas the MEMU will only let you swing 90°.

The MEMU weighs 50 pounds (22.7 kilograms), which would be only 20 pounds (9 kilograms) on Mars. This is very light, but imagine if you wore a suit weighing 20

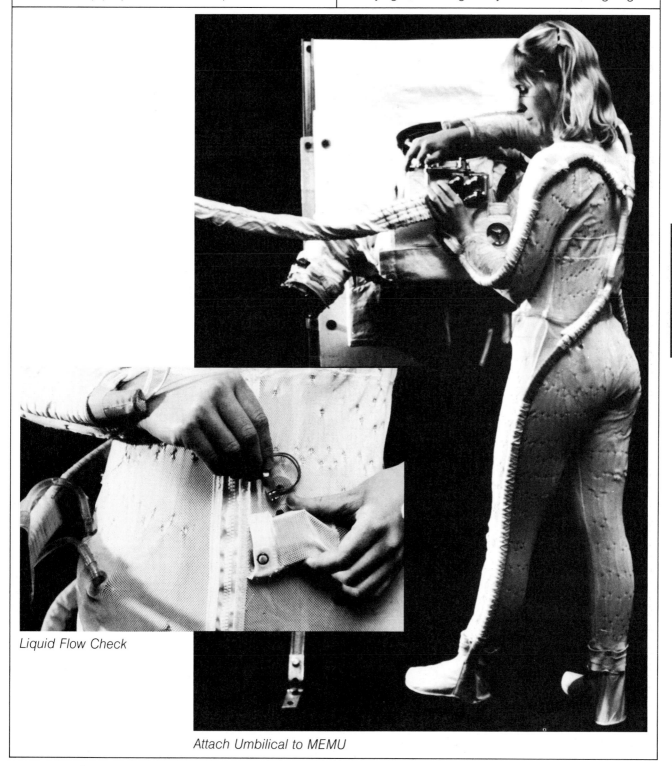

Liquid Flow Check

Attach Umbilical to MEMU

pounds on Earth. The weight would definitely be noticed, and would eventually have an effect on your comfort and stamina.

The MEMU can be hooked up with either a portable life-support system (PLSS) or with a long umbilical cord to carry supplies to the suit. The PLSS weighs 80 pounds (36.3 kilograms), 32 pounds (14.5 kilograms) on Mars, and can support you for up to eight hours. There is also a forty-minute reserve.

Arm Assembly

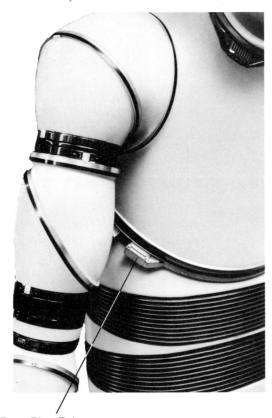

Torso Ring Release

The MEMU helmet is a Lexan bubble and has an ultraviolet-light-sensitive sunshade. The suit itself is made of a specially formed glass fiber, which is shaped over custom molds. Unlike the Shuttle EMU, which comes in small, medium, and large, these suits are mostly custom fit.

To don the suit, first put on your tubing suit or liquid cooling garment (LCG). This garment, by circulating warm or cool water, controls the temperature inside the suit. Second, put your arms overhead and slide them up into the sleeves of the upper torso. Then slide the lower torso on, making sure that your feet are comfortably inside the boots. Now attach the lower torso ring to the upper torso ring.

Having completed this, attach the flexible gloves to the suit and finally, the bubble helmet. The PLSS or umbilical cord is attached next, and you are ready to step outside. While the suit may look like a suit of armor, it has remarkable flexibility and toughness and should operate well on Mars.

4.5.12

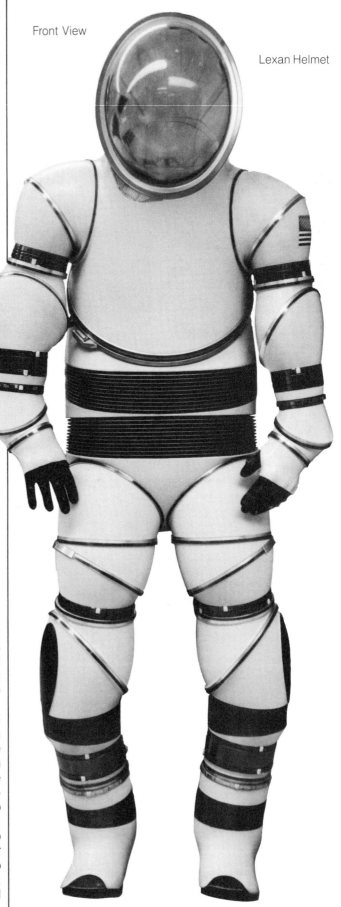

Front View

Lexan Helmet

Umbilical/PLSS Connector

Side View

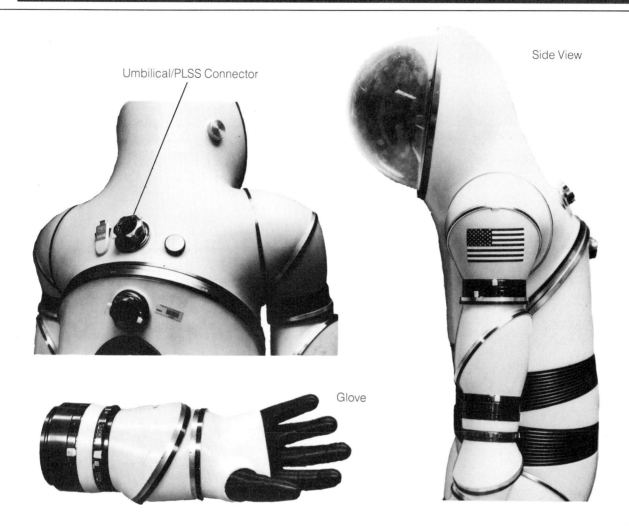

Glove

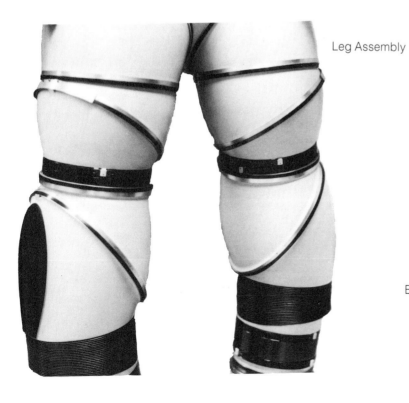

Leg Assembly

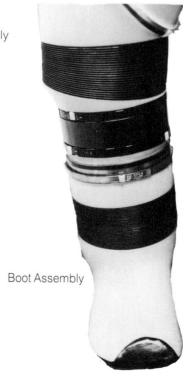

Boot Assembly

Your work on Candor mesa or on the long traverse involves the emplacement of certain surface experiments. You will first set up the Mars Science Station (MSS). This complex of instruments should continue to relay information for years.

The Mars science station consists of a central station and outlying experiments connected by cable. The central station is powered by a radioisotope thermoelectric generator (RTG). A power conditioning unit divides the RTG's 16-volt output to the necessary voltages

Transmitting Antenna

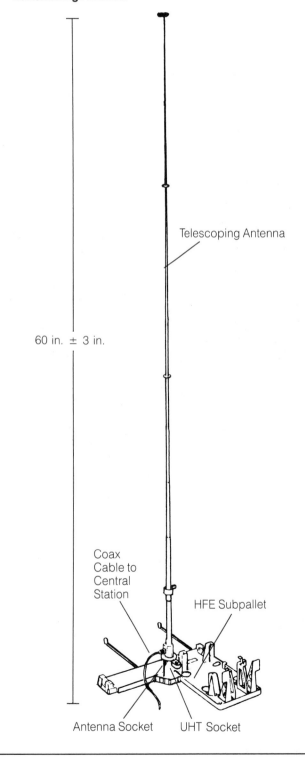

60 in. ± 3 in.

Telescoping Antenna

Coax
Cable to
Central
Station

HFE Subpallet

Antenna Socket   UHT Socket

Mars Surface Science Equipment List

Equipment Name	Average Power (watts)	Weight (lb)	Volume (cu ft)	Data Rate (bps)
Gamma ray spectrometer	10.0	85.0	2.0	3000
Downhole geophys. probe	34.0	57.0	4.0	1.1×10^4
Photomicrographic camera	60.0	15.0	2.0	film
Seismic amplifier	5.0	4.4	.028	**
Seismometer	1.0	22.2	.56	230
X-ray diffractometer	10.0	10.0	0.7	14
Antenna set (0.6 to 1.2 MHz)	**	440.0	10.5	**
Antenna set (5 to X.X MHz)	**	100.0	6.3	**
UV spectrometer	3.0	33.0	1.05	280.0
X-ray fluorescence spectrometer	0.5	15.0	0.7	14.0
IR spectrometer	0.3	33.0	0.9	1.0
Heat flow probe	**	.3	.01	**
Mass spectrometer (portable)	**	30.0	0.6	**
Gas chromatograph (portable)	**	55.0	2.0	**
Transmitter and antennas	40.0	22.0	.56	30
Magnetometer-fluxgate	3.0	15.0	0.2	10
Dipole ant. (2 km)	**	388.0	110	**
Whip antenna (10 m)	**	30.0	1.0	**
Data recorder	6.0	10.0	.15	**
Time base generator	5.0	1.1	.18	4000
Signal conditioning equipment	20.0	20.0	1.0	**
Electronics unit (heat flow)	3.0	8.8	.14	2000
Drill (30 m)	3000	200.0	36.0	**
Flashing light	neg.	10.0	30	**
Field bioscience kit	**	33.0	.40	**
Time-elapse camera	neg.	2.0	.20	**
Microscope	10.0	4.4	.50	**
Mapping kit	2.0	52.7	6.8	**
Geological tool kit	**	8.8	.2	**

** = not applicable

4.6.1

for each experiment. The data subsystem on the central station is responsible for the timing and control of the experiments, the collection and transmission of scientific and engineering data (telemetry), and the reception and decoding of instructional commands.

A high-gain axial helix antenna is also provided. It can be aimed at one of the communications satellites. To deploy the antenna, you should first level the entire unit, using the tubular bubble levels. You can then adjust the up–down axis of the antenna (elevation). Finally,

move the antenna along the left–right axis (azimuth) until the small signal-sensitivity gauge reaches a maximum. This indicates that the antenna is locked on to a comsat beacon and aimed correctly.

There are two switches on the side of the unit. Switch 1 permits you to select the second power conditioning unit should the first unit not function properly. If this is necessary, rotate the switch clockwise. Switch 2 is a safing switch that you must activate before your ascent from the surface. You rotate this switch clockwise also.

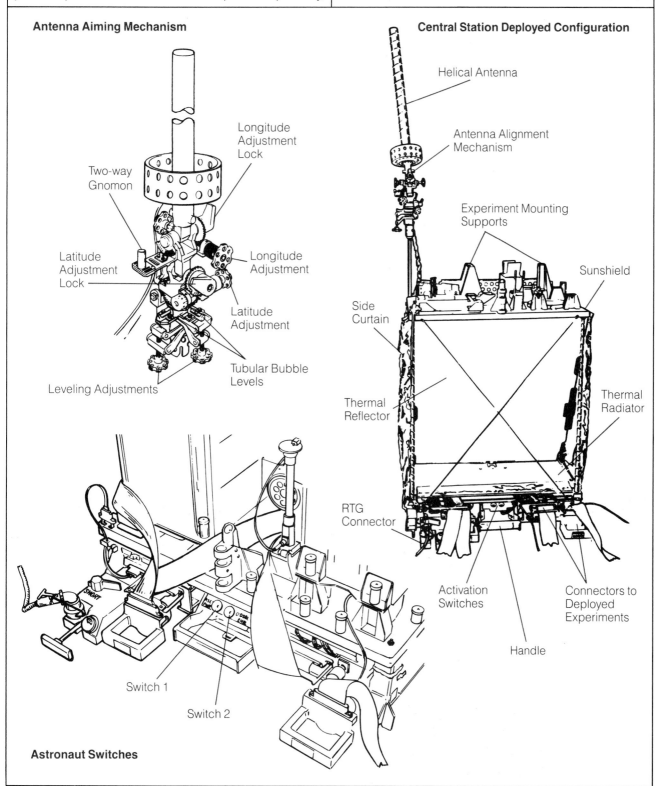

Antenna Aiming Mechanism

Longitude Adjustment Lock

Two-way Gnomon

Latitude Adjustment Lock

Longitude Adjustment

Latitude Adjustment

Leveling Adjustments

Tubular Bubble Levels

Central Station Deployed Configuration

Helical Antenna

Antenna Alignment Mechanism

Experiment Mounting Supports

Side Curtain

Sunshield

Thermal Reflector

Thermal Radiator

RTG Connector

Activation Switches

Connectors to Deployed Experiments

Handle

Switch 1

Switch 2

Astronaut Switches

4.6.2

Surface Experiments

The Heat Flow Experiment (HFE) is to provide information on the transfer of heat from the martian interior to the surface. The experiment will also provide accurate information on the thermal characteristics of the immediate subsurface. The experiment consists of two 10-foot (3 meter) probes set about 30 feet (9.1 meters) apart. Each probe senses temperature at four levels every 7.5 minutes. In addition to the temperature sensors, each probe has four heating elements. When the elements operate they produce a predetermined amount of heat. The temperature sensors detect this heat and can then determine the thermal conducting properties of the rock.

To set up the experiment, first bore two 10-foot (3 meter) holes 30 feet (9.1 meters) apart with your surface drill. Insert the two probes. Set up the electronics package about 30 feet (9.1 meters) from the central station and roughly between the probes. Attach the cables from the probe tops to the sockets in the electronics package. Then pull the flat cable from its reel in the electronics package to the central station and connect it to the port marked HFE.

4.6.3

Heat Flow Probes Deployed

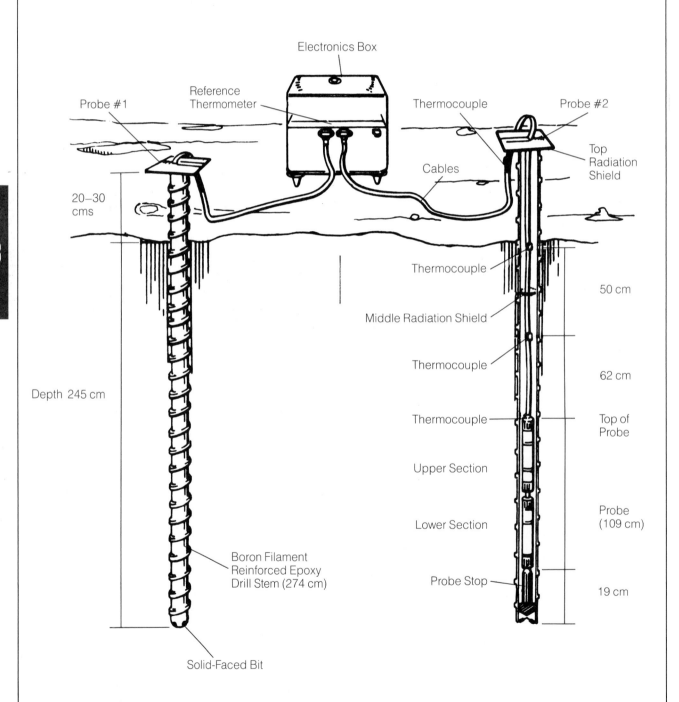

Electronics Box

Reference Thermometer

Probe #1

Thermocouple

Probe #2

Top Radiation Shield

20–30 cms

Cables

Thermocouple

Middle Radiation Shield

50 cm

Thermocouple

62 cm

Depth 245 cm

Thermocouple

Top of Probe

Upper Section

Lower Section

Probe (109 cm)

Boron Filament Reinforced Epoxy Drill Stem (274 cm)

Probe Stop

19 cm

Solid-Faced Bit

The Seismic Profiling Experiment (SPE) uses an old geologic technique for finding out what the subsurface structure is by creating tiny marsquakes and measuring the bouncing of the resulting seismic waves. The reflections of these seismic waves from various layers measured at various distances let you make a model of the subsurface layers. The experiment consists of a network of four detectors called geophones, which you deploy according to the diagram, and eight explosive packages, which will generate the seismic waves. The geophones detect seismic activity as deep as 1.9–2.5 miles (3–4 kilometers).

Geophone Module

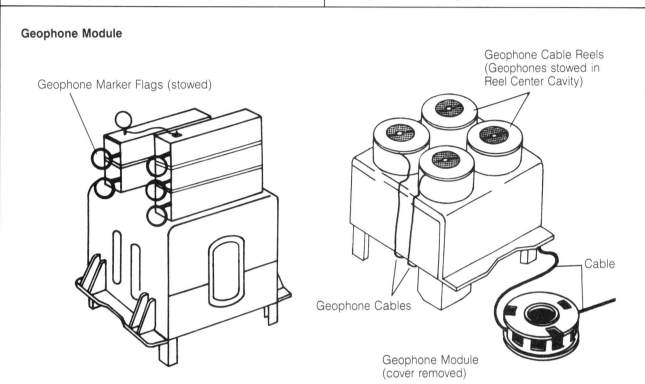

Geophone Marker Flags (stowed)

Geophone Cable Reels
(Geophones stowed in
Reel Center Cavity)

Cable

Geophone Cables

Geophone Module
(cover removed)

Seismometer Sensor Schematic

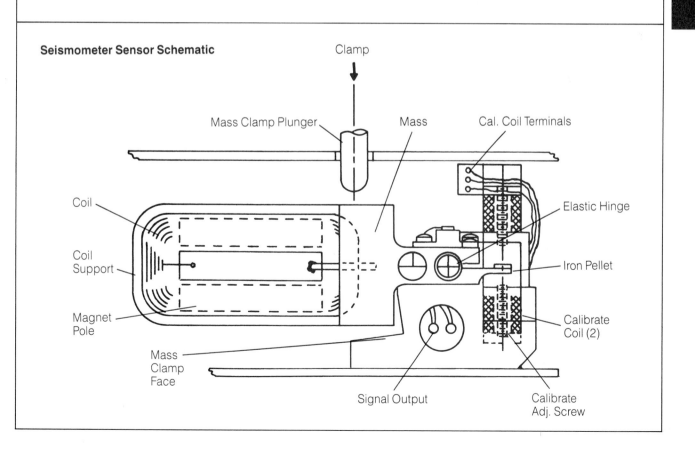

Clamp

Mass Clamp Plunger

Mass

Cal. Coil Terminals

Coil

Elastic Hinge

Coil
Support

Iron Pellet

Magnet
Pole

Calibrate
Coil (2)

Mass
Clamp
Face

Signal Output

Calibrate
Adj. Screw

Set up the geophone main module 30 feet (9.1 meters) from the central station, unwind the cable and connect it to the SPE port on the central station. Then deploy the geophones in a triangular pattern with 300-foot (91-meter) sides. Set the fourth geophone along the center cable in the center of the triangle 88 feet (26.9 meters) from the geophone main module.

The eight explosive charges are carried on two pallets. Each charge has a 6-foot (1.8 meter) antenna and three rings. IMPORTANT: FOLLOW ARMING PROCEDURE EXACTLY!

1. Pull Ring #1—swing up ring, rotate 90° counter-clockwise and remove.
2. Pull Ring #2—this releases SAFE/ARM plate.
3. Pull Ring #3—this frees firing pin.

Explosive Package

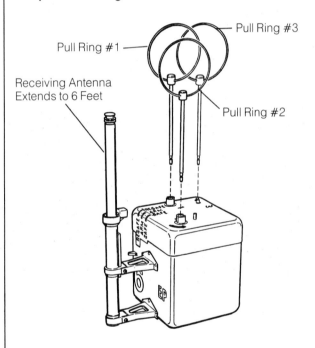

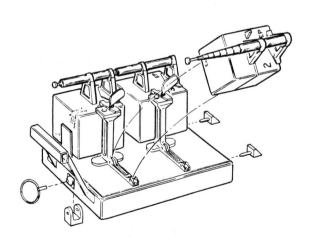

There are two explosive package pallets. There are four explosive packages on each pallet.

The deployment pattern of these charges will be along your walking traverse path.

Deployment Sequence

Mesa EVA #1	Mesa EVA #2	Long Traverse
EP #6 1 lb. charge 90-hr. Timer	EP #4 ⅛ lb. charge 90-hr. Timer	EP #2 ¼ lb. charge 92-hr. Timer
EP #5 3 lb. charge 91-hr. Timer	EP #1 6 lb. charge 91-hr. Timer	EP #3 ⅛ lb. charge 93-hr. Timer
EP #7 ½ lb. charge 92-hr. Timer	EP #8 ¼ lb. charge 93-hr. Timer	

Geophones Deployed

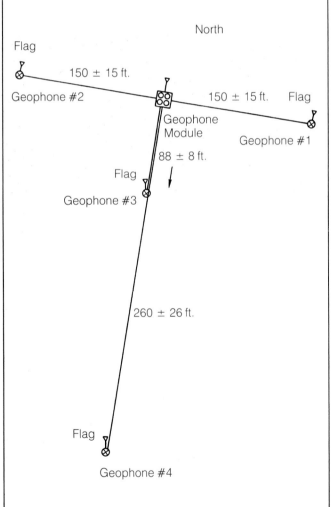

The sample return containers are 1000-cubic-inch (16,390-cc) capacity aluminum boxes measuring 19 x 11.5 x 8 inches (48 x 29 x 20 centimeters) on the outside. Each box has a mesh liner on the interior and a handle, latch pins, seals, and seal protectors. An additional strap/latch system provides further security. To open, rotate the handle. This opens the connecting latch pins. Three seals maintain the integrity of the sample until the cases can be opened in the containment chamber in the LAB module. The mesh liner helps to protect the samples from vibration and impacts.

Each container has a kit that includes Teflon-coated cloth Sample Collection Bags (SCBs). Each bag has slots for drive tube core samples and a special slit for small samples. The special Core Sample Vacuum Container (CSVC) is designed to isolate core samples in a pristine environment. To use an SCB, insert the sample and rotate the torquing handle to seal until it is tight. the core tube are sealed with Teflon caps, which are stored in the cubic dispenser. The drive tubes are used to collect core samples of the surface. The tube itself is a hollow aluminum cylinder 16 x 1.75 inches (40.6 x 4.4 centimeters) with a bit on one end. The tool extension is connected to the drive tube, which can be attached to another tube for deeper cores.

The hammer has an aluminum handle and a tool steel head for striking or chiseling surfaces. There is a tool extension rod that can turn the pick end into a hoe for digging.

The rake is used to obtain 0.5 to 1-inch (1.3 to 2.54 centimeter) rock and chip samples. The rake has 10-inch (25.4 centimeter) stainless steel tines with an aluminum handle.

The sample scale is used to weigh the sample return containers. The scale weighs in 5-pound increments and is calibrated to martian gravity to give an approximate Earth equivalent up to 80 pounds (36.6 kilograms).

The sampling scoop is a flat-bottomed container used to collect soil samples. The pan can be angled from 0° to 55° for scooping. For use as a trenching tool, the hinge can be set at 90°. The aluminum handle

Tool Carrier Stowed

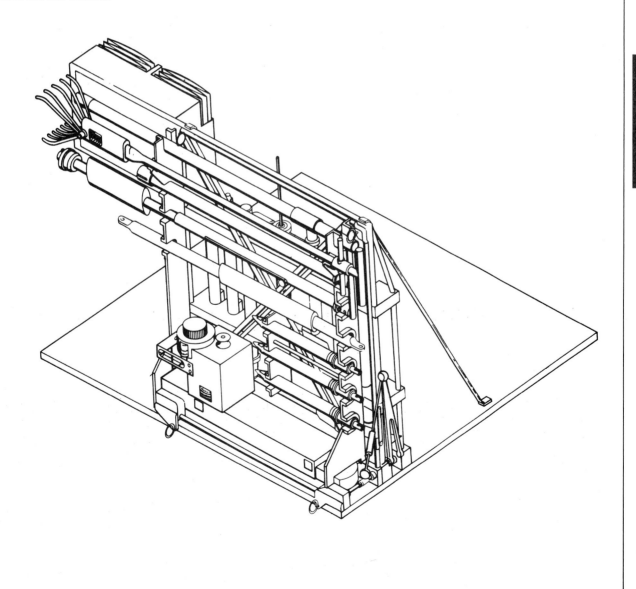

also fits the extension handle. The tongs are used to pick up pebbles and rock samples. The 32-inch (81-centimeter) tongs are stainless steel and are spring loaded. Squeezing the two handles opens the tongs, relaxing closes them.

The gnomon is a reference tool used for measuring. It is basically a tripod with a gimbaled (free-swinging) rod mounted through the top. As you set it up, the 18-inch (46-centimeter) rod will point downward, giving you a vertical reference. The rod is also banded in 1-inch (2.54-centimeter) lengths using a gray-scale. This will give you a size reference for photographs and a measure, for black and white images, of the reflectance of the surrounding rocks. On one of the tripod legs is a color chart. This will allow color pictures to be adjusted to their true color, because the laboratories on Earth have the same standardized chart. Also, the direction and length of the gnomon's shadow will indicate the Sun's direction and angle.

The surface drill (SD) is your tool for boring deep holes in the surface. It is used to deploy the heat flow experiment and to take deep core samples. The rotary-percussion drill is hand-held and has three major components: a powerhead assembly with battery; a rack assembly with bore and core stems; and a treadle assembly used for uncoupling and extracting stems as necessary.

The powerhead uses electrical energy to run a rotary-percussion motor. A thermal guard prevents you from accidentally touching the powerhead. To use the powerhead, attach the drill bit to the bore stem, and the bore stem to the powerhead. Should the bore stem get stuck, the treadle assembly can serve as a type of jackplate along with a handle to literally screw the stem out of the ground. Core stems with a cap dispenser for capping the enclosed core sample are provided. Each cap is lettered (A–H) and should be put on as the stem is removed from the ground and broken down. This will mark the extraction sequence.

Tool Carrier Setup

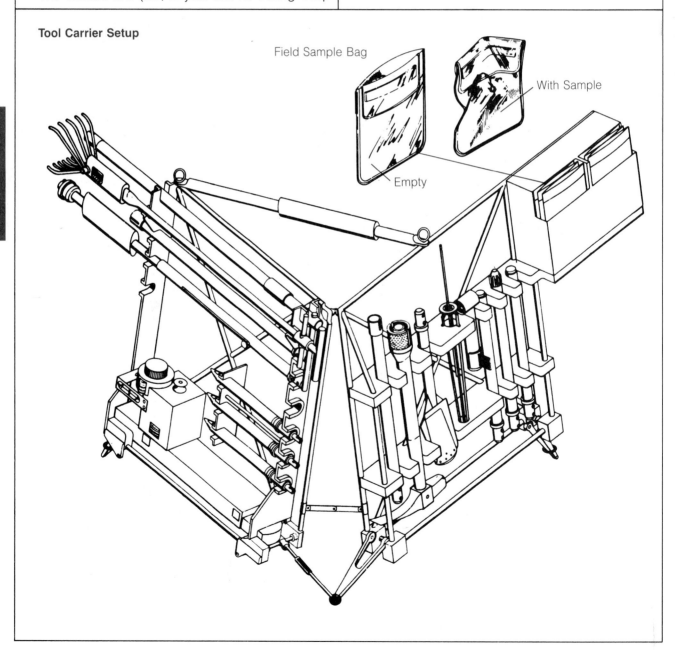

Field Sample Bag

With Sample

Empty

4.6.7

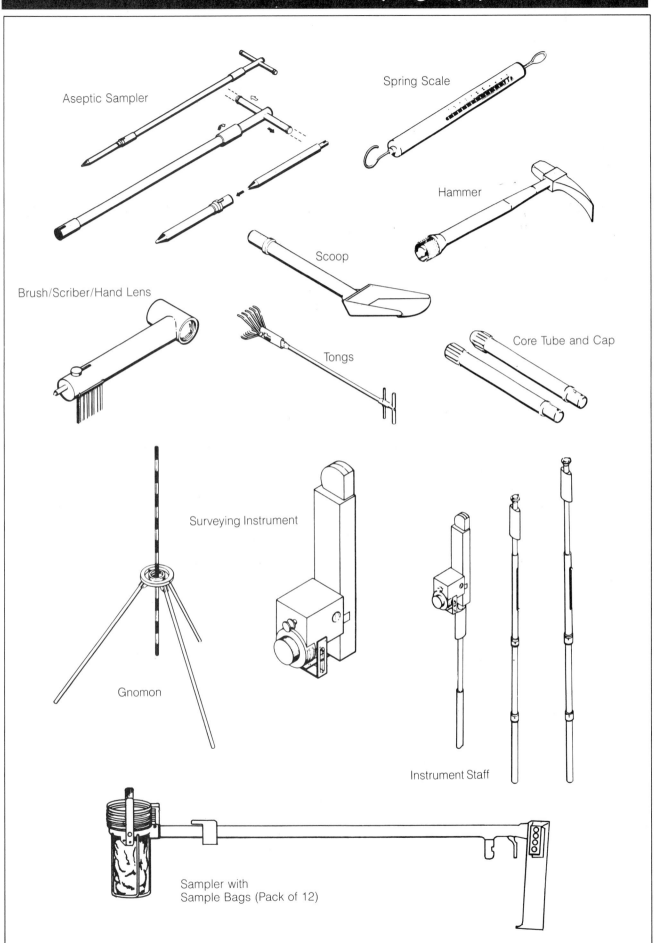

Aseptic Sampler

Spring Scale

Hammer

Scoop

Brush/Scriber/Hand Lens

Tongs

Core Tube and Cap

Surveying Instrument

Gnomon

Instrument Staff

Sampler with
Sample Bags (Pack of 12)

4.6.8

Gas Chromatograph/Mass Spectrometer (GC/MS)

One of the most powerful tools ever devised to identify unknown substances is the combined Gas Chromatograph/Mass Spectrometer (GC/MS). The gas chromatograph (GC) essentially spreads out elements and compounds by carrying them down a long column that contains tiny coated beads. Since compounds move through the column at different rates, the length of time a particular substance takes to make it through indicates what it is. To be sure of the identification, the stream, minus the helium gas used to carry the compounds down the column, is then smashed into ions (electrically charged atoms). Deflected by electromagnetic fields, these are scattered onto a detector, which determines which ions are present and in what proportion. This serves as a cross-check.

Operation of the GC/MS for surface field work is relatively simple. You can analyze different soil samples by putting them on a strainer and sifting smaller samples, or you can pulverize small rocks and strain them. Run each sample only in part and at different temperatures, first at 200° C (392° F), then at 500° C (932° F). This will cause both easily volatile materials and less volatile substances to evaporate.

A carbon dioxide gas carries the evaporated material to the column, where the helium carrier gas takes over. After the material passes through the column, the computer will display the chromatogram as it emerges. The helium gas is separated and the sample is fed into the mass spectrometer, which can detect elements from mass 12 to mass 200. The spectrometer produces a complete spectrum (cycle) every 10 seconds. This is too fast an accumulation of data to monitor, so the computer will store it for later analysis and give you a summary of the elements found. This will allow you to repeat the experiment if the results are poor or confusing.

You can also use the mass spectrometer to analyze the atmosphere. To do this, merely close the sample feeder to the gas chromatograph and open the valve marked ATM.IN. This allows the atmosphere to be fed directly to the ionizing chamber to be separated and analyzed by the spectrometer.

A sample gas chromatogram is shown below. The results you obtain should be similar.

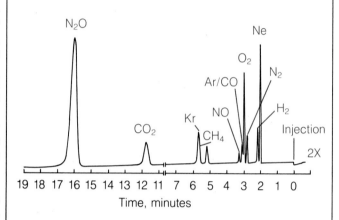

4.6.9

GCMS Instrument

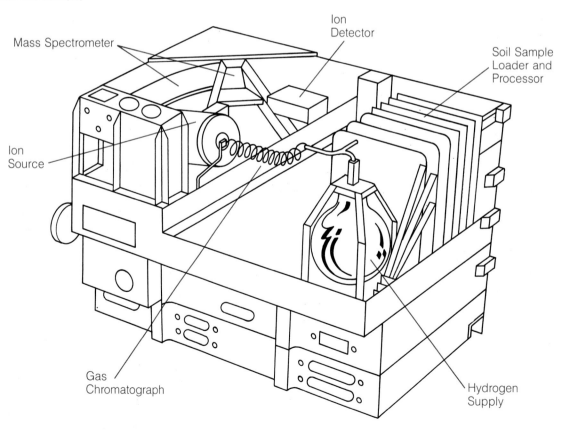

X-ray Fluorescence Spectrometer

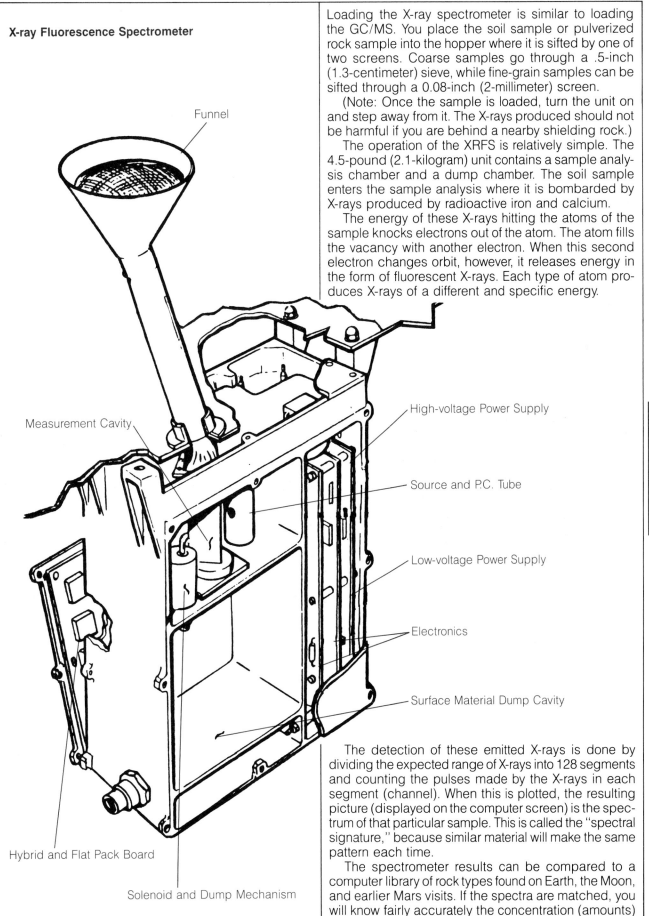

Funnel

Measurement Cavity

High-voltage Power Supply

Source and P.C. Tube

Low-voltage Power Supply

Electronics

Surface Material Dump Cavity

Hybrid and Flat Pack Board

Solenoid and Dump Mechanism

Loading the X-ray spectrometer is similar to loading the GC/MS. You place the soil sample or pulverized rock sample into the hopper where it is sifted by one of two screens. Coarse samples go through a .5-inch (1.3-centimeter) sieve, while fine-grain samples can be sifted through a 0.08-inch (2-millimeter) screen.

(Note: Once the sample is loaded, turn the unit on and step away from it. The X-rays produced should not be harmful if you are behind a nearby shielding rock.)

The operation of the XRFS is relatively simple. The 4.5-pound (2.1-kilogram) unit contains a sample analysis chamber and a dump chamber. The soil sample enters the sample analysis where it is bombarded by X-rays produced by radioactive iron and calcium.

The energy of these X-rays hitting the atoms of the sample knocks electrons out of the atom. The atom fills the vacancy with another electron. When this second electron changes orbit, however, it releases energy in the form of fluorescent X-rays. Each type of atom produces X-rays of a different and specific energy.

4.6.10

The detection of these emitted X-rays is done by dividing the expected range of X-rays into 128 segments and counting the pulses made by the X-rays in each segment (channel). When this is plotted, the resulting picture (displayed on the computer screen) is the spectrum of that particular sample. This is called the "spectral signature," because similar material will make the same pattern each time.

The spectrometer results can be compared to a computer library of rock types found on Earth, the Moon, and earlier Mars visits. If the spectra are matched, you will know fairly accurately the concentration (amounts) of the elements in the samples as well as their identities.

Meteorology Boom (MB)

Two small weather stations are included in the Mars One expedition. One is attached to the MEM and the other to the Rover. To deploy the boom on either vehicle, turn the knurled knob counterclockwise until the holding bolt snaps open. If the knob sticks, you can insert a screwdriver into the slot next to the knob and push the handle away from the knob (to your right). Then swing the boom away from the body of the MEM (or the MR) and tighten the knurled knob (clockwise) to hold the boom in place.

Like any good weather station, the meteorology boom can sense pressure, temperature, and wind speed. Temperature is measured by a device that looks like a cross between a small wrench and a cheese cutter. The three fine wires are called thermocouples and are gold plated to protect them from sand and solar heating. Each wire has two metals, which expand by different amounts when heated and contract by different amounts when cooled. Their motion induces an electric current, which can be measured to determine atmospheric temperature. When deploying the boom, be extremely careful not to break these fine wires. They do operate independently, however. So long as one wire is unbroken, you will get temperature data.

Measuring atmospheric pressure is equally simple.

**Meteorology Boom and Sensors
Deployed Configuration**

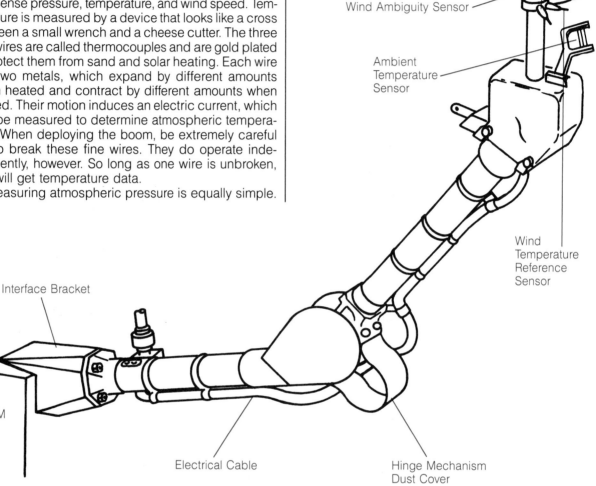

Active Wind Sensors

Wind Ambiguity Sensor

Ambient Temperature Sensor

Wind Temperature Reference Sensor

Interface Bracket

MEM

Electrical Cable

Hinge Mechanism Dust Cover

4.6.11

Mounted in the electronics box at the outer end of the boom is a thin metal diaphragm. On one side is a vacuum, on the other side is the martian atmosphere. Protected from the wind, the diaphragm will move only if the pressure on the atmospheric side changes. An electrical sensor picks up this movement; changes in voltage correspond to changes in pressure.

Wind measurements are a bit trickier to take. Two thin platinum-coated wires are mounted inside glass needles coated with aluminum oxide, which, in turn, are mounted on top of the boom. These two outer wires are at a 90° angle to a post at the end of the boom and to one another. They are called hot-film anemometers, and

they measure wind speed by recording the amount of energy necessary to maintain the temperature of the needles as the wind blows over them and cools them down. A third sensor mounted between the wires provides a temperature reference and controls the power levels. Together these sensors measure wind speeds between 4.5 and 340 mph (7.2 and 547 kph). A wind change sensor with a four-sided surface that gives speed and directional information is mounted above the needles. (Note: Like the wires in the temperature sensor, these wind-sensing glass needles are extemely delicate; contact with them should be very carefully avoided during deployment of the boom.)

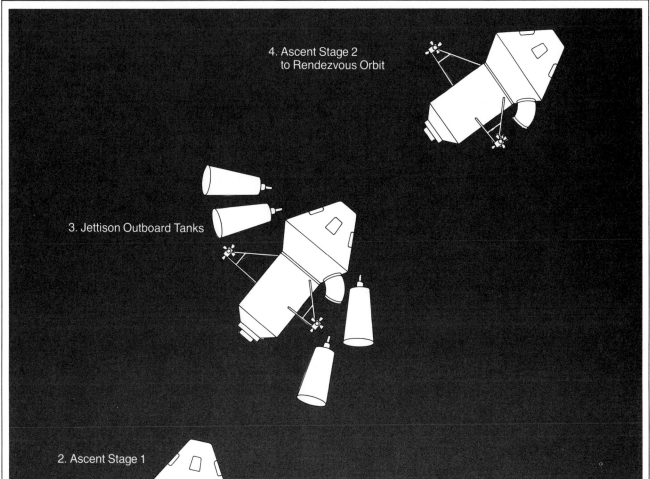

4. Ascent Stage 2
   to Rendezvous Orbit

3. Jettison Outboard Tanks

2. Ascent Stage 1

4.7.1

1. Ready for Ascent

The on-board computer controls the two-stage ascent and docking with the main ship. You depart from the Mars surface on March 20, 1997 (245-0528 JD), and ascend to MEM rendezvous orbit. After lift-off, you pass through a vertical rise phase, an arch-over, and then orbital insertion. You then fly three braking maneuvers to adjust your orbit to the MS orbit and dock. After the samples have been secured in the LAB and the MEM systems have been shut down, the ascent stage is jettisoned. Impact of the ascent stage on the martian surface creates a marsquake. The total effects of this modest quake are recorded by the hardlander/penetrator/science station network you left on Mars. This tests the system, which will continue to relay data until the power supplies on the comsats or the surface instruments run down.

You are now ready for a physical examination and debriefing before starting the journey home. The exam assesses the effects of thirty days of Mars's gravity on your body. Muscle tone, body mass, heart rate, red blood cell count, and other measurements are used to evaluate your condition. The debriefing includes a thorough set of interviews, an oral history, and annotations to transcripts of air-to-ground communication. The purpose of the debriefing is to extract as much information from you as possible while you are still close to the experience. Areas covered will include system performance, experiment deployment, general scientific findings, and research questions.

The period from the time you leave Mars orbit until you return to Earth involves many technical, physical, and psychological challenges. These are outlined in this section, which contains your routine for the inbound leg and quarantine procedures.

5.0.1

Inbound Daily Schedule

- Communication to/from Earth is accomplished on personal time

- Wednesday PM—Crew planning and assessment meetings

- Sunday schedule—free AM until exercise session PM—weekly physical, report/Earth readjustment session, intergroup meeting

5.1.1

HAB 1

Time (hrs.)	Length of Activity (hrs.)	Commander	Pilot	Chief Science Officer	Science Specialist #1	Science Specialist #2	Science Specialist #3
1–8	8	Sleep					
8:30	:30	Personal time					
9	:45	Breakfast					
10		System maint					
11–12	3	Research (Wednesday—Earth reorientation)					
13	1	Exercise A					
14	1	Exercise B					
15	:45	Lunch					
16–18	3:30	Research (Maintenance, extra exercise)					
19	1	Exercise and personal time					
20	1	Exercise and personal time					
21–22	1:15	Dinner					
23	1:30	Maintenance and housekeeping					
24	:45	Personal time					

HAB 2

Science Specialist #4 | Lander Commander | Lander Pilot | Lander Science Officer | Lander Science Specialist

Sleep

Personal time

Breakfast

System maint

Research (Wednesday— Earth reorientation)

Exercise A

Exercise B

Lunch

Research (Maintenance, extra exercise)

Exercise and personal time

Exercise and personal time

Dinner

Maintenance and housekeeping

Personal time

Your mission is not over. In fact, your most challenging weeks and months are yet to come. It is important to get back into your exercise and living routines. Over the coming months, your physical and emotional well-being will be as important as the samples and information you bring back with you.

Your daily schedule is very similar to the outbound schedule. There is still a small amount of training, but the training sessions are now primarily devoted to research, including reducing data from the MOSA phase and analyzing the results of your study.

You will monitor your diet closely, changing certain foods to study their effects on your body during prolonged weightlessness. Bone decalsification rate, red and white blood cell count, potassium and sodium levels, and your cardiovascular condition are also monitored.

By this time in the mission, psychological factors are even more important. Concern about reintegration into society, effects of the voyage on Earth relationships, etc., loom large. Group discussion sessions begin about one-third of the way home to allow the crew a chance to air and explore their feelings and to talk through potential problems.

For specific activities refer to the daily schedule in this section.

5.1.2

While you are away on your mission, the Quarantine Facility (QF) is being constructed in Earth orbit. When you return, you and your samples are processed through this facility. There are several important reasons for this. The first is protection for Earth. Although no evidence of organics or life was found by the Viking missions, this does not mean that life on Mars does not exist. Should the crew come in contact with life forms, or should the samples you are returning contain life forms, their existence would have to be detected and they would have to be contained and analyzed for their potential harm to the Earth's environment. The quarantine facility provides a significant level of protection.

The crew must also be checked for their own protection. Isolated communities can lose immunity to many diseases, and the physical well-being of the crew must be assured. The quarantine procedure is not new. The crews of the early Apollo landings were quarantined on Earth. But the Moon was an extremely unlikely place to find life, and they were only held for about ten days.

The quarantine facility is composed of several modules. A module weighing 30,000 pounds (13,600 kilograms) with extended solar panels powers the facility.

It connects to a central docking module. Directly opposite the power module is a 9,920-pound (4,500-kilogram) logistics module for storage of supplies, along with bulk and waste storage. A 30,000-pound (13,600-kilogram) habitation module contains the living quarters, a galley, a command operations center, and a medical support facility. Finally, the LAB module, also weighing 30,000 pounds (13,600 kilograms), is the location for sample storage, experiment control, and quarantine testing. The LAB module has a special sample acquisition port to receive the samples.

After transfer from the Earth arrival orbit to the QF orbit, the crew will rotate to the QF for medical checkups. During the first rotation, the samples are transferred by the remaining crew to the QF LAB.

The procedure for the analysis of the samples is performed in six stages. Once they are in the control areas, an analysis of the gases trapped in the sample collection containers and all individually sealed containers is carried out. Then, the radioactivity of all samples is tested for safe levels. Third, a complete chemical analysis is performed. Fourth, microscope and life-process (metabolic) analysis begins. Fifth, microbiological and

Planetary Positions at Earth Orbit Injection

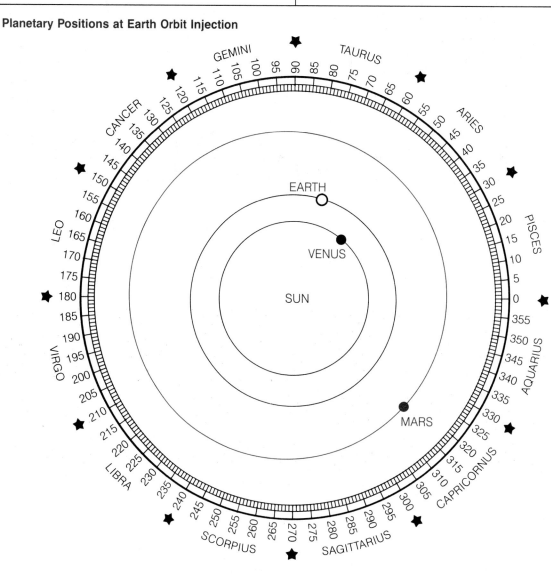

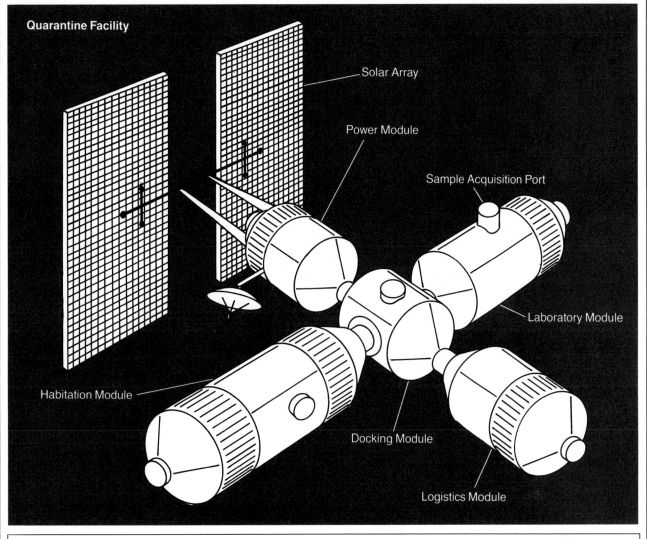

Quarantine Facility

Solar Array

Power Module

Sample Acquisition Port

Laboratory Module

Habitation Module

Docking Module

Logistics Module

Equipment List for the QF Laboratory

Item/Specifications	Power (W)	Weight (kg)	Item/Specifications	Power (W)	Weight (kg)
Alpha particle instrument	2	1.8	Micromanipulator	10	2.0
Autoclave	300	11.0	Microscope, compound, phase contrast, UV	25	5.0
Autoradiograph	0	1.0			
Camera, roll film	0	2.0	Microscope, scanning electron	500	70.0
Camera, video (color)	70	7.0	Microscope, stereoscopic	30	12.0
Centrifuge	2×10^3	100.0	Mixer/shaker	10	2.2
Dry heat sterilizer, drying oven	50	2.3	Plate scanner, counter	20	9.0
Electroanalytical apparatus, conductance bridge	10	9.1	Refrigerator	50	10.0
			Scintillation counter	10	4.5
Freezer, freeze dryer	300	15.0	Spectrophotometer, UV, visible	10	2.3
Gas bottles	0	68.0	Tissue culture chamber and maintenance system	10	15.0
Gas chromatograph/mass spectrometer	50[a]	10.0[a]			
Impedance bridge	1	1.0	Ultrasonic cleaner	30	10.0
Incubator	60	10.0	Vacuum cleaner	10	1.0
Kits, microbiology	0	1.0[a]	Vacuum dessicator	0	4.0
Liquid nitrogen dewar	0	50.0	Vacuum evaporator	0	4.0[a]
Mass measurement device, micro	1	2.0	Vacuum filter	0	4.0[a]

[a]Estimated.

[a]Estimated.

A longitudinal view of the Laboratory Module

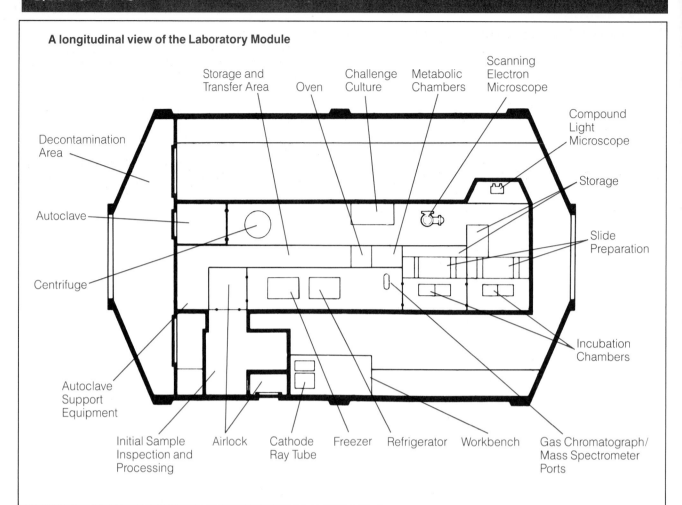

Decontamination Area

Storage and Transfer Area

Oven

Challenge Culture

Metabolic Chambers

Scanning Electron Microscope

Compound Light Microscope

Autoclave

Storage

Centrifuge

Slide Preparation

Incubation Chambers

Autoclave Support Equipment

Initial Sample Inspection and Processing

Airlock

Cathode Ray Tube

Freezer

Refrigerator

Workbench

Gas Chromatograph/ Mass Spectrometer Ports

challenge culture experiments occur. Finally, tests of all kinds are analyzed and a decision is made on the safety of taking the samples back to Earth.

These tests are extremely sophisticated. The radio-activity tests, for instance, are used not only to ensure the safety of the QF crew, but to act as a guide for evaluating the samples in a later phase of testing. In one of the tests a microbiological organism colony (a culture) is introduced into the presence of a Mars sample. This is called a challenge culture experiment. Since the effects of radiation on Earth organisms are known, knowledge of the Mars sample radioactive levels will also help explain the results of these culture challenge experiments.

The microscopic analyses are done after chemical tests for elements, amino acids, and organic materials are performed. A stereomicroscope is first used to study soil samples visually. Then a scanning electron microscope (SEM) is used to study the filters on which the soils were collected. In the third phase of this activity, light microscopes and the scanning electron microscope are used to study soil samples both in their natural state and stained with dye to bring out various features. Some of the other samples are then stained with fluorescent dyes and illuminated with ultraviolet light. This brings out additional detail and would also highlight the presence of chlorophyll, the chemical that turns plants green, because chlorophyll stimulates fluorescence.

The LAB module on the QF has several chambers.

The sample receiving area has a central set of containment compartments where samples are stored and treated. These sealed compartments have various robot arms and external arm inserts for technicians to do both precise and general work. On either side of the compartments are walkways lined with instrumentation and communications equipment.

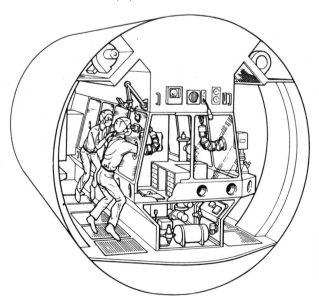

Laboratory personnel viewing slides with a light microscope.

At the end of the module is a decontamination chamber for humans. Before you can enter the area, you must disrobe and stow your clothing in the habitation module. You then move into the docking module through an airtight door, sealing that door behind you. Then you open the airtight door into the LAB module and enter the decontamination area. Here you have an air shower, a flow of fast-moving sterile air that blows loose particles off your body. The air is drawn out through filters. After the shower you wipe down your hands, neck, and face with a disinfectant towelette. Next, you don your laboratory garment and head cap after removing it from the moist-heat sterilizer. The outfit is completed with a face mask and surgical rubber gloves. When ready, you may enter the LAB. On leaving, you must do the entire process in reverse. During periods of non-use, the decontamination chamber is irradiated with ultraviolet lamps to kill any remaining microbes.

Equipment brought into the LAB area must also be sterilized and given an air shower. Then, after it has received ultraviolet radiation and disinfectant wiping, it may be taken into the testing area.

The Decontamination Area of the Laboratory Module (cross-section)

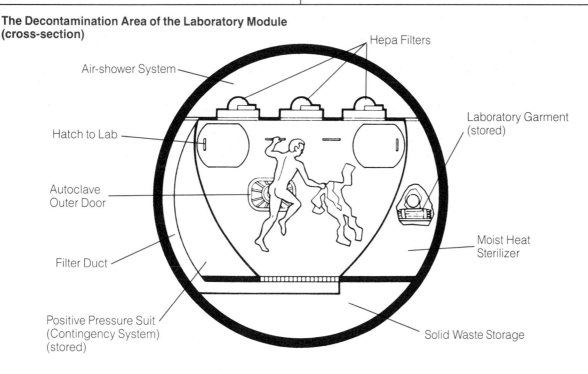

A cross-sectional view of the Laboratory Module

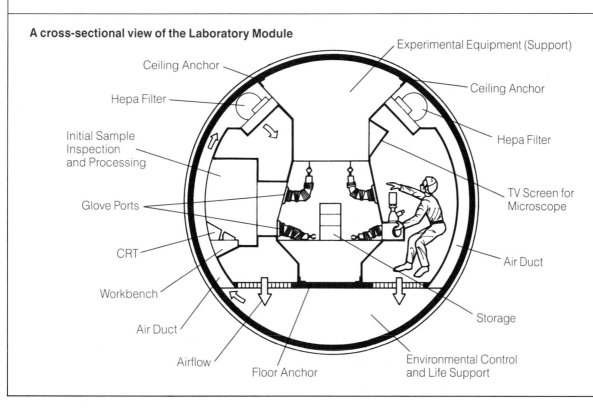

5.2.4

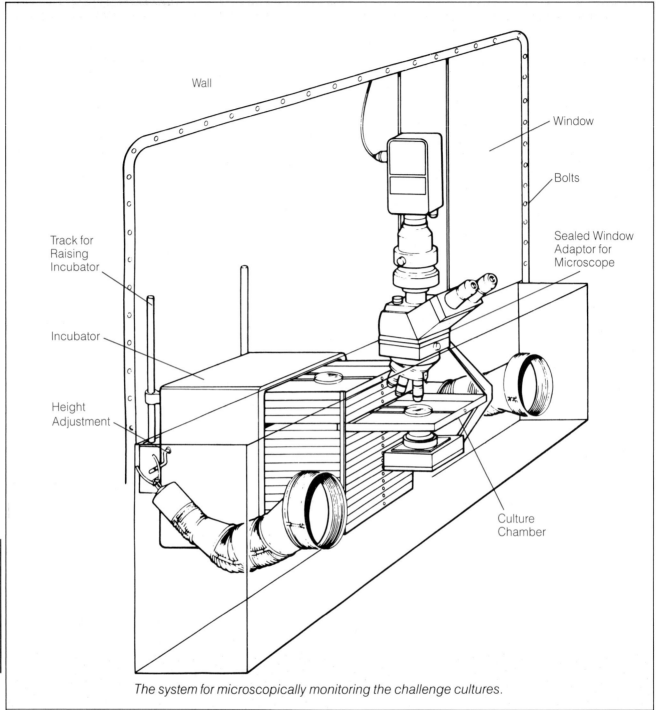

Wall

Window

Bolts

Track for
Raising
Incubator

Incubator

Height
Adjustment

Sealed Window
Adaptor for
Microscope

Culture
Chamber

The system for microscopically monitoring the challenge cultures.

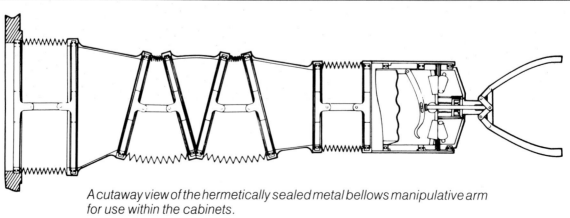

*A cutaway view of the hermetically sealed metal bellows manipulative arm
for use within the cabinets.*

5.2.5

Should containment be breached, whether by a broken seal or broken filter, several measures can be taken. By adjusting pressures of various compartments you can contain escaped microbes. In an emergency, you may have to evacuate the LAB, return to the decontamination area, and follow the decontamination procedures.

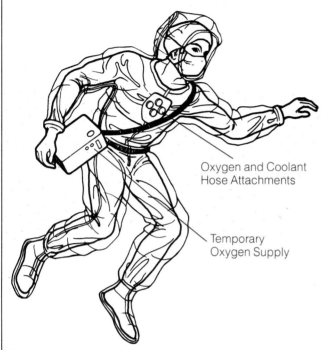

Oxygen and Coolant Hose Attachments

Temporary Oxygen Supply

The protective suit to be used during breaches of containment.

One member of the crew will then don a new laboratory garment and a special pressurized protective suit with its own separate oxygen supply. Only this crew member may reenter the area and make repairs.

During the containment breach, an automatic system floods the lab with formaldehyde gas to sterilize the area. Then a neutralizing gas makes the lab usable again.

Should a crew member become contaminated, a medical isolation chamber is provided where the individual can be contained for up to twenty-one days. The chamber is designed for zero-g operation. This chamber would be used if the patient had inhaled or swallowed particles or gas from martian samples.

The QF habitation area has crew accommodations, a galley, a small recreation and gymnasium area, and guest bunks. The QF crew consists of five members: the commander, who has an engineering background, and four scientists—a medical doctor, a research geobiologist, a biochemist, and a biologist with general background.

The QF will be used on future missions. An ambitious program of research is planned in the areas of weightlessness and biological systems; performance studies; effects of spaceflight on immunology, radiology, and social behavior; life-support systems; and bioinstrumentation development.

After quarantine, you are going home. Your work during this period is critical, and the process of readaptation to the 1-g Earth normal gravity environment requires patience. You will also suddenly be overwhelmed with people and obligations, so this first exposure to new people and a slightly new environment will be of some help.

An overhead view of the Habitation Module

Food Storage Area   Crew Quarter 1   Crew Quarter 2   Crew Quarter 3   Exercise Area   Waste Management Area   Workshop

Center Aisle

5.2.6

Dining Tables   Treadmill   Ergometer   Universal Machine   Isolators (collapsed)

Galley   Desk   Locker

Sleeping Bag   Shower   Sinks   Toilet

Pressure Hatch

Storage

Food Service Area   Command Console   Crew Quarter 5   Crew Quarter 4   Hygiene Area   Sick Bay

On December 19, 1997 (245-0802 JD), the Shuttle orbiter is launched. After a resupply stop at the space station, it changes orbits, makes a rendezvous, and docks with the QF. The entire crew then spends a full two days shutting down the main ship. A final decontamination of the main ship is followed by a crew transfer to the QF where each member is sent into the decontamination area one final time. You then transfer to the Shuttle and take your places in the passenger transport module.

Approximately 45 minutes later the orbiter performs the deorbit burn and leaves orbit. After another half hour, the orbiter enters the Earth's atmosphere. Five minutes later, the sheath of atmosphere surrounding the craft produces a blackout of radio transmission; five minutes later the orbiter reaches maximum heating. Seven minutes later the craft exits the blackout and completes the S-turns that help to dissipate the energy of its earthward plunge.

At this time you are experiencing up to 1.5-g forces. You may feel slightly woozy, since you have not felt this kind of force for such a long period. The orbiter now descends on a 22° glide slope. You can feel the banking turn around the Heading Alignment Circle (HAC), which lines you up on the runway. Thirty-two seconds before touchdown you feel the nose pull up as the orbiter goes through pre-flare. You hear the landing gear lock and, fourteen seconds later, you feel the touchdown and rollout. You have safely arrived at the Kennedy Space Center, Florida, U.S.A., Earth.

After you hear the signal WHEELS STOP, the ground crew comes aboard and prepares you for egress. You are assisted through the airlock into the flight deck, through the crew hatch, and down the steps to waiting wheelchairs. You and the other crew members are then loaded into a transport van and driven to the receiving site at the Vehicle Assembly Building.

The heads of state of all participating nations and the Secretary General of the United Nations are scheduled to be on hand to greet you, to offer congratulations, and to welcome you home. The date is December 21, 1997 (245-0804 JD).

Entry Flight Profile

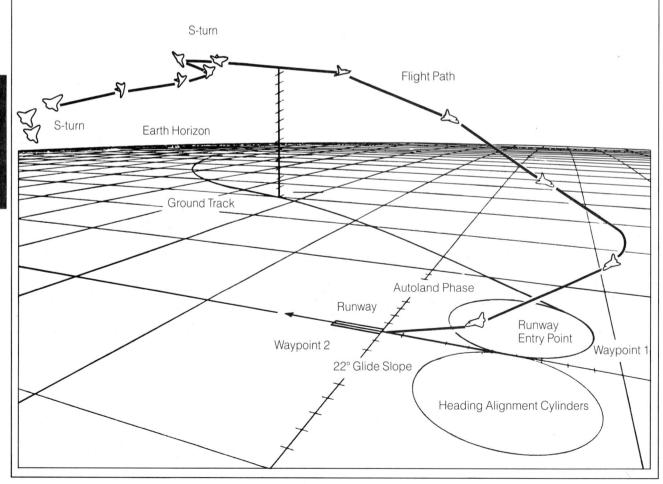

5.3.1

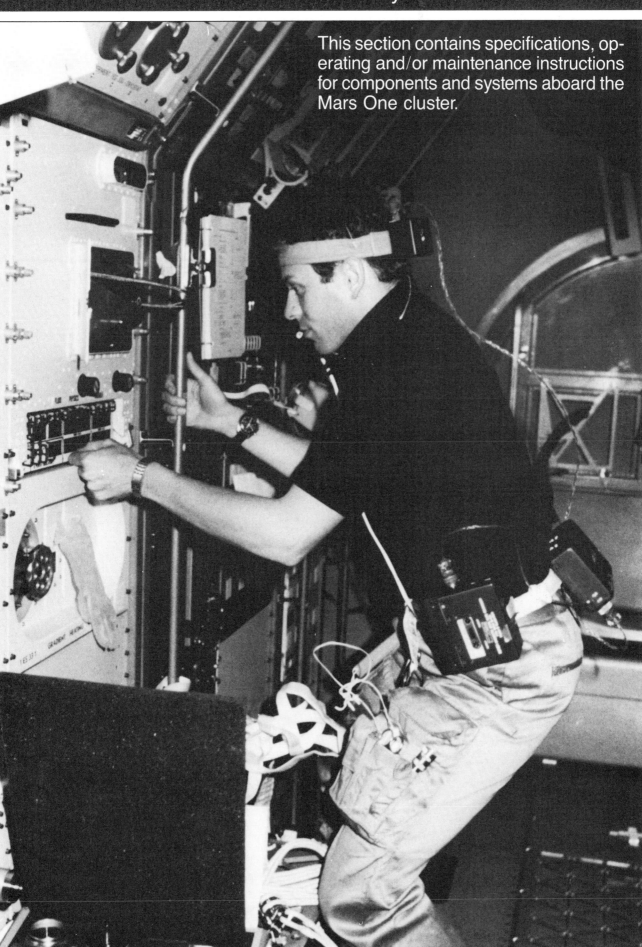

This section contains specifications, operating and/or maintenance instructions for components and systems aboard the Mars One cluster.

6.0.1

Computer systems are critical to your mission. A special computer configuration has been designed for the mission, called the Main Mission Computer (MMC). The MMC is a 64-bit parallel processing computer. It contains 10 megabytes (million bytes) of Read-Only Memory (ROM) and 30 megabytes of Random Access Memory (RAM). The MMC has a master program library stored partially internally and partially on a master disc. This master disc is read by a laser Data Recorder (DR). The DR is a read/write device capable of reading discs with storage capacity of 4.8 gigabytes (billion bytes).

The MMC can be programmed in three languages. HAL-S+ is a modified and enhanced version of the High-order Assembly Language—Shuttle +—that has become a standard for Shuttle and space station operations. The INFER language, developed in the late 1980s, is an artificial intelligence tool for developing expert systems. DANYET is a popular language for logic and simulation. It was developed by a team of scientists from the US, Japan, and the USSR, and many of the simulation exercises are written in this language. All displays can use either the Latin alphabet, the Cyrillic

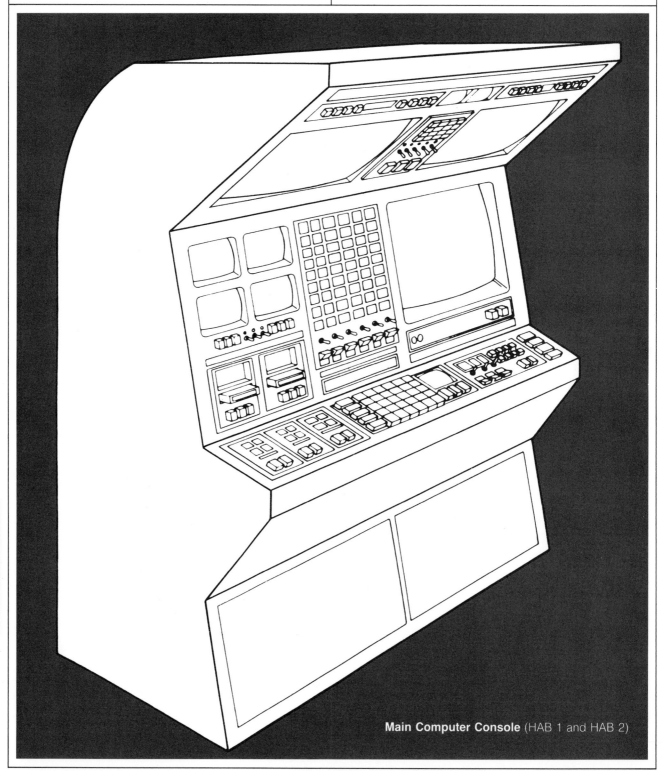

6.1.1

Main Computer Console (HAB 1 and HAB 2)

alphabet, or Japanese characters.

A portable version of the MMC is available. It contains only the basic operating system and must be used with the data recorders for RAM/ROM.

A pocket computer is also available. It runs simplified versions of many of the main mission programs.

There are 3 MMCs, 2 portables, 2 pocket computers, and 2 DRs in each HAB module. In the LAB module there are 2 MMCs, 1 portable, 1 pocket computer, and 2 DRs. In addition, there is a special Science Application Computer (SAC), which is specially configured for the scientific analysis, life science research, and other applications you require. The DRs also have reference discs with over 250,000 images of Mars and its moons.

The Mars excursion module has two special versions of the MMC, called Main Landing Computers (MLCs). These computers could actually be used as in-flight backups for the outbound leg, but contain special landing software in ROM. MEM has 2 MLCs, 1 SAC, 1 pocket computer, and 2 DRs. Finally, the Mars Rover has 2 MLCs, 1 SAC, 1 pocket computer, and 1 DR.

The series of software packages covers nine phases of the mission: 100 series—Outbound burn and midcourse maneuver (including Venus swing-by); 200 series—Mars orbit injection/Orbital operation; 300 series—Mars landing/Surface operations; 400 series—Earth return/Science operations; 500 series—System analysis and repair; 600 series—Mission simulation/Training; 700 series—Guidance and navigation; 800 series—Crew data/Entertainment; 900 series—Master control sequence/Master checklist/System supervisor.

Voice Recognition Commands

You say:	Response:
"EMCEE" (MMC)	
"EMCEE ON"	
"EMCEE LOAD (program name)"	
"EMCEE RUN (program name)"	
"EMCEE DATA' "(data file)" (e.g., "Commander's Log")	"WHAT FILE?" "Opening (data file)" (e.g., "Opening Commander's Log") then "Log open" then "(Appropriate prompts for numbers or text)"
"EMCEE LOAD (sequence name)"	
"EMCEE LIST DIRECTORY"	
"EMCEE HELP"	
"EMCEE MAYDAY"	

MMC Remote Terminal

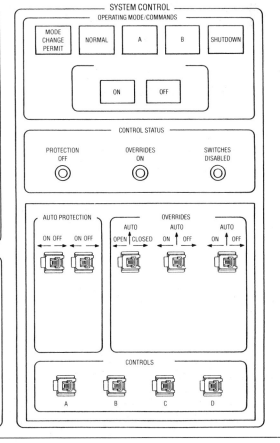
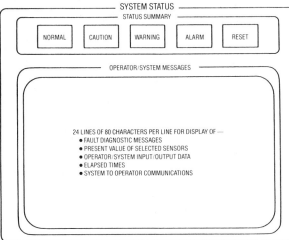
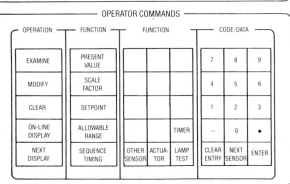

6.1.2

Illumination

The lights in all the modules are identical. They consist of floodlights for overall illumination and emergency lights that operate by rechargeable battery if primary power is lost. Each floodlight consists of a bulb and a protective housing. A standard fluorescent bulb, which should last at least six months, is encased in an aluminum cage which has a single switch control. The switch may be set to OFF-LOW-HI settings. The housing has a number on the bottom and on the end that identifies the location. The condition of the bulb, the number of times it is cycled (turned on and off), and its lifespan are all monitored by the main mission computer.

Sufficient lighting is provided to give an average illumination in the living areas of 5 foot-candles. This is similar to a living room. The waste management compartments and the LAB module work areas are lit at 9 foot-candles. This is like a bright kitchen. Each bulb is rated at 25 watts.

A portable light is provided for working in areas that need extra illumination. It uses a round housing with a handle and cable, and a standard bulb.

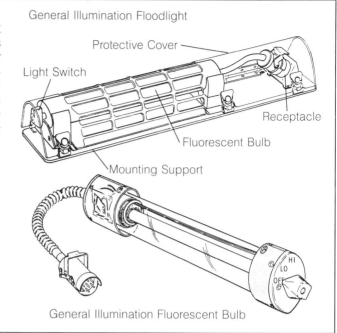

General Illumination Floodlight

Protective Cover

Light Switch

Receptacle

Fluorescent Bulb

Mounting Support

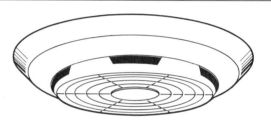

General Illumination Fluorescent Bulb

Fire sensors

Fire sensors are located in each compartment of each module. The alarm is sounded by a claxon through the communications station. The readout displays the location of the activated sensor and the temperature at that sensor. Punching in the sensor number will cause the computer to check all other sensors and report status.

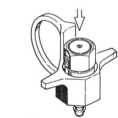

Latches and fasteners

There are several types of latches and fasteners used on cabinets, storage containers, boxes, housings, etc. They are outlined here so you can be familiar with their operation and repair. They include: magnetic latches, handle and trigger latches, lift-handle latches, suitcase latches, and rifle bolt latches.

Restraint Straps   Astro Pin

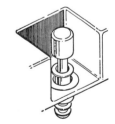

Squeeze Spring (Dog Ear) Latch

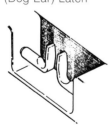

Rifle Bolt Latch

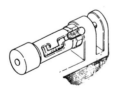

T-Bar Latch

Lift Handle Latch (Adamsrite)

Push Button Latch

Film Access Door Lock

Twist Strap and Hook Latch

Springed Slot Screw

Thumb Screw and Dog Latch

Knob Handle Screw

Restraints

To be able to work at various work stations, foot restraints and hand holds are provided. These are either fixed or portable. The portable foot restraints can be anchored to the floor or walls using pins and pre-drilled mounting holes. The foot restraints can also be mounted on the outside of the craft for EVA repairs. Several platforms with built-in restraints are provided for servicing major components.

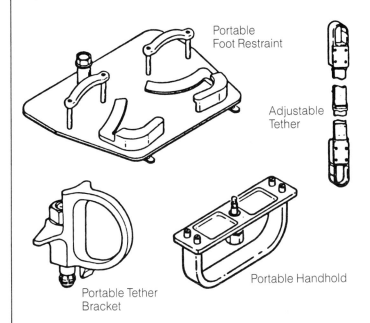

Portable
Foot Restraint

Adjustable
Tether

Portable Tether
Bracket

Portable Handhold

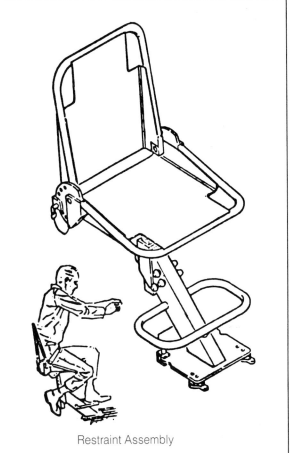

Restraint Assembly

Hatches

All hatches are circular and have a handle for opening and closing, a two-panel window, a lock, and a hand hold. To use a hatch, rotate the handle to the desired position (opened or closed). Be sure the small pressure equalization valve near the window has been checked, then pull the handle.

Hatch Handle
Lock Assembly

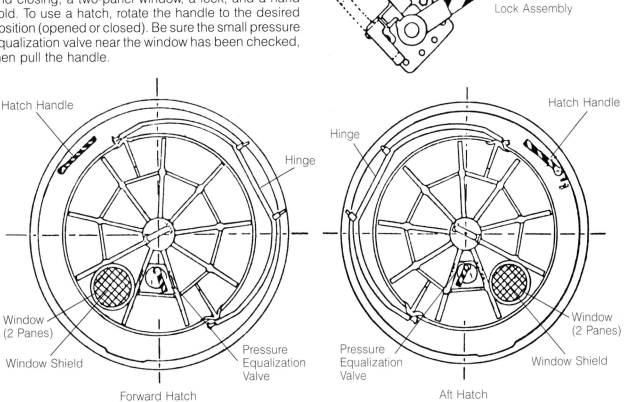

Hatch Handle

Hinge

Hatch Handle

Hinge

Window
(2 Panes)

Window Shield

Pressure
Equalization
Valve

Pressure
Equalization
Valve

Window
(2 Panes)

Window Shield

Forward Hatch

Aft Hatch

6.1.4

Containers

Wall, floor, and ceiling containers are built into the ship. These containers have hinged doors and use several types of latches. Don't forget to wipe around the doors, and inside empty containers, with biocide wipes during the mission to retard growth of microorganisms. You will be transferring supplies into and out of the containers. Most compartments have been modularized with standard sizes and shapes to make transfers easier.

D400 Series Stowage Compartments (6 ft³ ea)

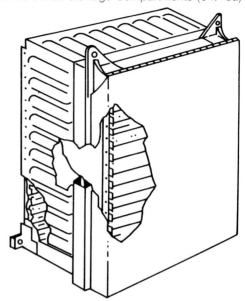

3 ft³ Stowage Compartment

1.5 ft³ Stowage Compartment

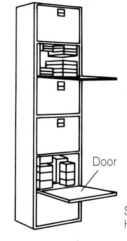

Door

Stowage Compartment Interior (TYP)

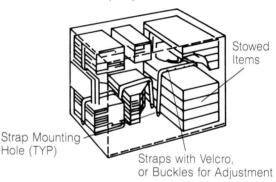

Stowed Items

Strap Mounting Hole (TYP)

Straps with Velcro, or Buckles for Adjustment

1 ft³ Stowage Compartments

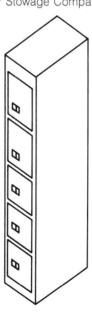

5 ft³ Stowage Compartment

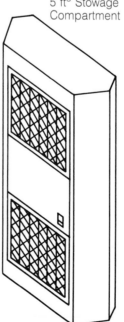

5.5 and 6.5 ft³ Stowage Compartment

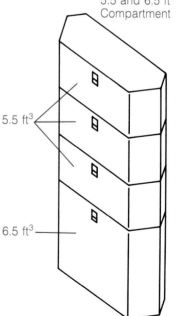

5.5 ft³

6.5 ft³

6.1.5

While much of the information you gather can be analyzed onboard, communication with Earth to transmit surplus and backup data is essential. In addition, the flight controllers, designers, scientists, engineers, and governments supporting this mission have a huge reserve of information that can be tapped in an emergency.

Telecommunication for this mission is the most sophisticated of any in history. The main ship can communicate with both Earth and the martian surface. The MEM and the Rover communicate through relay satellites placed in orbit.

The information to be transmitted is divisible into three categories—information (digital data), voice, and video. The first category, digital data, carries all of the telemetry, scientific information, and engineering data. Scientific data from the impressive array of instruments is transmitted via relay satellites, collected and sorted by computers aboard the main ship, and relayed to Earth. Engineering data, information on all systems (life support, propulsion, navigation, communications, etc.) is sent in a steady stream from every piece of hardware. The MMC continually monitors all of this data for any non-nominal (abnormal) behavior. This information too is sent back to Earth as a history of flight hardware performance.

Voice data is taped as a matter of record, and blocks of voice transmission are routinely relayed to Earth. Due to the distance, two-way communication is lengthy, but requests for information can be sent, and replies can be available in twenty minutes.

Video is extremely limited. This is largely due to the enormous amounts of power and information required. One channel of Mars One television can carry 4,000 voice channels or 50 million bits of data per second. Although video is used sparingly, you can make a daily televised report; the Mars surface activities are also televised "live" to Earth.

High-gain and low-gain antennas are used on this mission. A high-gain antenna is usually directional in nature. It emits its signal in a narrow beam, so that the receiver will get a good deal of that power. As a receiver, it collects information from a specific point, allowing maximum signal strength. A high-gain antenna is generally steerable and is used to lock on to targets that

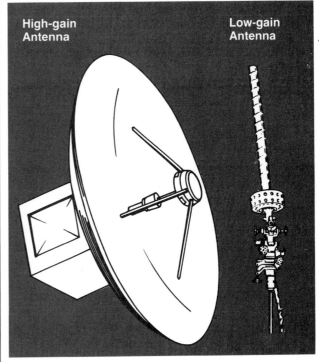

High-gain Antenna

Low-gain Antenna

change position. It can carry more information with greater clarity.

Low-gain antennas are usually omnidirectional, radiating their signal in all directions. This causes a weaker signal. When a low-gain antenna is used as a receiver, a more powerful transmitter is required.

The main ship uses several frequency bands. High-gain antennas communicate with Earth using transmission frequencies of 1.4 gigahertz (ghz—billions of cycles per second) and 2.6 ghz. They receive on 1.6 ghz and 2.4 ghz. Four low-gain antennas are also used to maintain continual contact with Earth, even when the high-gain antennas lose "Earth point."

The MEM uses a high-gain antenna to transmit video, voice, and data to the relay satellites, and a low-gain antenna to receive commands and data updates. The Rover also uses both a high-gain and a low-gain antenna. The remote control instructions to steer the Rover from orbit can be received through the low-gain antenna.

Communication Links

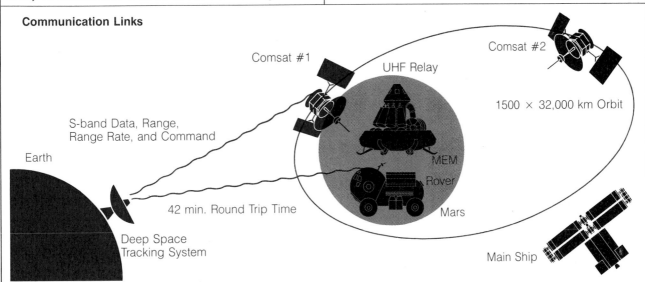

Comsat #1

UHF Relay

Comsat #2

1500 × 32,000 km Orbit

S-band Data, Range, Range Rate, and Command

Earth

MEM

Rover

Mars

42 min. Round Trip Time

Deep Space Tracking System

Main Ship

Space Shuttle Uprated Engine (SSUE)

The primary engine for TMI stage and the main ship is the Space Shuttle Uprated Engine (SSUE). This engine has been a standard in the Shuttle program since its introduction in 1989. The SSUE generates 450,000 pounds (2,043,000 newtons) of thrust using liquid oxygen and liquid hydrogen fuels. The engine is extremely efficient and has regenerative cooling. Liquid hydrogen, which is stored at a temperature of −18.4° F (−28° C), is used to cool the nozzles of the engine. It is also mixed with liquid oxygen, which is stored at −297.4° F (−183° C), to power the turbo-pumps, which, in turn, pump the huge quantity of fuel necessary to create the engine's thrust. This is a two-stage process using both low- and high-pressure turbo-pumps, four in all, for the fuel (LH_2) and oxidizer (LO_2).

The SSUE achieves its improved performance by increasing the fuel flow and the pressures attained in the turbo-pumps. The size of the engine has changed little. It is 13.9 feet (4.23 meters) high. The nozzle is 9.4 feet (2.86 meters) long and 7.8 feet (2.38 meters) in diameter.

The TMI stage has two engines, which provide a 50 percent safety factor against premature shutdown or an engine failure. The main ship has only one engine. This engine performs three burns: Mars Orbit Injection (MOI), Trans-Earth Injection (TEI), and Earth Orbit Injection (EOI). As the mass of the main ship decreases through the loss of the MEM, deployable packages, and used-up fuel, shorter burns are required to achieve the necessary changes in velocity. These burns are well within the capability of this engine.

SSUE Controller Side

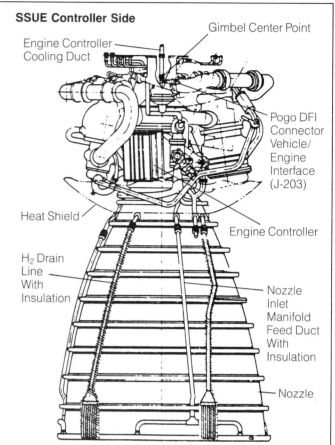

Engine Controller Cooling Duct
Gimbel Center Point
Pogo DFI Connector Vehicle/Engine Interface (J-203)
Heat Shield
Engine Controller
H_2 Drain Line With Insulation
Nozzle Inlet Manifold Feed Duct With Insulation
Nozzle

Reaction Control Engines

The Reaction Control Systems (RCS) for this mission include the RCS for the main ship and for the Mars excursion module.

The main ship RCS is used primarily to change the orientation of the craft for communications, heat distribution, deployment of experiment packages (probes, hardlanders, etc.), and rendezvous and docking operations. The system consists of twelve clusters of engines. Each cluster has twelve engines and is oriented to provide rotation and translation of the entire main ship. The ship can be rotated around three axes—the length, width, and height axes running through the center of each cluster—and the entire ship can be translated or moved along the same three axes without rotating or changing its orientation.

6.3.1

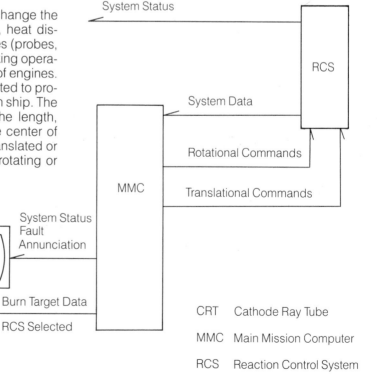

System Status

RCS

System Data

Rotational Commands

Translational Commands

MMC

System Status Fault Annunciation

CRT

Burn Target Data

RCS Selected

Keyboard

CRT — Cathode Ray Tube
MMC — Main Mission Computer
RCS — Reaction Control System

These maneuvers are performed primarily by the MMC. Desired motions are requested on the menu. Motions are plotted with respect to sun angle and star (Canopus) point. Major maneuvers have been preprogrammed, but variations and adjustments can be programmed manually.

The main RCS engines are fueled by monomethyl hydrazine (N_2H_4) and nitrogen tetroxide (N_2O_4). The hydrazine is also the source of nitrogen for the cabin atmosphere. Each engine, capable of 50,000 starts, can be used in a pulse mode with a minimum of 80 millisecond pulses, or in continuous thrusts of 1 to 150 seconds. Each engine generates 1,000 pounds (4,540 newtons) of thrust.

The MEM uses 32 smaller reaction control engines. Sixteen are used in the descent stage and sixteen in the ascent stage. The descent RCS engines produce 740 pounds (3360 newtons) thrust each, while the smaller ascent stage RCS engines produce 185 pounds (840 newtons) thrust each.

Reaction Control Engine

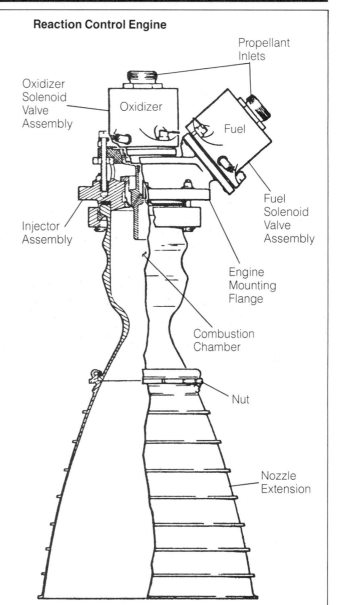

Reaction Control Engine Housing

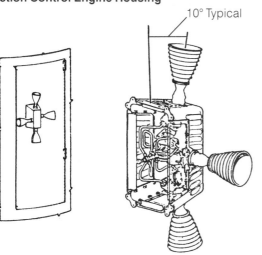

Mars Excursion Module Engines

The descent and ascent engines for the MEM are somewhat exotic. They are called plug nozzles and were chosen over the traditional bell-shaped nozzle for their thrust-to-weight ratio (the power generated from the weight of the engine). The plug nozzle has injectors on the outside of a ring. The flow wraps around the flattened surface. This exerts a force on the nozzle, like the force produced on the inside of a conventional nozzle.

The descent engine weighs 2,020 pounds (1,178 kilograms) and produces 140,000 pounds (635,600 newtons) of thrust. The ascent engine weighs 490 pounds (222 kilograms) and produces 35,000 pounds (158,900 newtons) of thrust. The fuel is a mixture of fluorine/oxygen (FLOX) and methane (CH_4) combined in a ratio of 5.75 units of FLOX to 1 unit of CH_4.

The five solid-fuel rocket deorbit motors have a combined thrust of 46,000 pounds (208,840 newtons) for a burn time of 46 seconds. The deorbit motor cluster weighs 7,400 pounds (3,357 kilograms).

Plug Nozzle

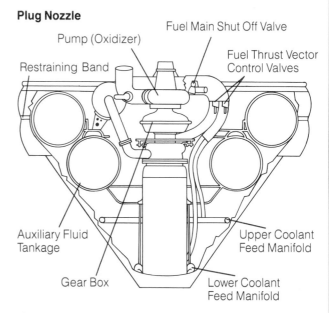

6.3.2

Environmental Control Systems

This section contains schematics and drawings for the identification and servicing of life-support system components. Step-by-step instructions can be found in the MMC Series 500, Sections 530 to 550. Field-stripping of various valves and parts may be necessary during the mission, but all parts were designed to exceed mission requirements by a factor of two in length of service, capability, and reliability.

Potable Water System Schematic

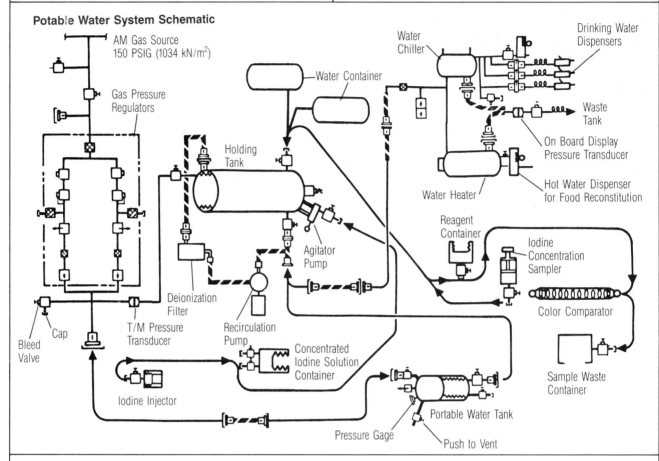

Water Heaters

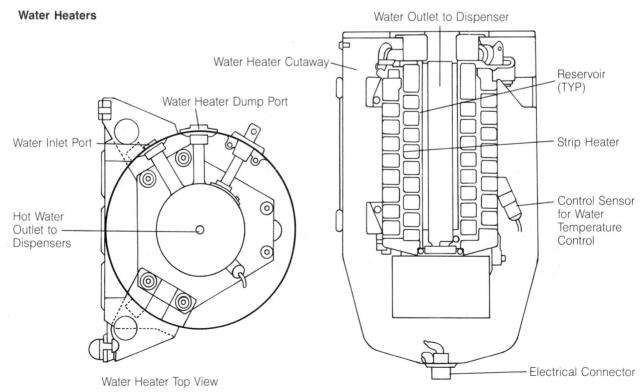

Water Chiller

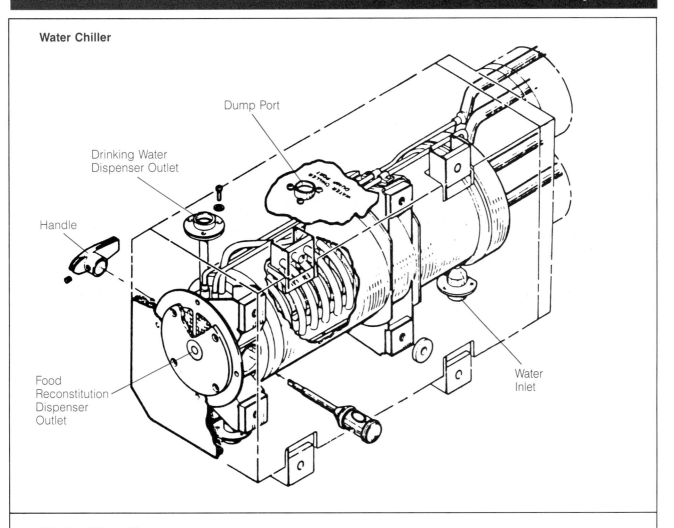

Dump Port

Drinking Water
Dispenser Outlet

Handle

Food
Reconstitution
Dispenser
Outlet

Water
Inlet

Drinking Water Dispensers

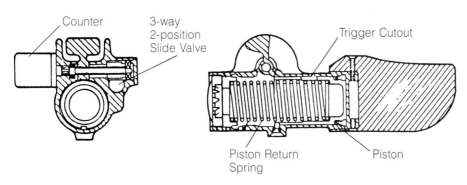

Counter

3-way
2-position
Slide Valve

Trigger Cutout

Piston Return
Spring

Piston

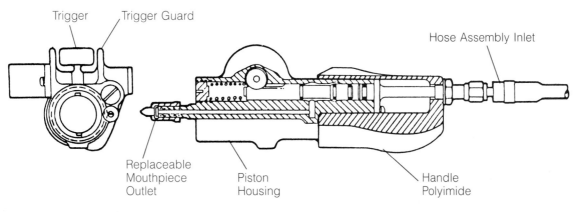

Trigger   Trigger Guard

Hose Assembly Inlet

Replaceable
Mouthpiece
Outlet

Piston
Housing

Handle
Polyimide

6.4.2

Water Pressurization Panel

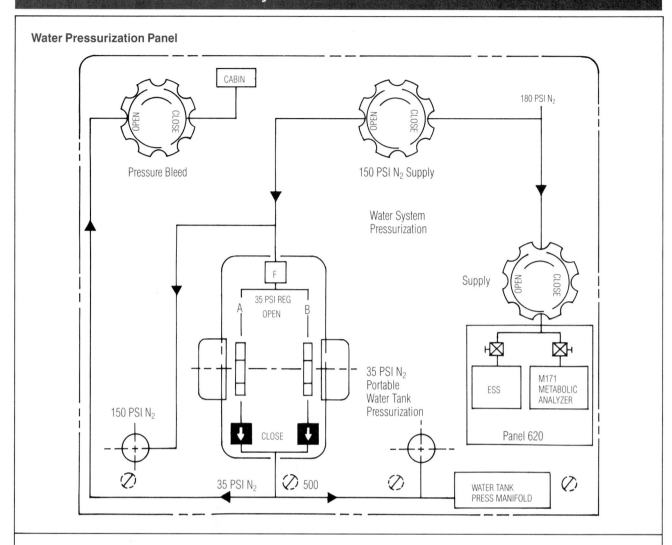

Shower Flow Diagram

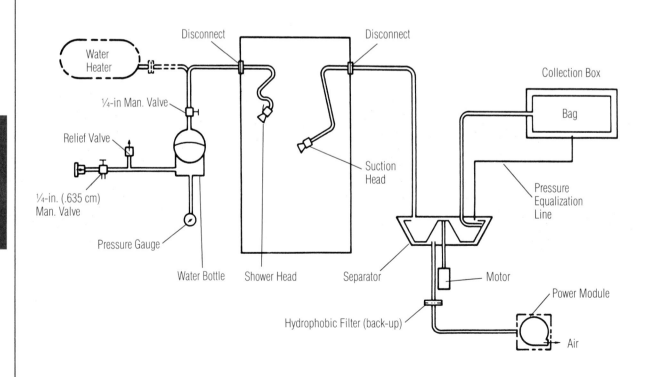

Pressure Regulator

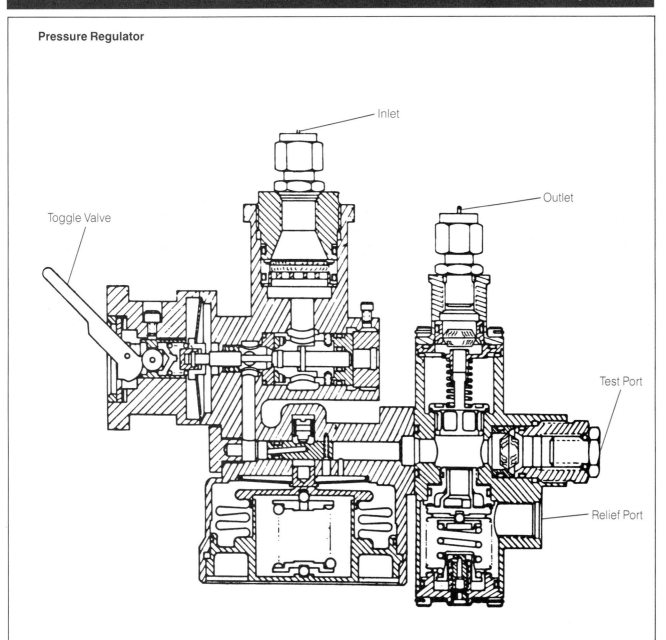

Toggle Valve

Inlet

Outlet

Test Port

Relief Port

In-Flight Maintenance

There are several pieces of apparatus that require regular attention in order to assure proper operation. The schedule in this section lists maintenance procedures and the frequency with which you must perform them in order to keep the ship running smoothly. There are, of course, many other checks to be run, but computer analysis of sensor data monitors these for you and provides servicing requirements and instructions as needed.

Emergency repair procedures, schematic diagrams, emergency and backup operational procedures, and maintenance training information are available in the MMC Series 500.

In-Flight Maintenance

Task Description	Planned Frequency (days)
Vacuum clean inlet screens	6
Vacuum clean air mixing chambers	6
Vacuum clean fan inlet screens	
Vacuum clean vent upstream filter (coarse)	6
Replace waste management vent unit upstream filter (fine)	6
Replace shower filter	6
Lubricate Chibis garment waist seal	7
Replace sieve solids traps	11
Replace inlet CO_2 detector cartridges	14
Replace waste management vent unit upstream filter (coarse)	28
Replace fecal collector filter	28
Replace urine separator filter	28
Replace sieve charcoal canister	28
Replace waste management filter and charcoal cartridge	28
Replace outlet CO_2 detector cartridge	28
Replace PPO_2/PPN_2 sensor (partial pressure)	90
Replace cooling water filter	90
Replace EVA/IVA gas coolant separator	90
Replace urine separator	120
Vacuum clean solenoid vent filter	120
Replace batteries	120

6.5.1

This section is a summary of the known scientific information about the planet Mars. It supplies physical data on Mars and its moons, Deimos and Phobos, and describes surface and atmospheric characteristics. It also includes brief descriptions of earlier unmanned missions. A list of frequently used acronyms and a glossary complete this section.

7.0.1

Mars, fourth planet from the Sun, is located in an elliptical orbit averaging about 141.6 million miles (227.8 million kilometers) from the Sun. The planet gets as close to the Sun as 128.3 million miles (206.5 million kilometers) and as far away as 154.8 million miles (249.1 million kilometers). It can get as close as 40 million miles (64.4 million kilometers) to Earth and as far away as 250 million miles (400 million kilometers) from Earth.

Mars completes one orbit of the Sun every 686.97964 Earth days (668 sols). Mars and Earth have close approaches about every 780 days. The planet rotates on its axis in 24 hours 39 minutes 35.238 seconds (1 sol), and the axis is tilted at an angle of 25° with respect to the plane of the Sun and the planets. This angle changes for Mars from 14.9° to 35.5° over a cycle of 1.2 million years. The Earth rotates in 24 hours, of course, and is itself tilted at an angle of 23.5°. Like a spinning top, both Earth and Mars wobble, or precess. Earth precesses in 26,000 years, but Mars takes 175,000 years. Curiously, this causes the Mars orbit to rotate every 72,000 years and causes the climate to change in cycles of 51,000 years.

Because of its axial tilt, Mars has seasons divided by hemispheres. The northern hemisphere summer lasts 178 days and northern hemisphere winter only 154 days. The winters are longer and more severe in the southern hemisphere since the planet is farther from the Sun during the southern winter.

The planet itself has an equatorial diameter of 4221.96 miles (6794.4 kilometers). Like the Earth's, the equatorial region bulges slightly. The diameter through the poles is only 4,195 miles (6751 kilometers). Mars is also less dense than the Earth, so its mass (the total amount of material in the planet) is only 10.74 percent of Earth's. This means that its gravitational pull is less. In fact, martian gravity is 12.16 feet per second squared (ft/sec^2) compared to 32 ft/sec^2 on Earth (372.52 cm/sec^2 versus 980 cm/sec^2 on Earth). This weaker

Dynamical Properties

Parameter	Value	Comments
Semi-major axis	13.68 x 10^7 mi 22.794 x 10^7 km	1.523691 AU*
Perihelion distance	12.40 x 10^7 mi 20.665 x 10^7 km	1.381398 AU
Aphelion distance	14.95 x 10^7 mi 24.918 x 10^7 km	1.666984 AU
Eccentricity	0.093387	Earth: 0.017
Orbit inclination	1°50'59.28"	
Mean orbital velocity	14.48 mi/hr 24.129 km/sec	
Year	686.97964 days	
Solar day (1 "sol")	24^{h}39^{m}35.238^s	noon to noon
Tilt angle of rotation axis	25°	Earth: 23.5°

*1 AU = 93 million miles (149 million km)

North Polar Region

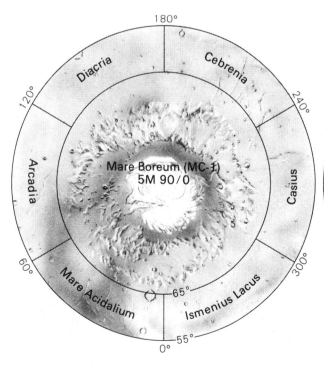

South Polar Region

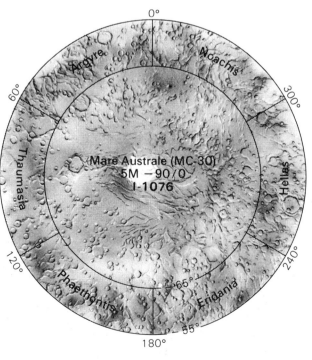

gravitational pull has its advantages. With less than 40 percent of the Earth's gravitational force to work against, you can heft your suit and portable life-support system, which together weigh over 150 pounds (68 kilograms), with relative ease.

Also, the needed escape velocity for your return to Earth is only 11,214 mph (18,047 kph), compared with 25,000 mph (40,000 kph) for the escape from Earth.

Mars has a very weak magnetic field, only about .0001 of the Earth's field strength. This raises some interesting questions. Because Mars rotates at a rate about equal to Earth's, if it has a liquid core, it should have a far stronger magnetic field. The presence of volcanoes on Mars proves that it had to have had a molten core at some point in its geologic history, so the weak field remains something of a mystery. The rock samples you return will tell the story. If residual magnetism is found in rocks of various ages, we will be able to piece together a sort of magnetic history of Mars.

Mars's two moons, Phobos and Deimos, are discussed further in Section 7.3.6. For now, suffice it to say that they are in fairly circular equatorial orbits. Phobos orbits at a distance of 2.76 Mars radii (5,827 miles or 9,378 kilometers) and at the slight tilt of only 1.02° with respect to Mars's equator. Its orbital period is 7 hours 39 minutes 13.85 seconds. Phobos is irregular in shape and is about 8.4 miles (13.5 kilometers) long, 6.65 miles (10.7 kilometers) wide, and 5.96 miles (9.6 kilometers) high.

Tiny Deimos orbits at 6.9 Mars radii (14,577 miles or 23,459 kilometers) and is inclined or tilted only 1.82° from the planet's equator. Its orbital period is 30 hours 17 minutes 54.87 seconds. This small, asteroid-like body is only 4.66 miles (7.5 kilometers) long, 3.73 miles (6 kilometers) wide, and 3.4 miles (5.5 kilometers) high.

Physical Data

Parameter	Value	Comments
Radius		
Equatorial	2,038.32 mi	
	3,397.2 km	
Polar	2,025.30 mi	
	3,375.5 km	
Mass	1.415×10^{24} lb	0.1074 that
	6.418×10^{23} kg	of Earth's mass
Mass ratio: Sun/Mars	3,098,700:1	
Mean density	245 lb/ft³	Earth: 337.75 lb/ft³
	3.933 g/cm³	5.21 g/cm³
Gravity at surface	12.2 ft/sec²	Earth: 32 ft/sec²
	372.52 cm/sec²	980 cm/sec²
Escape velocity	3.01 mi/sec	Earth: 7 mi/sec
	5.024 km/sec	11.2 km/sec
Surface temperature extremes	−225 to 80°F	
	130 to 300 °K	
Surface atmospheric pressure	5.9 to 15.0 mb	varies seasonally

Equatorial Region

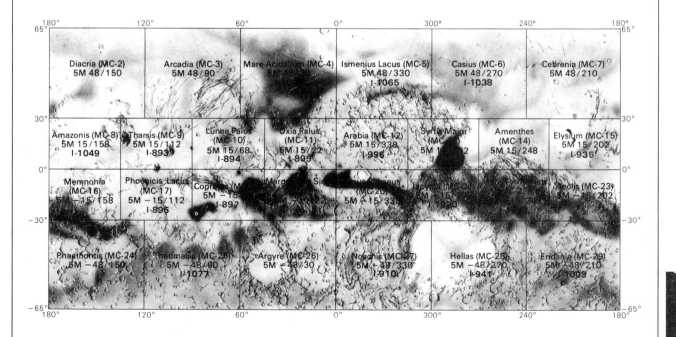

Shaded areas indicate Lowell Observatory Albedo map. Maps show quadrangle areas. Refer to quadrangle name for computer reference.

The first probe to send back useful data from Mars was the Mariner 4 fly-by. On July 14, 1965, Mariner 4 passed within 7,800 miles (13,000 kilometers) of the martian surface and transmitted 22 images back to Earth. These pictures were thirty times more detailed than those from Earth-based telescopes and, though they covered only 1 percent of the surface, they changed our thinking about Mars.

Craters, ranging from 2.5 to 75 miles (4 to 120 kilometers) in diameter, were identified. Rather than canals built by martians, Mars's surface appeared more like that of the Moon. Mariner 4 did detect a magnetic field that was only .0003 that of Earth's, but Mars seemed barren and perhaps disappointingly simple in geology. This, of course, is an excellent example of why you must view preliminary and limited results with a good deal of skepticism.

The next two missions to reach Mars were also fly-bys—Mariners 6 and 7. Each came within 2,175 miles (3,500 kilometers) of the surface. Mariners 6 and 7 also recorded mostly cratered terrain, but the small craters were now seen to be bowl-like, and the larger ones were flat-bottomed. These differences hinted that erosion might have taken place. Some of the 126 Mariner 7 images showed somewhat linear features, and revealed a southern polar cap frost over 33 yards (30 meters) thick. Rough terrain also discovered began to suggest a more interesting geology.

On November 14, 1971, Mariner 9 went into orbit around Mars. On November 27 and December 2, the Soviet orbiters Mars 2 and 3 arrived and deployed two landers. Touching down during a global dust storm with winds of 200 mph (320 kph), the landers learned little. Their positions were 44.20° S, 313.2° W (Mars 2 lander) and 44.90° S, 160.08 W (Mars 3 lander). The major finding of these missions was of traces of water vapor.

Mariner 9 imaging, however, was a scientific bonanza. The major finding, after the dust storm subsided, was of volcanoes. The largest volcano, Olympus Mons, was measured as 15.5 miles (25 kilometers) high and 435 miles (700 kilometers) across.

Another startling feature found during the Mariner 9 mapping was Valles Marineris, a huge fracture in the martian surface that is more than 1,550 miles (2,500 kilometers) long, about 125 miles (200 kilometers) wide, and about 2.2 miles (3.5 kilometers) deep. Valles

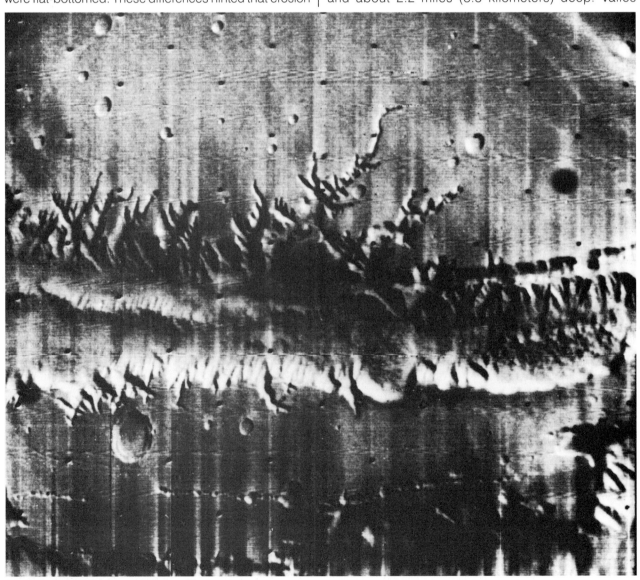

Mariner 9 photo: part of Valles Marineris.

Mariner-Mars 1971

Viking 1975

Marineris's length is about the distance from Chicago to California; the Grand Canyon in Arizona would fit in one of its small tributaries. Erosion forces have caused slumps and landslides along the canyon walls, so many rock samples accrue in the talus along the valley floor. In fact, the floor area of Valles Marineris and its huge branch canyons are excellent places to find a large variety of martian rock and soil samples. This is certainly a major consideration in the landing site selection for the Mars One mission.

Mariner 9 also revealed that the planet's southern hemisphere was much more cratered than the northern half. Streaks of lighter material downwind from many craters showed that dust, deposited around and behind the craters, was probably the major cause of slow erosion on Mars.

Mariner 9 revived some hope that there might be, or might have been, some life forms on Mars. Mariner 9 images revealed a whole series of features that looked like river channels. All the formations typical of a region

7.2.2

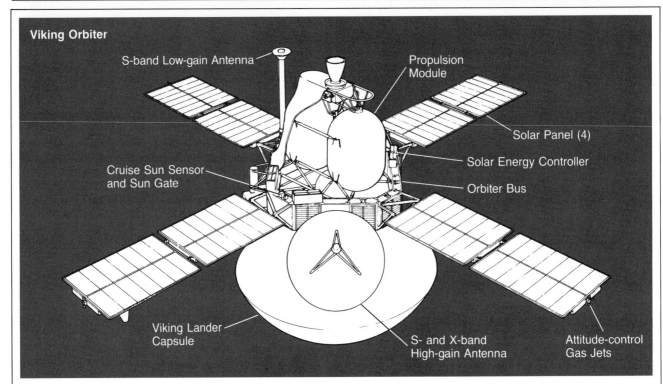

Viking Orbiter

S-band Low-gain Antenna

Propulsion Module

Solar Panel (4)

Cruise Sun Sensor and Sun Gate

Solar Energy Controller

Orbiter Bus

Viking Lander Capsule

S- and X-band High-gain Antenna

Attitude-control Gas Jets

through which water flowed were there: channels, sandbars, feeder stream beds, etc. While there are other possible causes for these types of features, water is the most interesting theoretical cause. For if Mars had flowing water, it had the basic requirement for life.

Of course, it is possible that permafrost in those regions suddenly melted and flooded the area, causing the formations. If this is the case then the possibility of life forms becomes more remote since such forms require continuous availability of water for an extended period of time.

The Mariner 9 pictures of the northern polar cap revealed a layered terrain that seemed to vary on a seasonal basis. Radio contact with Mariner 9 was lost after 698 orbits. On October 7, 1972, the attitude (orientation) control gas was exhausted and, after 7,329 pictures, Mariner 9 became silent.

In 1973, the Soviet Union launched an ambitious four-spacecraft barrage toward Mars, Mars 4, 5, 6, and 7. Mars 4 and 5 were to be orbiters and Mars 6 and 7 were to be direct-entry landers. Mars 4 failed to achieve orbit, but did transmit 12 images. Mars 5 did orbit the planet, operating for twenty orbits. Mars 6 landed 24° S, 20° W, but transmissions lasted only 2.5 minutes and were cut off .3 of a second before touchdown. Unfortunately, Mars 7 missed the planet altogether. This arrival activity took place within about one month, from February 10 to March 12, 1974.

The next missions to reach Mars were the Vikings. Each Viking craft was comprised of an orbiter and a lander. The plan was to orbit, evaluate landing sites, release the lander, and then conduct both orbital and surface science tests. Viking 1 arrived at Mars on June 1, 1976. The lander reached the Martian surface at Chryse Planitia (Plains of Gold) on July 20, located 22.4° N, 47.5° W. The Chryse site, near one of the large channel systems, was chosen in order to provide the best chance of finding moisture, or the effects of past

moisture. Viking 2 arrived in Mars orbit on August 7, 1976, and its lander touched down September 3 at 47.59° N, 225.86° W in Utopia Planitia.

Viking orbital analyses revealed many features related to water or subsurface ice. Many craters, for instance, seemed to show a flow after the initial impact. By comparison, the Moon's craters are surrounded by a dry spatter of material. Viking found that the planet's polar caps were definitely made of water and carbon dioxide ice, and found that terrain on Mars previously thought to be smooth was quite cratered, fractured, and eroded.

The channels observed by Mariner 9 were indeed found to resemble water erosion, and they were seen to be even more extensive. Other evidence of water included extensive cracked areas or collapsed areas that could have been caused by permafrost melting underneath the surface.

Because of the remoteness and complexity of the Viking landers' operation, a great deal of artificial intelligence had to be built into the crafts. The landers were said to be as intelligent as dragonflies; not impressive by human standards, but, considering how complex a creature a dragonfly is, an impressive feat for the computer technology of the early 1970s. The landers also went through the most extensive sterilization procedures of any spacecraft in history. Considering that they would be looking for evidence of life on Mars, it was essential that they not contaminate the immediate environment with Earth organisms.

The landers were equipped to measure atmospheric temperature, pressure, and composition. One surprise was the fixing of the argon proportion of the atmosphere at 1.6 percent. The Mars 6 probe mentioned above had recorded a 30 percent reading. This new figure settled what had been an interesting discrepancy about argon levels. Nitrogen gas was also discovered. This was significant because nitrogen is one of the four basic atomic building blocks of life, along with carbon, hydrogen, and oxygen. The carbon dioxide gas and the water in permafrost and polar caps provided an abundance of the other three elements.

The life-detection experiments, of course, riveted public attention. Everyone wanted to know if there was life on Mars. The clues had been building. While Mars was incredibly arid, permafrost and water ice were known to exist, and evidence of liquid water flow in the past seen in geologic formations was abundant. Nitrogen was discovered, completing the minimum atomic requirements for life as we know it.

The Viking life-detection package consisted of three biology experiments: pyrolytic release, gas exchange, and labeled release. These experiments assumed that microorganisms, if present, would act the way their counterparts on Earth did. In the pyrolytic release (PR) experiment, for example, it was presumed that any martian organisms might be able to assimilate carbon

dioxide (CO_2) from the atmosphere as Earth plants do. The availability of solar energy (ultraviolet radiation) also suggested that plant-like forms might exist.

In the PR experiment, a sample of martian soil was incubated in an atmosphere with radioactive CO_2. After five days, the sample was heated (pyrolyzed) to 1,160° F (625° C) and a radiation detector measured to see if the CO_2 (or carbon monoxide, CO) had been retained by the sample. This would indicate a probable biological activity. Little assimilation was observed, certainly much less than would have been found in an Earth soil sample.

The gas exchange (GEX) experiment looked at samples to determine if biological processes occur where water vapor is present, or if nutrients are available. One cubic centimeter of soil was loaded into the GEX test cell and sealed. The soil was then incubated in a carbon dioxide, helium, and krypton atmosphere at a pressure of about 2.9 psi. Then a nutrient solution made up of amino acids (the building blocks of proteins),

Viking Lander

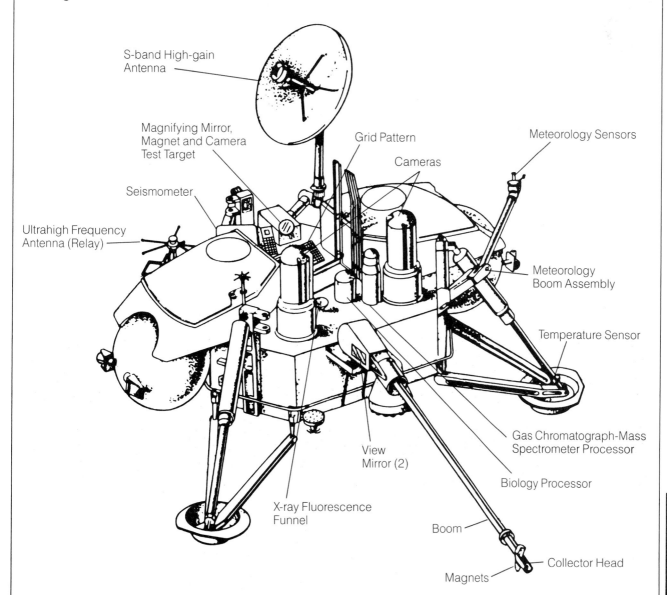

- S-band High-gain Antenna
- Magnifying Mirror, Magnet and Camera Test Target
- Seismometer
- Ultrahigh Frequency Antenna (Relay)
- Grid Pattern
- Cameras
- Meteorology Sensors
- Meteorology Boom Assembly
- Temperature Sensor
- Gas Chromatograph-Mass Spectrometer Processor
- Biology Processor
- View Mirror (2)
- X-ray Fluorescence Funnel
- Boom
- Collector Head
- Magnets

7.2.4

vitamins, salts, and other organic compounds was added. A gas sample of the test cell's atmosphere was taken after 1, 2, 4, 8, and 12 days, and sent through a gas chromatograph (See Section 4.6.9). The procedure was then repeated at temperatures up to 320° F (160° C).

An initial release of oxygen and some carbon dioxide proved very exciting, but organisms would normally produce a build-up of oxygen, just as a human would gradually fill a sealed room with carbon dioxide. The oxygen released in the Viking GEX experiments behaved more like a chemical reaction. When humidity was introduced into the test cell, it triggered the oxygen release, but the nutrient in solution, which should have had a similar result, actually slowed down the oxygen accumulation.

The labeled release (LR) experiment was still another variation on the theme of detecting life processes of microorganisms. One-half cubic centimeter of soil was sealed and incubated. Then a radioactively labeled nutrient solution was added. This was prepared by introducing radioactive carbon into the nutrient compounds. After the radioactivity of the solution was measured (called a count), it was added to the soil sample. Another detector measured any radioactivity in the atmosphere above the soil sample: the release of radioactive CO_2 would indicate biological activity in the soil.

Again the results were interesting. Radioactivity was detected, and analysis indicated that one of the nutrients was conserved. After the sample was sterilized at 320° F (160° C) the release stopped. But the analysis of the chemical composition of the martian soil by other experiments, like the gas chromatograph/mass spectrometer, offered good non-biological explanations for this behavior.

The Mars Geoscience/Climatology Orbiter (MGCO) arrived at Mars in August, 1991, about the time the first launches for the Mars One mission were being readied. The orbiter was placed in a near-circular 217.5-mile (350-kilometer) orbit. The orbit was Sun-synchronous. This means the spacecraft was at the same latitude at 2:00 each day, which permitted comparison of images with similar Sun angles. The spacecraft worked successfully for both its one-Mars-year life expectancy and its one-Mars-year extended mission. In fact, it is still partially operational and may be available to you during your mission.

The geoscience instruments included a gamma-ray spectrometer to measure the radioactivity emitted from the planet and an infrared spectrometer, to measure the ferrous and ferric (iron) content of the surface along with sulfur-, hydrogen-, and carbon-bearing compounds (sulfates, hydrates, and carbonates). In addition, a global map of carbon dioxide and water ice was prepared for you from MGCO data. An additional ultraviolet spectrometer provided studies of atmospheric ozone and dust, and the radar altimeter has been used to generate accurate topographical maps.

The MGCO also carried a magnetometer to help solve the riddle of Mars's weak magnetic field. It is hoped that this data coupled with the rocks you collect will settle the question.

The climatology portion of the MGCO mission studied

Mars's seasonal behavior, along with the transportation and deposit of carbon dioxide, water, and dust. This experiment helped to tie together the relationship between Mars's climate and its surface and crustal structure.

Pyrolytic Release Experiment

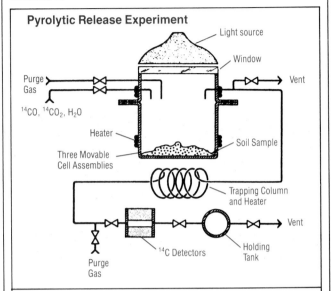

Labeled Release Experiment

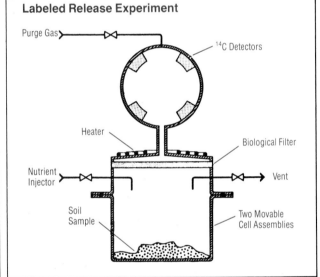

Gas Exchange Experiment

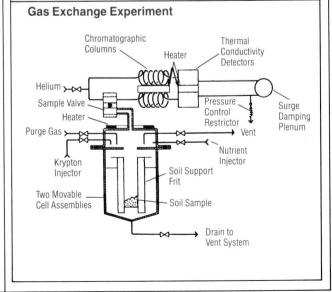

Your preparation for this mission has required intensive study in the areas of geology, atmospheric science, laboratory and tests procedures, and comparative planetology. This section is a discussion of major features and findings you will need to know as you explore the surface and study the martian environment.

Geomorphology

The geomorphology, or overall surface geologic features of the entire planet, need to be understood to fit the exploration you will do into the proper perspective.

First, consider the equatorial regions. The terrain of equatorial Mars is divided into four basic types or units: (1) heavily cratered old regions, (2) wind-blown volcanic plains with few craters, (3) circular features like volcanoes, craters, and domes, and (4) erosional features like channels and canyons.

The major division of features on Mars occurs at a near-equatorial line between north and south. The south-ern hemisphere is generally very heavily cratered and made up of old regions. It is thought that this region may reflect Mars's early history and would be in the neighborhood of four billion years old. There is a large number of shallow craters over 12.4 miles (20 kilometers) in diameter. This represents a type-1 unit as mentioned above. One large cratered area does extend north-ward from the major cratered region but stops at about 45°N, 330°W.

The northern hemisphere consists mostly of plains, with few craters (unit 2). These plains, while not as cratered, do have many features that indicate the re-sults of volcanic, wind, and water erosion. Other features, like cracks, show the presence of ground ice.

There are three extensive regions of volcanoes (unit 3). The oldest is south of the Hellas Basin (40°S, 290°W). This region is in a pocket of unit 2-type terrain with sev-eral old volcanoes. The Elysium region, around 25°N, 215°W, is the smallest unit-3 region, with three major

Argyre Planitia and cratered terrain.

7.3.1

volcanoes. Each of these volcanoes is over 93 miles (150 kilometers) wide. By far the most extensive volcanic region is Tharsis. Located north of the equator and centered at about 115°W, this gigantic area has influenced a major part of the martian surface. Cracks in the surface radiating from the Tharsis region run almost halfway around the planet. These cracks are faults, like those on Earth. Many form in pairs with ditches in between and are called graben. All this activity shows Tharsis to be the youngest of the three volcanic regions.

Tharsis is also the highest region on Mars. The whole area is referred to as the Tharsis Bulge, and it is like a huge bump on the martian surface. There is no sea level on Mars, so an atmospheric pressure level (6.1 millibars) was chosen instead. It so happens that above this pressure, liquid water could exist if the temperature were right. Below this pressure water cannot liquefy. With this artificial "sea level," called a datum, selected, Tharsis averages about 4.3 miles (7 kilometers) above datum.

The Tharsis volcanoes extend above this level. Olympus Mons and the three aligned volcanoes Arsia Mons, Pavonis Mons, and Ascraeus Mons, are all about 16.8 miles (27 kilometers) above Mars datum. There are also smaller (younger) volcanoes scattered throughout the region.

The fourth major equatorial geological unit is the canyon/channel system. Many canyons and channels have already been noted as radiating from the Tharsis Bulge.

Arsia Mons on the Tharsis Bulge.

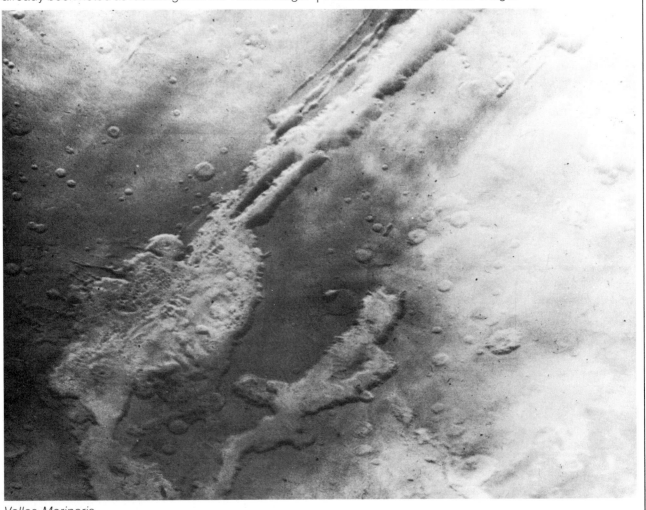

Valles Marineris.

The largest of these, Valles Marineris (see Mariner 9 above), is over 1,550 miles (2,500 kilometers) long. Valles Marineris includes Capri Chasma, Eos Chasma, Coprates Chasma, Melas Chasma, Ophir Chasma, and your primary landing site—Candor Chasma. Nearby are Hebes Chasma, Juventae Chasma, and Ganges Chasma. Valles Marineris is part of a whole system of canyons extending 2,500 miles (4,000 kilometers) eastward. In the central sections, this canyon system is over 4.35 miles (7 kilometers) deep. This is 3.5 times deeper than the Grand Canyon. Unlike canyons on Earth, these canyons have no tributaries, but start and end quite abruptly.

The bottoms of the canyons show evidence of faulting, and the slumped walls mentioned earlier show that the canyons are expanding. The canyons, unlike the channels, do not seem to show much water-type erosion, but the proximity and relation to the channels indicates that there may be a common origin.

least 3 billion years ago, although some channel floors have extremely few craters, suggesting a much lower age. Actually, several of the ideas on how they formed could be correct. There may well be a number of contributing causes.

The polar regions are as fascinating as the equatorial regions. In 1666, Giovanni Cassini made drawings of Mars that noted the existence of polar caps. Later, astronomers noted that the polar caps changed seasonally. These early observers assumed that the polar caps were made of water ice, but the discovery that the atmosphere was 95 percent carbon dioxide suggested that they might contain dry ice, frozen CO_2, as well.

The polar regions consist of a series of layers that range from a few yards to tens of yards thick. These layers suggest the whole history of the polar regions. They extend out about 10° in latitude and are roughly circular. The poles are higher than the surrounding ter-

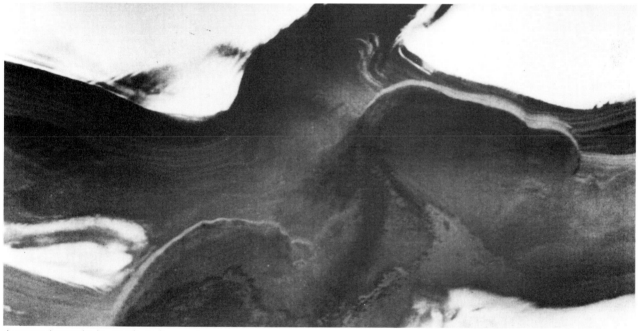

Layered terrain in north polar region.

To the northeast are three distinctive parallel channel systems—Simud Vallis, Tiu Vallis, and Ares Vallis, and to the north the huge Kasei Vallis. All these channels surround Chryse Planitia, the site of the Viking 1 lander. Like the canyons, these channels start fairly abruptly in canyons or in what is called chaotic terrain —the cracked and broken areas mentioned above.

All the channels have distinct flow lines that move around higher objects and form cuts and what appear to be islands. Evidence of many changes in direction of flow further add to the mystery of channel formation. Getting that much water to arise, flow, and disappear is hard to imagine. Some scientists feel the flow came from pressure causing a slurry of flowing water and rocks. Others feel that trapped water under pressure was released at different times. Geothermal ice melting, glacier formation and retreat, wind erosion, and even lava erosion have all been given as other possible causes for the martian channels.

The channels all appear to be quite old, formed at

rain and have few craters. This tells us that they are very young and seem to be always changing. The layers appear to be made of dust, water ice, and dry ice.

The northern polar cap forms under a cloud, called the polar hood, during the fall and onset of northern winter. The CO_2 condenses onto the caps from the thick clouds. The polar cap reaches a maximum of 65°N, but ground frost has been observed at the Viking 2 landing site, which is at 48°N.

The south pole is obscured by thinner clouds during the southern autumn; it is expected that the layers of the polar cap in the south would be thinner. The south pole has its winter when the planet is farthest from the Sun and moving the most slowly in its orbit. The longer winter and the hotter summers make the southern polar cap expand and contract more than the northern polar cap.

When the poles melt back, the residual caps exhibit a modified terrain. The northern residual cap has swirled ridges. The smaller southern residual polar cap is surrounded by a terraced surface created by eons of such

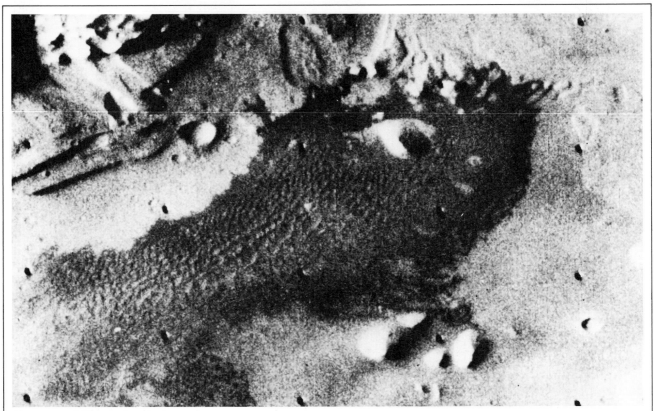

Huge sand dunes (center).

movement. Both the north and south poles are surrounded by dust. The north polar cap is especially surrounded by an extensive dune field.

The layers around the residual caps tell the climatic history of Mars. When they are decoded, we will know much more about martian environmental history. The causes of the layering, whether deposits, wind erosion, or a combination, will also provide an insight into global wind patterns and erosion processes.

The global dust storm observed by Mariner 9 left no doubt that dust is a major part of the martian environment. You will deal with dust during your surface stay. Viking surface images have shown that dust is continually being shifted on the surface. Some of the dust is light enough to be picked up by the atmosphere. Slightly larger particles are skipped or bounced along. This process is called saltation. Finally, these airborne particles collide with slightly heavier particles, propelling them slowly along the surface in a process called creep.

The velocity near the surface would have to be 5.3 mph (2.4 meters per second) to move the finest grains; this means the velocity just above the surface would be 100–280 mph (45–125 meters per second). During saltation, particles would rise 18–39 inches (0.5–1 meter) high and travel 3–11 yards (3–10 meters).

All this activity produces mass movement of dust. On Mars most dust moves near the poles, unlike on Earth, where most sand moves near the equator. The patterns the martian dust makes, however, are remarkably similar to sand patterns on Earth. Two major types of dunes form. Transverse dunes, formed where there is a good supply of dust, form wave-like patterns in many regions. Barchans, which look like crescents of sand, form where dust is scarce.

Unlike Earth, Mars has an abundance of craters. Aerodynamic theory says that sand blowing over a round, flat crater should form a tail or streak on the downwind side. This has been observed consistently on Mars.

The Atmosphere

Earth observations have determined the atmosphere of Mars to be mostly carbon dioxide (CO_2) but its pressure at the surface has been found to be only about .01 that of Earth's. Like Earth's, the martian atmosphere has clouds, winds, water vapor, and seasonal changes. The primary elements are given in the table below.

Composition of the Martian Lower Atmosphere	
Gas	Percent Volume
Carbon Dioxide (CO_2)	95.32 percent
Nitrogen (N_2)	2.7 percent
Argon (Ar)	1.6 percent
Oxygen (O_2)	0.13 percent
Carbon Monoxide (CO)	0.07 percent
Water Vapor (H_2O)	0.03 percent variable
Neon (Ne)	2.5 ppm
Krypton (Kr)	0.3 ppm
Xenon (Xe)	0.08 ppm

The atmosphere is driven by seasonal temperature changes, which move it from pole to pole. The atmosphere is thickest over each pole during winter, the prevailing wind direction is westerly, and winter storms are produced. Summer in the south is still subject to dust storms, but the northern hemisphere is comparatively quiet for most of the year.

Temperatures on Mars can vary by as much as 90°F (50°C) daily. Imagine waking up to 0°F temperatures, going to work in subfreezing weather, going outside to a blistering 90° day at 1:00 P.M., then donning your parka to go home. This would be the situation if you lived on Mars. Mars's extremely thin atmosphere heats and cools very rapidly. On Earth, it is usually colder at the top of a mountain than at the bottom, but on Mars, the temperature is dominated by the amount of sun and the amount of energy reflected by the surface. This leads to temperatures that may be the same anywhere on the mountain. This climatic situation tends to produce winds as well. Generally, such winds move up the mountain during the day and down at night.

Martian atmospheric pressure varies with the seasons. In the winter, pressure might reach 10 millibars; in late summer, it might only be 7 millibars. Water vapor also varies with the season. During the winter, the water vapor "freezes" out and goes into the polar cap or ground frost. In the summer, however, water vapor goes back into the atmosphere but remains mostly in the northern latitudes.

As mentioned above, the clouds are also a part of the martian atmosphere. The polar hood, discussed earlier, is a haze of water ice. Other clouds are visible around the planet. Wave clouds are produced on the downwind side of obstacles, while orographic clouds, which form mostly in spring and summer, develop around high features on a daily basis. High clouds at altitudes of 2.5 to 3.7 miles (4 to 6 kilometers) are common, and temperature changes from day to night can create both high-altitude clouds and ground hazes. Ground hazes form mostly during the morning, especially in the canyons. You may experience this phenomenon at Candor Chasma.

The Surface

Despite the sophistication of orbital sensing instruments, you don't absolutely know what is on Mars until you actually get there and look. Even environmental satellites around Earth require on-site inspection to assure

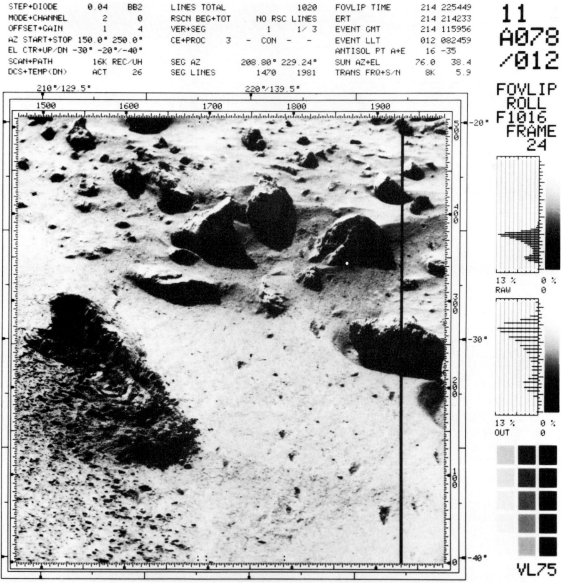

Viking lander surface image.

7.3.5

that what you thought you saw in the photo was actually there. Your visit to the martian surface is the same type of investigation and verification. It is referred to as obtaining "ground truth." You will be collecting a wide variety of rock samples from very different locations. So far, we have sample analyses only from the two stationary Viking landers. The landers each had an arm with a scoop shovel at the end to feed surface samples to the analyzing instruments inside the craft. An X-ray fluorescence spectrometer similar to the MEM instrument analyzed the chemistry of the martian soil. Iron oxides and quartz were found to be the main compounds in the soil (62.9 percent of the total). The percentages of compounds in the analyses did not add up to 100 percent, suggesting that water, carbon dioxide, and carbonate compounds were driven off during the analysis.

What do you find as you step onto the surface? As you are landing in a canyon and not on a plain, like Viking, there may be some important differences, but some features should be similar. The surface is most probably littered with blocks of rock. Many were probably formed by meteor impact or the movement of water across the surface. They are irregular in shape and show signs of weathering. Rocks may exhibit graininess, with other rocks and minerals imbedded in them. These rocks are most likely pitted from wind and sand. There is considerable debate about rock types. There may be only one or two, or there may be ten or more. We won't know until you have collected and analyzed your samples.

The Viking sites revealed dunes and drifts of dust not unlike Earth deserts. Fine-grained material regularly coats rocks and then is blown away. Sediments or layers have also been observed. Some of this may be due to the carving or sculpting of rocks by dust particles, and some by actual layering or irregularities in the rocks themselves. Dust layering, when examined closely, reveals the changes in wind conditions that produced the different drifts.

The Viking arm dug several trenches in the soil to obtain samples. The soil was fairly easy to dig; this indicates that footing in the rock-strewn soil could be dangerous and tiring. This factor must be considered as you make final determinations of your Mars surface exploration workload.

The Martian Moons
The gross physical characteristics of Phobos and Deimos have been treated in Section 7.1.2, but these complex bodies deserve some special consideration. The orbital science team will be performing imaging experiments to learn more about them.

Interest in Phobos and Deimos has always been high. Even when first discovered, they were surrounded in controversy. Asaph Hall first observed them in 1877, but there is a reference to two moons orbiting Mars in Jonathan Swift's *Gulliver's Travels*, written 150 years earlier. Astronomers on Swift's imaginary floating island of Laputa tell Gulliver about them and even give the orbital period for the inner moon as about 10 hours. Phobos's actual period is 7 hours, 39 minutes. One possible explanation dates back to Johannes Kepler, an early-seventeenth-century astronomer. Besides being

a scientist, Kepler was somewhat of a mystic. At that time, it was known that Venus had no moons, Earth had one, and Jupiter had four (the Galilean satellites). It stood to reason then, that Mars should have two. It could well be that it was Kepler's 1610 hypothesis that Swift was using in 1726.

Phobos, which means fear, and Deimos, which means terror, are interesting for several scientific reasons. Phobos, for example, has a surface streaked with grooves that may be the crack marks of meteor impact or may be the result of tidal action by Mars. Both moons are heavily cratered. Phobos is accelerating and will eventually either fall into Mars or break up into smaller pieces and form a fine ring around the planet, perhaps a smaller version of the rings discovered around Jupiter and Uranus.

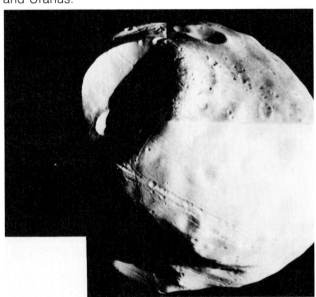

Phobos showing impact craters and fractures.

The origin of the two moons is also a puzzle. It is possible that they are made from debris left over after the formation of the planet, or that they are captured asteroids. Their density is very low and their dark gray appearance is quite similar to that of a class of meteors and asteroids known as carbonaceous chondrites. These moons are interesting for yet another reason. Meteorites of similar material found on Earth have been found to contain organic compounds including the twenty basic amino acids that make up life on Earth. Finding these compounds on Phobos or Deimos would be a confirmation of the theory that organic molecules (not life, just building blocks) can evolve in extremely non-Earthlike environments.

Phobos and Deimos have surfaces that are apparently covered by the debris of their many collisions with meteors. This loose material, called regolith, may be tens of meters deep. There is keen interest in mining not only on our Moon, but the asteroids as well, and the two martian moons could be excellent candidates for mineralogical exploration. Also, it appears that oxygen (O_2) and other compounds could be easily synthesized from the regolith and turned into fuel and supplies for further manned exploration of Mars and, perhaps, beyond.

7.3.6

Acronyms and Abbreviations

APU	auxiliary power unit
CH$_4$	methane
CO	carbon monoxide
CO$_2$	carbon dioxide
CRT	cathode ray tube
CSVC	core sample vacuum container
D/D	decontamination/debriefing
DR	data recorder
EC/LSS	environmental control/life support system
EOI	Earth orbit injection
ESA	European Space Agency
EVA	extravehicular activity
FLOX	fluorine/oxygen (liquid fuel)
g	gravity force
GC/MS	gas chromatograph/mass spectrometer
GET	ground-elapsed time
GEX	gas exchange experiment
ghz	gigahertz
GMT	Greenwich mean time
H & H	health and hygiene deck
H$_2$	hydrogen
HAB	habitability module
HAC	heading alignment circle
HAL-S+	high order assembly language—Shuttle plus
HFE	heat flow experiment
HGA	high-gain antenna
HMF	health maintenance facility
IR	infrared
JD	Julian day
kg	kilogram
kph	kilometers per hour
lb	pound
LAB	laboratory module
LCG	liquid cooling garment
LGA	low-gain antenna
LH$_2$	liquid hydrogen
LiOH	lithium hydroxide
LO$_2$	liquid oxygen
LR	labeled release experiment
m	meter
mb	millibars
MB	meteorology boom
MC	mission control
MEM	Mars excursion module
MEMU	Mars extravehicular mobility unit

MGCO	Mars geoscience and climatology orbiter
mhz	megahertz
ml	milliliters
MLC	main landing computer
MMC	main mission computer
MMU	manned maneuvering unit
MOI	Mars orbit injection
MOSA	Mars orbit and surface activities
mph	miles per hour
MR	Mars Rover
MS	main ship
MSS	Mars Science Station
MTK	master tool kit
N$_2$	nitrogen
O$_2$	oxygen
PLSS	portable life support system
ppm	parts per million
PR	pyrolitic release experiment
psi	pounds per square inch
QF	quarantine facility
RAM	random access memory
RCS	reaction control system
ROM	read-only memory
rpm	revolutions per minute
RTG	radioisotope thermoelectric generator
SAC	science applications computer
SAM	silicone ablative material
SCB	sample collection bag
SD	surface drill
SEM	scanning electron microscope
SPE	seismic profiling experiment
SRB-X	solid rocket booster—extended
SSME	Space Shuttle main engine
SSUE	Space Shuttle uprated engine
STS-C	space transportation system—cargo
TCM	trajectory correction maneuver
TEC	Trans-Earth coast
TEI	Trans-Earth injection
TIG	time to ignition
TMC	Trans-Mars coast
TMI	Trans-Mars injection
TPS	thermal protection system
UAMS	upper atmosphere mass spectrometer
UNMEA	United Nations Mars Exploration Authority
UV	ultraviolet
XRFS	X-ray fluorescence spectrometer

Glossary

aerobraking   Using the drag of an atmosphere to slow a craft.

aerocapture   Achieving an orbit around a planet using atmospheric drag for some or most of the braking.

albedo   The fraction of light reflected by a planet, moon, or other object.

altimeter   An instrument for accurately determining altitude.

anode   The positive terminal of an electrolytic circuit.

aphelion   The point in an orbit where the object is at maximum distance from the sun.

apoapsis   The point in an orbit at which a satellite is at maximum distance from a planet.

argon   An inert gas found in tiny quantities in the atmosphere of both Earth and Mars.

assimilation   The absorption of elements or nutrients.

azimuth   The angle between a fixed point and an object.

barchan   Crescent-shaped sand dunes that form in regions where sand is scarce.

boil off   Evaporation of fuels during a mission. This requires taking extra fuel to compensate for losses.

burn   A rocket motor firing, used to leave, enter, or adjust orbits.

carbonaceous chondrites   A class of meteorites with high carbon content and simple organic molecules.

cathode   The negative terminal of an electrolytic circuit.

climatology   The study of weather and climate changes.

contamination   Impurities which can be dangerous biologically or chemically.

creep   The movement of heavy particles of dust or sand.

datum   A basis for measurement or calculation (e.g., the selection of an artificial "sea level" on Mars determined by an atmospheric pressure rather than an actual water level).

dock   Joining two spacecraft.

drag   The slowing (friction) produced on a body as it moves through an atmosphere, a fluid, or over a solid surface.

electrolyze   To separate a compound into simpler compounds or elements by applying an electric charge.

elevation   The angle between an object and the horizon.

extravehicular activity   Work done outside a spacecraft.

fault   A fracture in the crust distinguished by the movement of the strata.

fuel cell   A device that mixes oxygen and hydrogen in a non-explosive process to produce electricity and water.

g   The symbol for the force equivalent to the acceleration of Earth gravity.

gas chromatograph   An instrument which separates elements and compounds by their rate of movement through a long column of helium gas.

geothermal   Heat caused by geologic pressure.

graben   A ditch or depressed area with a fault on either side.

ground truth   Verification on the surface of data obtained by remote sensing.

heliocentric   A view seen in relation to the Sun.

hydrazine   A nitrogen-hydrogen compound used for propellant and life support.

jettison   To cast away or drop from a vehicle.

krypton   A rare gas found in planetary atmospheres.

magnetometer   A device that measures the presence and strength of a magnetic field.

mass spectrometer   An instrument which measures the relative amount of elements in a sample.

module   An individual component of a spacecraft. Modules are usually divided by function—propulsion, habitation, storage, docking, etc.

orbit   An elliptical path produced when a body's tendency to fly inertially into space is balanced by the gravitational attraction of a central body.

orographic clouds   Clouds which form around mountains.

partial pressure   That part of the total cabin pressure contributed by each gas in the atmosphere.

periapsis   The point in an orbit at which the satellite is at minimum distance from a planet.

perihelion   The point in an orbit at which the object is at minimum distance from the sun.

permafrost   A permanently frozen subsurface layer.

pounds per square inch (psi)   A pressure measurement in the English system. The metric equivalent is the kilopascal. 1 psi $\times$ 6.895 = 1 kilopascal.

precession   The wobble of a rotational planet, like that of a spinning top.

pyrolyze   To use heat to cause a chemical change.

rendezvous   Piloting two craft into near proximity with each other.

saltation   Movement of particles of dust or sand by windblown lighter particles.

seismometer   A device for measuring subsurface vibrations (quakes) on a planet.

slumping   Down-sliding of rock at the base of a higher geologic feature; collapsed formation.

sol   The martian day measured from noon to noon; equals 24 hours 39 minutes.

solar flares   Immense bursts of energy produced by the Sun. These flares release streams of particles (mostly protons).

spectrometer   A device which spreads a sample (light, atoms, compounds) into an array, and measures that array.

trajectory   The path of an object in a gravitational field.

tranverse dunes   Wavelike patterns of sand dunes formed in regions of heavy amounts of sand.

umbilical   A cable that carries wiring and life support from a craft to an astronaut during extravehicular activity.

Velcro   A nylon fabric that can be fastened to itself.

voice recognition   The ability of the computer to accept input from human speech.

Epilogue and Apology

This book is dedicated to the men and women of the planet Earth: to those who will ultimately make the journey to Mars and beyond, to the thousands who will help them, to the millions who will support the massive effort required to take humanity's baby steps to the stars, and to the billions who will watch; watch with a spirit of kinship for those who desire to know what is over the next hill.

The voyage to Mars is only the next step in a trek that apparently began in West Africa a million years ago. It is no more daunting than the voyages of the Polynesians setting out in small boats to settle the islands of the Pacific, or the migrations of our forebears, however they traveled, from Africa to Mongolia or from Alaska to Tierra del Fuego.

What is perhaps most compelling about a voyage to Mars is that we have, today, the technology to accomplish it. We lack only the will.

Much has been made of the cost and practicality of such missions. Even though Mars beckons as a great mystery, why go there at all? The answer, to those who colonized the New World, to the Japanese fishermen who made incredible journeys around the Pacific, to the Eskimos who survive in seeming trackless wastes, is that survival depends on adaptability. And humans are better at it than any species in Earth's history. Although we haven't been around as long as the dinosaurs, there is every indication that we could survive that long if we put our minds to it.

In fact, if we never achieve a speed greater than that necessary to get to Mars, we could colonize half the galaxy in a period of time equal to about five times the dinosaurs' stay on Earth, or about 700 million years.

It is difficult to write a science book that you know has errors. While the technical information in the book is correct, no one can predict now how we will actually go to Mars, even if it could be done within the next decade or so. New forms of propulsion that are only experimental today could fantastically reduce travel times; new technologies may substantially improve reliability, reduce weight, and lower cost. Yet the orbital positions, the basic activities, and many of the details should happen as they have been described here.

While the cabin atmospheres, precise weights, actual orbital dimensions, or some equipment may change, the basic mission requirements for propulsion, life support, training, and the like will still remain. The information for this book was drawn from over twenty years of studies sponsored by the National Aeronautics and Space Administration, aerospace companies, universities, and think tanks. These studies are based on different assumptions, so information derived from one set of data may not mesh completely with information derived from another set of data, creating some minor inconsistencies. For this the author apologizes. Yet the fact remains that all the numbers are within the "ballpark" of an actual mission, if not precisely so, and most of the numbers in the book—trajectory dates, scientific data, life-support data, experimental equipment information—are all based on things we already know.

The research for this book led through an almost bewildering maze of both obscure and available technical documents. Colleagues at NASA Headquarters, Washington, D.C., the Johnson Space Center, Houston, the Ames Research Center in California, the Jet Propulsion Laboratory, Pasadena, Lockheed Missiles and Space, Sunnyvale, California, and many other places, provided documentation and valuable advice.

In the 1930s, the British Interplanetary Society conducted a study on the best ways to travel to the Moon. At a time when little was known about liquid-fueled rockets or advanced materials, they came up with a scenario that was very similar to the lunar orbit rendezvous technique actually used on Apollo.

Designing hardware that does not yet exist is always a risky venture, but someday, when the main ship is orbiting overhead, or when the MEM is on Mars, whatever the configuration, the crew may be people who read this work in the 1980s and said, "Someday I'm going to do that."

Mr. Gagarin, Dr. von Braun, Mr. Kennedy, Mr. Shepard, Mr. Clarke, Dr. Shatolov, Mr. Heinlein, Mr. Grissom, Dr. Ley, Dr. Armstrong, Mr. Leonov, Mr. White, Dr. Low, Mr. Webb, Dr. Sagan, Mr. Burroughs, Dr. Ride, Mrs. Tereshkova, thank you. We will never stop wanting to know what is over the next hill. We will, with intelligent effort and a keen sense of the future, move patiently and persistently toward our highest sense of what the human species can achieve. A leading science writer once imagined that if Werner von Braun were alive today, he would be stalking the halls of power and asking, "When are we going to Mars?"*

---

*Robert C. Cowen, *Christian Science Monitor,* January, 1983.

About the Author

Coauthor of the *Space Shuttle Operator's Manual*, Kerry Mark Joëls holds degrees in physics, aerospace education, and history of science. He has served on university faculties, worked at the NASA/Ames Research Center, was a curator at the National Air and Space Museum, Smithsonian Institution, and serves as curriculum director for the national Young Astronauts program. A fellow of the Royal Astronomical Society of England, Dr. Joëls lives with his wife, daughter, Norwegian Elkhound, and six computers in Alexandria, Virginia.